The Sopranos Scriptbook

The Sopranos Scriptbook

Created by David Chase

First published in October 2001 by Channel 4 Books, an imprint of
Pan Macmillan Ltd, 20 New Wharf Road, London N1 9RR, Basingstoke
and Oxford.

Associated companies throughout the world.

www.panmacmillan.com

ISBN 0 7522 6157 6

9 8 7 6 5 4 3 2 1

A CIP catalogue record for this book is available from the British Library.

Designed by Dan Newman/Perfect Bound Ltd
Printed by Mackays of Chatham PLC, Chatham, Kent

Picture acknowledgements:
Cover – Michael O'Neill/HBO; p1 – (top) Barry Wetcher/HBO, (below) HBO;
p2 – Anthony Neste/HBO; p3 – Anthony Neste/HBO; p4 – Anthony Neste/HBO;
p5 – Anthony Neste/HBO; p6 – (top) Anthony Neste/HBO, (below) Barry Wetcher/HBO;
p7 – Barry Wetcher/HBO; p8 – Barry Wetcher/HBO.

Contents

"The Sopranos" 13
Pilot
Written by David Chase

"College" 57
Season 1
Written by James Manos, Jr. and David Chase

"The Legend of Tennessee Moltisanti" 95
Season 1
Written by Frank Renzulli and David Chase

"The Happy Wanderer" 133
Season 2
Written by Frank Renzulli

"The Knight in White Satin Armor" 173
Season 2
Written by Robin Green & Mitchell Burgess

"Proshai, Livushka" 213
Season 3
Written by David Chase

Introduction

David Chase

In 1996, Lloyd Braun, then an executive at Brillstein-Grey Entertainment, asked me about doing a TV version of "The Godfather." I wasn't interested but Lloyd's suggestion triggered a movie idea I'd had years earlier – funnily enough, during one of my own psychotherapy sessions – about a mobster in therapy who was depressed. That idea eventually became the first season of "The Sopranos."

The Mob has been a lifelong interest of mine – perhaps because I grew up an Italian-American kid, first in Mount Vernon, New York, and later in North Caldwell, New Jersey. (Coincidentally, the same town where Tony Soprano lives.) Over the years, I've picked up details about mob guys – how they live and talk, what they value – from many sources, and a fair portion of my education came from movies and from the books but particularly from the local newspapers I devoured. In high school, I knew the sons of some wiseguys, and an older cousin of mine was married into it. We've also gotten lots of insights from a contact in a DA's office who prosecuted mobsters, and I believe in doing research. Frank Renzulli, one of our writer/producers for the first season and a half, is another great source of wiseguy information. He grew up in East Boston.

When it came time for casting, we knew that we needed actors with New York-New Jersey roots, and, whenever possible, theater experience as well. James Gandolfini, Michael Imperioli, Nancy Marchand, and Edie Falco all have extensive stage credits. (Being Italian also helped. But Nancy Marchand, Jamie-Lynn Sigler and Robert Iler have done okay despite their tragic handicap.) On the other hand, I just knew that Stevie Van Zandt, who had never acted before, was a natural. He's Calabrese. The audition process also provided inspiration for other characters. Tony Sirico, who read for the roles of "Big Pussy" and "Uncle Junior," inspired me to create the character of Peter "Paulie Walnuts" Gualtieri.

I had a fairly good sense of who Tony was from the beginning, perhaps because I personally relate to his anger and anxiety. Other things in our lives are similar as well – we both have smart wives, difficult mothers, love history and old gangster films, have nightmares and often feel like outsiders.

Originally, Tony was to be named Tommy Soprano – perhaps an unconscious homage to the character of Tom Powers (played by James Cagney) in one of my favorite films, "The

Public Enemy." (Coincidentally again, also one of Tony's favorite films!) But we couldn't get clearance on that name and so, with disappointment, I agreed on Tony. Now, of course, I can't imagine Tony's character with any other name. Tommy seems ridiculous.

Livia, as many fans know, was modeled *somewhat* on my own mother – an acerbic and fearful woman. Though Livia, fittingly, is also the name of Tiberius's scheming mother in "I, Claudius," it was also the name of one of my maternal aunts. One of my therapists, in trying to explain the reason for my mother's unrelenting pessimism and critical nature, once described her as having a "borderline personality disorder." Whatever the diagnosis, she was quite a character. Many of Livia's gestures, facial expressions and dialogue are exactly as I remember my mother talking and behaving. I'm not sure if it was ever my mother's intention – and I didn't see this at the time – but she was, in retrospect, a very funny woman – perhaps, as I say, knowingly.

Some of the other character names also were chosen based on personal connections. A cousin of mine was married to a woman named Carmela, which I always thought was a lovely name. Dr. Melfi, who is patterned on a therapist I've known, was named for someone very dear to me, Teresa Melfi, my paternal grandmother. And one day, years before I began work on the series, my wife, Denise, and I were having lunch in the Rita Flora coffee shop/florist shop in Los Angeles and our young waitress was wearing a tag with the name Meadow on it. I remarked to Denise about how unusual the name was and mentally filed it away.

The six scripts I've selected for this book were chosen because they each represent and deal with different aspects of the show. "College" is the one that comes closest to achieving my personal goal of making episodes that could have been made as a stand alone feature film. It is self contained.

The pilot would, of course, have to be included in this book. It not only introduces the characters, but also establishes the tone, style and soul of the series, as well as laying the groundwork for future episodes. It's the only episode that used voice over. When scenes are moved in editing, that's an intuitive, subjective decision, based on what a director believes makes the story more coherent or flow better. In the pilot, some excisions, both of scenes and dialogue, were made due to time constraints (it could only be 60 minutes long) or to tighten the story, while others, such as Meadow's teenage martyr fantasy – being burned at the stake – just didn't . . . work. It also became clear that the scene of Tony kissing Dr. Melfi wasn't appropriate at that point in their lives. However, a similar scene was reconceived and used in a much later episode, "Pax Soprana."

Astute fans may also have noticed some differences in the Soprano's kitchen from the one in the pilot. That's because the pilot was shot on location, while in later episodes, all interior house scenes (as well as the office in the Bada Bing strip club and Dr. Melfi's office) were shot on our set in Queens, New York, at the Silvercup Studios. After the pilot was picked up, we could afford to build sets. All exteriors are shot in New Jersey – Lodi, North Caldwell, Verona, Newark and other towns. In "Commendatori," (the episode where Tony and the crew go to Italy), exterior scenes were shot on location around Naples.

So, how to describe the actual Sopranos writing process? It essentially works like this: Before meeting with the writers, I outline some story arcs or milestones for the season, but we're not bound by them. Getting a final script is a fluid and organic process, and script changes are made up until the end – sometimes even during shooting. Before starting a season, I don't really consciously think, for example: 'Oh, this season is going to be about Tony and his dysfunctional relationship with his mother.' However, after the first season was finished, that was the theme that emerged.

I believe the main theme of season 2 essentially is "plateau therapy" – it deals with what Tony discovered and acknowledged in therapy during season 1 – and the feelings these insights evoked. Though as a child he was shaped by forces over which he had no control (his parents), he's now an adult and must struggle to take responsibility for who he is. He has to stop blaming his mother and own up to his actions. (It is a very compressed version of what actually would be years of therapy.) Focusing more on Tony and Carmela and their role as parents, as we've done in season 3, is a theme that just seemed to assert itself.

For any given season of 13 shows, once the broad outline has been established, we begin to fill in 13 episodic stories. Each episode usually has three strands – what we call an A, B, and C, or even D, storyline. ("College" is an exception with only 2.) The A and B stories basically are of equal importance, while the C story is less important, and D is usually a comic runner. For example, in "The Happy Wanderer," the A strand of the story is the spider-fly relationship between Tony and David Scatino and how they both behave according to their true natures: David is a compulsive gambler and Tony, ever the spider, can't resist taking his money though it spells his friend's doom. The B story is the relationship between Meadow and Eric Scatino – their performance at Talent Night and their concerns about getting into college. The C strand is Tony finding out he has a retarded uncle, and the D story is the funeral for the father of Tony's brother-in-law.

Once in the writing room, we (the writer/producers) begin to flesh out the story for each episode, listing the 'beats' (i.e. scenes) for the A, B, and C stories, one story at a time, on a wipe-off board. Each story – A, B, C, D – has a beginning, middle and end, and *could* stand alone as films. Each script has approximately 35 beats – 13 or so in the A and B stories, usually 5 to 6 in the C story, and sometimes a D story with just a few beats. A writer's assistant then types up everything that's been written on the board – in that same A, B, and C storyline system. The A, B, C, and D stories are then literally cut apart with scissors and then all "married" together – actually scotch-taped (and re-taped) in the order of the whole script. For example, a scene from story A could be followed by a scene from B, then back to A, then C, and so on. Once satisfied with the scene order (aka story), the taped pages are retyped and this version becomes the script outline for the episode. How a story is assigned to one of the core group of writers is often determined simply by who's available at the time, or who expresses an affinity for a particular story. On occasion, when none of the writers/producers have the time to write a script, the story will be assigned to an outside writer. But no matter who writes an episode, they all are based strictly on the outline that's been given to them.

According to the Writer's Guild code, a writer must submit at least two drafts. Usually we ask that the first one be delivered in two or three weeks after the assignment is accepted. (Our schedule allows for approximately three months from initial writing to shooting.) Usually, the executive producers – Robin Green, Mitchell Burgess (writers I worked with on "Northern Exposure") and I – see this version. We review it as soon as possible and then generate our notes – comments about what we like and dislike, suggestions for changes, what's funny, not funny, etc.

There could be ten drafts of a script, either revised by the original writer or reassigned at some point to another writer. Once a script is finished, polished and approved, it becomes the formal production draft and is given scene numbers. This is the first time that any of the cast or crew see a script.

Something that I *think* is unusual for a drama show on television is that we have a read through (also called a table read) with the cast, so we can hear what the written words sound like when spoken. This is done toward the end of preproduction. Production includes 2 stages – 1, prep or pre-production and 2, shooting. A writer/producer is always on set through prep and shooting. (We take turns.) When an episode is being shot, the remaining writers are working on the next outlines, stories, scripts, rewrites, etc. Prep (meetings with department heads such as casting, location, wardrobe, etc.) requires eight days, while actual shooting averages nine days. Before shooting even begins, however, we meet with the director and we discuss the meaning of every scene, both what's apparent and what's unspoken – the essence of the overall story, and how to best interpret this vision. This is called a "tone meeting" and it invariably sucks. It's long and tedious.

In production, many takes and angles are shot of each scene, so there are always numerous performances to choose from when editing. The film editor assembles an episode and it then goes to the director who makes his cut. This is his opportunity to replace angles with a different camera angle or performance, but, in general, the director doesn't change the order of scenes or omit scenes that were in the script. After the director's cut is made, the film comes to me and I generate many cuts, all the way to the final – which could include reordering and omitting scenes. This process can take months, and I always, selfishly, use as much time as the schedule allows. I firmly believe that the more time a filmmaker has to edit, the better a piece will be.

Music has always been a big part of my life. (I used to want to be a rock and roll musician.) I sometimes see the music as another character, the lyrics of songs functioning as a Greek chorus, sometimes – but not always – summing up or commenting on events in the story. Or not. Mostly the music fosters a feeling or mood. There's no question that the music and working with this particular cast of actors are my favorite parts of "The Sopranos."

The pilot for "The Sopranos," which was originally developed for Fox, was rejected, then was rejected by all the major networks. This turned out to be the best thing that could have happened because there's no way that the show we now see would have wound up on the screen of network television. And it wasn't the nudity, profanity or violence that bothered the networks – it was the details, the complexity, the different pacing. I also believe that, often, network television is about people saying *exactly* what's on their minds. This show is about people acting in a passive-aggressive – or aggressive – way. "The Sopranos" turned out to be a show that you could not put on anywhere but HBO. The fit with a network just wasn't there. Networks usually only want what's familiar. I think they would agree with that statement.

HBO has consistently demonstrated its commitment to innovation – probably the bravest thing you can do in TV – and their choices show a respect for the audience. Sopranos is an example of a gamble HBO was willing to take: Chris Albrecht, president of original programming and original movies, not only allowed me to direct (a big risk) and cast a relatively unknown actor in the lead, but authorized spending additional money per-episode because he understood that shooting on the New Jersey location was vital to the show's authenticity. Anytime I'd talked with a network about the show, they'd say, "Yeah, yeah, it's New Jersey, but you're really going to shoot it in LA or Canada, right?"

What Tony Soprano shows, I guess, is that rarely is anything black and white in life. Life is difficult, messy, disappointing. Things don't work out the way we'd like – our kids make bad choices, our parents are a burden, our friends disappoint or betray us. In that sense, I hope it's similar to the foreign films I loved as a young adult for their ideas, their mystery and their ambiguity – for not having the endings spelled out or telling the audience what to think or feel. What *I* love most when I'm watching something is a feeling of strangeness, suspense, poetry – things happening that you can't predict. I hope we've achieved that with "The Sopranos." We're continuing to learn. I remember Akira Kurosawa saying at age 80-something, that the great thing about filmmaking is you're constantly learning. He was still learning, he said.

Working on "The Sopranos" with so many talented people has been a joy. I realize how very lucky I am. I thank all of our fans. I hope you like this book.

David Chase

David Chase, April 2001

"The Sopranos"

Pilot

Written and Directed by
David Chase

Soprano Productions, Inc.

Production Draft	7/16/97
1st Revision (Blue)	7/18/97
2nd Revision (Pink)	7/29/97
3rd Revision (Yellow)	8/4/97
4th Revision (Green)	8/7/97
5th Revision (Goldenrod)	8/19/97
6th Revision (Salmon)	8/25/97

CHARACTER LIST

TONY SOPRANO
CARMELA SOPRANO
DR. JENNIFER MELFI
CHRISTOPHER MOLTISANTI
MEADOW SOPRANO
ANTHONY SOPRANO JR.
LIVIA SOPRANO
CORRADO "JUNIOR" SOPRANO
BIG PUSSY BONPENSIERO
SILVIO DANTE
HERMAN "HESH" RABKIN
HUNTER SCANGARELO
ARTHUR BUCCO
CHARMAINE BUCCO
ALEX MAHAFFEY
SECRETARY/YOUNG WOMAN
DICK BARONE
PETER "PAULIE WALNUTS" GUALTIERI
FATHER PHIL

Emil Kolar
Irina
Beppy
Nursing Home Director
Nils Borglund
Owner
Hostess

SETS

INTERIORS
Dr. Melfi's Waiting Room
Dr. Melfi's Office
Soprano House – Kitchen
Soprano House – Family Room
Soprano House – Hallway
Soprano House – Pantry
Soprano House – Meadow's Room
Soprano House – Bedroom
Bucco's Vesuvio
Bucco's Vesuvio – Kitchen
Livia's House
Christopher's Car
MRI Center – MRI Machine Room
The Pork Store
The Pork Store – Butchering Area
Airport Area Topless Bar
Green Grove Retirement Community
Il Granaio
Cabin Cruiser – Below Decks
Cabin Cruiser – Top Deck
Apartment Bedroom
Cathedral
Junior's Lincoln
Soprano House – Garage

EXTERIORS
Soprano House
Soprano Backyard
Soprano Backyard – Pool
Street – US/HMO
Parking Lot
The Pork Store
Bucco's Vesuvio
Elm Parkway/Livia's House
Construction Site
State Park
Pitch 'n' Putt
Barone Sanitation
Manhattan
Il Granaio
Marina
Inner City Parochial School
Cathedral
Plastic Mound
Parochial School Ball Court

FADE IN:

1: INT. DR. MELFI'S WAITING ROOM – DAY

ANTHONY SOPRANO, 40, sits and waits. Uneasily. Staring confusedly at a vaguely erotic Klimt reproduction. Inner door opens. DR. JENNIFER MELFI (attractive, 35) appears.

> **MELFI**
> Mr. Soprano?

2: INT. DR. MELFI'S OFFICE – DAY

Melfi gestures Tony to a choice of seating.

> **MELFI**
> Have a seat.

She seats herself in a facing armchair. She looks at him with a polite, expectant gaze. He stares back, waiting. There is utter silence. Nothing happens. Such is psychotherapy. Finally –

> **MELFI (cont'd)**
> My understanding from your family physician, Dr. Cusamano, is you collapsed? Were unable to breathe? Possibly a panic attack?

> **TONY**
> They said it was a panic attack – because all the neurological work and blood came back negative. They sent me here.

> **MELFI**
> You don't agree you had a panic attack?

He laughs – too loud.

> **MELFI (cont'd)**
> How are you feeling now?

> **TONY**
> Now? Fine. I'm back at work.

> **MELFI**
> What line of work are you in?

> **TONY**
> Waste management consultant.

> **MELFI**
> Any thoughts at all on why you blacked out?

Tony shrugs. Fidgets. Then –

> **TONY**
> I don't know. Stress, maybe?

> **MELFI**
> Stress? About what?

3: DAWN

The first rays over the post-industrial landscape.

> **TONY (V.O.)**
> Well, I once heard some guy use this expression, 'The sun setting over the empire...?'

4: EXT. SOPRANO HOUSE – DAWN

Split-level. New Jersey. The only thing distinguishing it from its neighbors is high security fencing and mercury vapor lamps that make the lawn bright enough for night baseball. A sensor reels the dawn's rays and the lamps switch off and –

5: INT. SOPRANO HOUSE – BEDROOM – DAWN

Tony's EYE slams open from sleep. He stares soberly up at the ceiling.

> **TONY (V.O.)**
> That morning of the day I got sick? I'd been thinking: it's good to be in a thing from the ground floor. I came too late for that, I know. But lately I'm getting the feeling I might be in at the end. That the best is over.

6: EXT. SOPRANO HOUSE – DAY

Bathrobed Tony reads his morning paper in the gated driveway: CLINTON WARNS MEDICARE COULD BE BANKRUPT BY YEAR 2000. Tony goes to the Sports, ambles down the driveway.

> **MELFI (V.O.)**
> Many Americans, I think, feel this.

> **TONY (V.O.)**
> Take my father. He never reached the heights like me. But in ways he had it better. He had his people – they had their standards. They had pride. Today what do we got?

> **MELFI (V.O.)**
> Did you have this feeling of loss more acutely in the hours before you collapsed?

7: EXT. SOPRANO HOUSE – BACKYARD – DAY

An expanse of lawn, then a pool with Tropitone furniture. Tony gathers speed, excited. But reaching the pool, he looks around, worried. The water is like glass. The morning is too still.

> **TONY (V.O.)**
> I dunno. Couple months before all this these two wild ducks had landed in my pool. Amazing. From Canada or someplace, I don't know. It was mating season.

DUCK FAMILY

Wild mallards, mother and babies, come waddling from the bushes, QUACKING. Tony beams, takes feed from a bin and drops down on both knees. He feeds them.

> **TONY (cont'd)**
> Yum. Yum.

8: INT. SOPRANO HOUSE – KITCHEN – DAY

CARMELA SOPRANO (mid 30's), in bathrobe, makes breakfast for her kids. She is a dark-eyed, dark-haired, pretty woman with blonde hi-lites. Hi-lites and nails are a priority. At the table are MEADOW SOPRANO, 15, and her friend, HUNTER SCANGARELO.

> **TONY (V.O.)**
> My daughter's friend was there to drive my daughter, Meadow, to school.

> **HUNTER**
> *(staring out window)*
> Meadow, your father with those ducks.

> **CARMELA**
> Have something more than just cranapple juice, ladies. You need brain food for school.

ANTHONY JR. enters. He's thirteen. He sits, starts spooning cereal in. Carmela smooches him. Everyone ad-libs happy birthdays. He acknowledges, his mouth crammed with food.

> **HUNTER**
> The male and female duck just made a home in your pool and 'did it'? Weird.

> **CARMELA**
> *(crosses with pastry)*
> Girls, you want some of last night's sfogliatell'?

> **MEADOW**
> Get out of here with that fat.

> **CARMELA**
> Oh, have a bite.

> **MEADOW**
> Wait – like Italian pastry is <u>brain</u> food?

> **HUNTER**
> Bon Jovi? Hello?

They laugh. Anthony Jr.'s hand goes in the box; he dunks the Italian pastry in his cereal milk and eats. The girls 'ee-ew'.

> **HUNTER (cont'd)**
> How do you stay so skinny, Mrs. Soprano?

Carmela isn't listening. She is staring out somberly.

9: EXT. SOPRANO HOUSE – BACKYARD – POOL – DAY

Tony has waded into the pool to adjust a plywood launching ramp he has constructed for the ducks. His robe floats on the water; he doesn't care. He talks to the ducks.

> **TONY**
> Don't you worry. I'll make you a better ramp.

The ducklings suddenly furiously flap their wings in protoflight, following their mother's lead.

> **TONY (cont'd)**
> Kids! Come here!

10: INT. SOPRANO HOUSE – KITCHEN – DAY

> **TONY (V.O.)**
> Hey, kids!

The teenagers trudge dutifully to the door.

11: EXT. SOPRANO HOUSE – BACKYARD – POOL – DAY

> **TONY**
> Look! They're trying to fly.

> **KIDS**
> *(bored, humoring)*
> Nice, dad. *National Geographic.* [ETC.]

They go back inside.

12: INT. SOPRANO HOUSE – KITCHEN – DAY

> **HUNTER**
> It is so cool you're going to be able to come to Aspen with my family at Christmas. Last year at Aspen? I saw Skeet Ulrich. As close as from where you're sitting.

> **MEADOW**
> Omigod.

13: INT. DR. MELFI'S OFFICE – DAY

> **TONY**
> My wife feels this friend of Meadow's is a bad influence.

14: INT. SOPRANO HOUSE – KITCHEN – DAY

> **CARMELA**
> Miss Meadow, we made a deal – you keep your school grades up and you keep your curfew between now and Christmas – then you get to go.

> **MEADOW**
> *(edge)*
> I know that.

Tony enters, robe gone, his lower torso wrapped in a beach towel. He claps Anthony Jr. on the back.

> **TONY**
> Happy Birthday, son.

He runs his hand on Carmela's butt, but she seems not to notice. So he starts slap fighting with Anthony Jr.

> **CARMELA**
> You're going to be home tonight for Tony Jr.'s party, right?
> *(to his grunt)*
> Birdman. Hello?

Tony is reaching for The Audubon Society "Master Guide to Birding" and getting engrossed.

> **TONY**
> I'll get home from work early.

> **CARMELA**
> I wasn't talking about work.

She moves off sullenly. As he watches her –

15: INT. DR. MELFI'S OFFICE – DAY

Tony – in the present – a strained silence. She stares.

> **TONY**
> This isn't going to work. I can't talk about my personal life.

> **MELFI**
> It's hard for everybody.

> **TONY**
> You don't understand.

> **MELFI**
> Finish telling me about the day you collapsed.

16: INT. CHRISTOPHER'S CAR – DAY

Back to the past. Brand new Lexus 400.

> **TONY (V.O.)**
> I rode to work with my nephew, Christopher...he's learning the business.

CHRISTOPHER MOLTISANTI (25) is in cool-ass cruise mode. Good looking – almost pretty – wears an earring, a Jersey Shark's ball cap. He is chuckling at Howard Stern on the radio. Tony rides passenger, engrossed in his Audubon book.

Rust-belt New Jersey floats by: the Meadowlands – mile after mile of marsh, iron bridges, and raw honking trucking. The skyline of Manhattan beckons from the distance.

> **TONY (V.O.) (cont'd)**
> He's an example of what I was saying before –

> **TONY (cont'd)**
> You call whatisname at Triboro Towers about the hauling contract?

> **CHRISTOPHER**
> I got home too late last night. I didn't want to wake the man up.

> **TONY**
> You get up early this morning and call? He's always in the office at six.

> **CHRISTOPHER**
> I was nauseous this morning. My mom told me I shouldn't even go in today.

> **TONY (V.O.)**
> Bear in mind, this is a kid who just bought himself a 60,000 dollar Lexus.

They are now in a business district. Christopher's head whips around.

17: EXT. STREET – BUSINESS DISTRICT – US/HMO – DAY

> **CHRISTOPHER**
> It's that guy. Mahaffey.

> **TONY**
> Get out.

> **CHRISTOPHER**
> Back there. See? With the boo-boo in red?

> **TONY**
> Back up.

ON MAHAFFEY

a forty-four-year-old executive, walking with a YOUNG WOMAN, a secretary. They carry lattes and bagels.

The Lexus pulls up. Tony gets out –

18: INT. DR. MELFI'S OFFICE – DAY

Tony has stopped talking.

> **TONY**
> There was an issue of an outstanding loan –

> **MELFI**
> Let me stop you a second.

> **TONY**
> Sure.

> **MELFI**
> I have no idea where this story is going...but there are a few ethical ground rules we should quickly get out of the way.

He waits. She smiles nervously.

> **MELFI (cont'd)**
> You said you were in waste management...

> **TONY**
> Recycle. The environment.

> **MELFI**
> Dr. Cusamano, besides being your family physician, is also your next door neighbor. See what I'm saying?

> **TONY**
> I get it. Yeah.

> **MELFI**
> *(dry mouth)*
> What you tell me in here falls under doctor/patient confidentiality. Except – if I was, for example, to hear that a... say a... murder?... was about to take place –
> *(quickly)*
> – not that I'm saying – but, it. Well, anything like that... where a patient tells me someone is going to be hurt? I'm supposed to go to the authorities. Technically.

> **TONY**
> *(long beat)*
> Oh.

> **MELFI**
> I don't know what happened with this Mahaffey fellow. I'm just saying.

> **TONY**
> I see.
>
> *(beat)*
> Nothing. We had coffee.

19: EXT. STREET – BUSINESS DISTRICT – US/HMO – DAY

When Mahaffey sees Tony, his latte spatters the sidewalk as he takes off running! Christopher takes after him.

THE PURSUIT

Christopher and Mahaffey burn up the sidewalk. Bystanders peer curiously.

Tony calmly gets behind the Lexus wheel, makes a U-turn.

Mahaffey runs toward a sleek five story office building, US/HMO. He cuts across the lawn making for the front entrance.

> **MAHAFFEY**
> Security!

Christopher closes, grabs him by his neck, tries to swing him to the ground. Christopher loses his footing on the slippery grass and Mahaffey twirls free. But Christopher is now between him and the door; Mahaffey cuts for the parking lot, panting, full out, grabbing in his pocket for his car keys. Christopher runs after him into the lot.

20: EXT. PARKING LOT – DAY

Tony suddenly draws abreast of Christopher in the Lex, gives a cheerful TOOT, then accelerates down the parking aisle.

Mahaffey's legs churning.

THE LEXUS

deliberately clips Mahaffey. He hurls over the car about thirty feet, crashes to the ground. Tony calmly gets out.

> **MAHAFFEY**
> My leg! It's broken! Oh fuck, oh fuck, the bone's coming through!

Tony starts punching him in the face briskly and efficiently.

> **TONY**
> *(punching)*
> I'll give you a fuckin' bone. Where's my money?

The secretary comes up, watches in horror. One of the Lexus' headlights hangs by its wires and Christopher broken-heartedly tries to put it back in.

> **MAHAFFEY**
> I'll get the money!

> **TONY**
> *(punching, but tiring)*
> I know you'll get the –
> *(sees Christopher fussing over the car)*
> The fuck you doing? Get over here.

Christopher crosses, takes over the physical labor – kicking Mahaffey in chest and stomach while Tony catches his breath and picks up where he left off –

> **TONY (cont'd)**
> I know you'll get the money. What you ought to fuckin' get is a fuckin' cork to put in your mouth.

US/HMO employees watch from windows.

> **TONY (cont'd)**
> *(as he and Christopher kick in Mahaffey's ribs)*
> Huh? You tell people I'm nothin' to worry about compared to who used to run things?

> **MAHAFFEY**
> I'm sorry, I'm sorry.

Tony heads back to the car. Christopher's eyes rest on the eyes of Mahaffey's young, horrified secretary. Christopher gets in the car.

> **MAHAFFEY (cont'd)**
> *(screaming)*
> My leg. Ohmigod! Fuck!

> **TONY**
> *(sees US/HMO sign)*
> HMO. What are you fuckin' crying about? At least you're covered.

21: INT. CHRISTOPHER'S CAR – DAY

Christopher drives. Tony massages his knuckles.

> **CHRISTOPHER**
> What you thinking about?

> **TONY**
> HMO's.

> **CHRISTOPHER**
> Homos?

> **TONY**
> HMO! HMO! It's a medical care provider. Read a fuckin' paper once in a while, Christopher.

22: INT. DR. MELFI'S OFFICE – DAY

Tony and Melfi are looking at each other in the psychiatric silence.

> **MELFI**
> So you had coffee.

> **TONY**
> Right.

> **MELFI**
> Go on.

> **TONY**
> Next? Let's see, I had a breakfast meeting.

23: EXT. THE PORK STORE – DAY

Italian-American inner city neighborhood; an Italian butcher shop with a plaster pig on top. At a little table out front under the Stell D'Oro umbrella sit Tony, Christopher, a large man, BIG PUSSY BONPENSIERO, PETER "PAULIE WALNUTS" GUALTIERI and trash hauling company owner DICK BARONE. A young butcher in a blood-stained apron serves espresso.

BIG PUSSY BONPENSIERO should not be confused with LITTLE PUSSY MALANGA, of whom we shall learn more shortly.

> **TONY**
> So what's going on at Triboro Towers?

> **BIG PUSSY**
> The site manager wants to renew his contract with Dick. But this Kolar Sanitation...

> **DICK BARONE**
> Nationwide company.

> **BIG PUSSY**
> The Kolar brothers, they're some kind of Czechoslovakian immigrants or some shit – these Polacks'll haul the paper, plastic and aluminum for seventy-five thousand a month less than Dick.

> **TONY**
> So Kolar pays you the regular forty times the monthly for stealing your stop.

> **BIG PUSSY**
> That's the thing – he won't. Says if he could tell the Commie bosses back in Czechoslovakia to go fuck themselves, he can fuckin' tell us.

> **TONY**
> Fucking garbage business.

> **BIG PUSSY**
> I know. It's all changing.

> **CHRISTOPHER**
> Let me see what I can do.

> **TONY**
> You sure? You over your stomachache?

A black STS has pulled up and nattily dressed SILVIO DANTE heads for the Pork Store. Tony spots him. All ad lib hellos all around.

> **SILVIO**
> Gabriella sends me down here for the gabagool.

> **PAULIE WALNUTS**
> Best in the area.

> **SILVIO**
> Tony, I'm thinking: did you go to elementary school with a guy named Artie Bucco?

24: INT. DR. MELFI'S OFFICE – DAY

> **TONY**
> So this situation came up. It involves my uncle. I can't go into detail on this one.

> **MELFI**
> *(relieved)*
> That's fine.

TONY
But I'll say this — my uncle adds to my general stress level.

25: BACK TO THE PORK STORE

SILVIO
Probably none of my business, but down at the club, the word is your Uncle Junior is going to whack Little Pussy Malanga...

26: EXT. BUCCO'S VESUVIO – DAY

Christopher's Lexus drives up to the restaurant.

SILVIO (V.O.)
...in your friend Artie Bucco's restaurant.

27: INT. BUCCO'S VESUVIO – DAY

A cozy Italian eatery for politicians, wise-guys. Tony and Christopher stop at a booth ruled by Tony's uncle, CORRADO "JUNIOR" SOPRANO, and other geriatric mobsters in cheap cardigan sweaters. Junior is smallish with coke-bottle lenses. His muscle, BEPPY, sits beside him.

TONY
(pats his neck)
Uncle Jun', how you doing?

JUNIOR
(warm hug)
I was just talking about you. Tony Jr.'s birthday dinner tonight, right?

TONY
Don't buy him anything big. We overindulge him.

Tony and Christopher move on to ARTHUR BUCCO – an affable restaurateur Tony's age. They hug.

TONY (cont'd)
Arthur! What's the word at land of a thousand clams?

ARTHUR
Jefe.

CHARMAINE, Arthur's wife, watches sourly from the cash register. Tony blows her a big kiss. He and Christopher sit at a prime booth.

CHRISTOPHER
You know what that means for Arthur, one of these old mutts gets wet in here?

TONY
Ruin his business.

CHRISTOPHER
You better sit down with your uncle.

TONY (V.O.)
Uncle Junior is my father's brother. A good guy, but old now and crabby. He used to take me to Yankee games when I was a kid. I love my uncle.

28: EXT. ELM PARKWAY/LIVIA'S HOUSE – DAY

A middle-class street of three-story clapboard homes.

TONY (V.O.)
At the same time, Uncle Junior also told our girl cousins I would never be a varsity athlete. I found out he'd said that and, frankly, it was a tremendous blow to my self-esteem.

Christopher waits in the Lexus as Tony carries a Bose carton to a large three-story home, pats himself down for a key, RINGS bell. Presently...

> **VOICE**
> Who's there?

> **TONY**
> It's me, mom.

> **VOICE**
> Who are you?

> **TONY**
> Ma, open the door!

> **VOICE**
> Tony?

> **TONY**
> Ma, open the door!

> **CARMELA**

Four locks operate, the door squeaks open a crack and Tony's mother, LIVIA SOPRANO, warily peers out. Tony enters.

29: INT. LIVIA'S HOUSE – DAY

> **TONY**
> Jeez, Ma, get some air in here.

He flings open a window. Livia looks older than her sixty-nine years. She's wearing a housecoat and slippers.

> **LIVIA**
> Did you lock the door behind you?

> **TONY**
> *(wearily)*
> Yes.

> **LIVIA**
> Somebody phone me last night. After dark.

> **TONY**
> Who?

> **LIVIA**
> You think I'd answer the phone? It was dark out.

> **TONY**
> Ma, that I will never get. The phone is an auditory thing. Dark is an eye thing. Some people won't go out after dark – okay – get jumped from the shadows – but not answer the phone after dark?

> **LIVIA**
> Listen to him. He knows everything. You want some lunch? I got eggplant.

> **TONY**
> I just ate.

She goes into the kitchen and starts fixing him food anyway. Tony takes a new table-top CD player from the carton.

> **TONY (cont'd)**
> Know who I just saw? Uncle Junior.

> **LIVIA**
> That one. Think he ever comes to see his sister-in-law?

TONY
Remember Artie Bucco? My friend in elementary school?

LIVIA
I still see his mother. She tells me he calls her every day.

TONY
(doesn't rise to the bait)
Thing is...Uncle Junior...he's gonna make a problem for Arthur. It would impact on Arthur's livelihood.

LIVIA
(eyes CD player)
What's that?

TONY
CD player.

LIVIA
(put upon)
For who? For me? I don't want it.

TONY
You love music. All the old stuff's being reissued on CD, your favorites.
(shows CDs)
Look... Connie Francis... 'Pajama Game'...

He puts a CD on. Steam Heat from 'Pajama Game' fills the room. He tries to waltz her around.

TONY (cont'd)
Ma, you need something to occupy your mind. When dad died you were going to do all kinds of things–

LIVIA
(tears up)
He was a saint.

TONY
I know, but he's gone. You were going to do volunteer work, travel. You've done nothing.

LIVIA
Don't you tell me how to live. You shut up.

TONY
I worry about you.

LIVIA
Don't you start with that nursing home again!

TONY
It is not a nursing home. How many times I have to say it? It's a 'retirement community'. You're with active seniors your own age. They do things. They go places.

LIVIA
(crying)
I've seen these women in these nursing homes. In these wheelchairs. Babbling like idiots. Eat your eggplant.

TONY
I told you I just ate lunch! Maybe you could talk to Uncle Jun' about Artie Bucco. He respects you...

LIVIA
If your uncle has business with Arthur – then he knows what he's doing.

TONY
And I don't?

LIVIA
All I know is girls take better care of their mothers than sons.

TONY
I bought CDs for the broken record lady. I didn't drive my sisters out of state.

He gets up. Moves toward front door.

TONY (cont'd)
I expect to see you at Tony Jr.'s dinner tonight with the baked ziti.

LIVIA
Only if someone picks me up and drives me home. I don't drive when they're predicting rain.

30: EXT. LIVIA'S HOUSE – DAY

TONY
You're a healthy girl. It's good for you to drive. Use it or lose it.
(kisses her on cheek)
I have to get back to work.

LIVIA
Sure. Run off.

31: EXT. SOPRANO HOUSE – BACKYARD – DAY

Carmela has generated an astounding array of food, yet she still looks, as Christopher once remarked "eminently fuckable." Tony is taking off his jacket, she hands him a platter of steaks and sausage.

TONY (V.O.)
That night it was my son's birthday party.

TONY (cont'd)
Maybe I should go get my mother.

CARMELA
No way. She's jerking your chain.

She lets him kiss her. Just then –

FATHER PHIL
You had a recipe for creme anglais all the time, Carmela. Right here in 'Julia Child'.

FATHER PHIL, thirtysomething priest, wanders out of the house carrying a cookbook, wearing an apron. Tony immediately chills.

FATHER PHIL (cont'd)
Oh, hi, Tony. You like creme anglais?

TONY
You bless it, I'll eat it.

ANTHONY JR.
(enters with portable phone)
Grandma's not coming. She started crying and hung up.

TONY
She needs a purpose in life.

CARMELA
Your mother's tougher than you think.

> ANTHONY JR.
> *(bummed)*
> No fucking ziti now?

> BOTH PARENTS
> *(sharply)*
> Hey!

> VOICE
> Where's everybody?

32: INT. SOPRANO HOUSE – HALLWAYS – DAY

Uncle Junior wanders, his eyes swimming in the thick lenses. He carries a huge birthday present and a wrinkled paper bag.

> JUNIOR
> I brung fresh arugula from my garden.

33: EXT. SOPRANO HOUSE – BACKYARD – DAY

Tony stands at a top-of-the-line barbecue kettle, lights fluid-soaked charcoal. Whoosh. He is moving the lighter fluid out of the way to make room when –

The duck family are all beating their wings in the pool. CAMERA slows to dreamlike slo-mo as the mother levitates. The first duckling becomes airborne... then the second... then the others... they follow their mother up into the air.

Tony watches with both joy and horror as they circle his yard once, then fly off forever, their QUACKS receding.

> TONY (V.O.)
> At first it felt like ginger ale in my skull.

Suddenly Tony's eyes roll, he clutches his head, crashes into the kettle. The lighter fluid can drops from his hand onto the coals. He falls to the grass.

Carmela and family rush out.

> CARMELA
> Oh, my God –

Silvio Dante and family, just arriving, react in alarm.

Carmela is moving toward Tony. Is driven back as the can of lighter fluid explodes – a ball of orange flame that completely destroys the kettle. Tony, unconscious, has no awareness. Silvio grabs a fire extinguisher and starts shooting hot coals that have blown out of the grille.

34: OMITTED

35: INT. MRI CENTER – MRI MACHINE ROOM – DAY

The magnetic oracle hums. Tony lies alone and naked on a tray, about to be served to the machine.

> TONY (V.O.)
> Dr. Cusamano put me in the hospital. I had every kind of test.

A speaker in the room clicks on.

> VOICE
> When you're in the machine, there's a microphone by your head if you get claustrophobia and have to come out. Only we suggest that you don't do that 'cause we'll only have to start over again from the beginning.

> TONY
> Okay.

No answer. Moments pass. Nothing happens. A door opens.

> **TONY (cont'd)**
> Carmela...?

She brings a chair over from the wall. Sits beside him.

> **CARMELA**
> I thought maybe you'd want some company.

> **TONY**
> *(surprised)*
> Thanks. Six-thirty in the morning? How are the kids?

> **CARMELA**
> Worried about you – I told Tony Jr. we'd rain check his birthday.

> **TONY**
> Carm', you think I have a brain tumor?

> **CARMELA**
> Well, we'll find out.

> **TONY**
> *(pissed off)*
> What a bedside manner. Very encouraging.

> **CARMELA**
> What are you gonna, not know?

Beat.

> **TONY**
> We've had some good times, some good years.

> **CARMELA**
> Here he goes now with the nostalgia.

> **TONY**
> What I'm saying – no marriage is perfect.

> **CARMELA**
> But having that goomar' on the side helps.

> **TONY**
> I don't see her anymore, I told you. How do you think I like it, having that priest in my house all the time?

> **CARMELA**
> *(eyes narrow)*
> Don't even go there. Father is a spiritual mentor – he's helping me to be a better Catholic.

> **TONY**
> We all have different needs.

> **CARMELA**
> What's different between you and me is you're going to Hell when you die.

That about kills the conversation. The machine hums. A technician enters and Tony tenses up. Carmela unhesitatingly takes his hand. The technician gives Carmela prism eyeglasses which she places on Tony.

TONY'S POV

A weird prism look ninety degrees past his own head that allows him to keep tenuous visual contact with Carmela as he goes into the machine.

Carmela smoothes his hair, says something loving. But the MRI machine makes its hellish hammering which drowns everything out and continues into –

36: INT. THE PORK STORE – NIGHT

Christopher, alone, does a Kung Fu dance in the glow of the meat cases.

> **TONY (V.O.)**
> My nephew, Christopher, was handling the garbage contract problem while I was in the hospital. On this here also you don't need to know the details.

A Ford van with KOLAR SANITATION on its door pulls up outside. EMIL KOLAR, 24, gets out. He comes to the Pork Store, knocks. The door is opened a crack by Christopher.

> **CHRISTOPHER**
> Yeah?

> **KOLAR**
> Emil. Kolar.

Christopher lets him in. The two cross to a door toward the rear –

> **CHRISTOPHER**
> Money, hope this don't give you indigestion. It's private here like we need. To talk.

This as they go into –

37: OMITTED

38: INT. THE PORK STORE – BUTCHERING AREA – NIGHT

Lamb's heads, pigs' trotters, hanging carcasses.

> **KOLAR**
> In the Czech Republic, too, we love pork. You ever have our sausages?

> **CHRISTOPHER**
> I thought the only sausages were Italian and Jimmy Dean's. See what you learn when you cross cultures and shit?

> **KOLAR**
> My Uncle Uvzen doesn't know I came. But if we make any progress here tonight I will have to tell him.

> **CHRISTOPHER**
> We have to make progress, Email. We must stop the madness. The garbage business is changing. We're the younger generation. We have issues in common.

> **KOLAR**
> Emil.

> **CHRISTOPHER**
> Where'd you go to high school? Poland?

> **KOLAR**
> *(angry)*
> I'm not Polish.

> **CHRISTOPHER**
> Well, what's Czechoslovakian? Isn't that a type of Polack?

> **KOLAR**
> We came to this country when I was nine. I went to West Essex.

> **CHRISTOPHER**
> Yo, money. My cousin Anthony's school used to play you in football. He went to Boonton.

> **KOLAR**
> *(impatient)*
> Where's the...?

CHRISTOPHER
Ah, yes, the reason for the visit.

He beckons Kolar to a table where lines of coke are arranged on a cleaver blade.

CHRIS
Taste the wares, Email.

Kolar takes the straw, leans over to dose. Christopher places a Glock 9mm to the back of his head and fires. Kolar sprawls forward onto the butcher block. Christopher fires three more times. One of the severed lamb's heads appears to be watching. Christopher addresses it.

CHRISTOPHER
Can you see him yet? Has he arrived where you are?

39: EXT. BUCCO'S VESUVIO – DAY

Couple of days later. Tony, Uncle Junior and his bodyguard, and Beppy, a crony, emerge from the restaurant laughing, kidding.

TONY (V.O.)
The doctors kept me hanging about the neurological tests. My Uncle Junior and I played a round of golf and then had lunch.

MELFI (V.O.)
In what way is your uncle a problem for you?

JUNIOR
Who do you think you are?

TONY
The guy who says how things go is who I think I am. Artie's dinner business is nice upscale people from the suburbs. Don't ruin his life.

BEPPY
Vesuvio is where Pussy feels safe! He's been eating there for years.

TONY
Kill him someplace else.

JUNIOR
You may run North Jersey, but you don't run your Uncle Junior – how many fuckin' hours did I spend playing catch with you – ?

40: OMITTED

41: INT. SOPRANO HOUSE – FAMILY ROOM – NIGHT

MELFI (V.O.)
You keep bringing up this uncle. What about your immediate family? They're more important to the work here.

TONY (V.O.)
(sighs)
My wife and daughter aren't getting along.

Father Phil is sunk deep in the cushions with his feet up, wiggling his toes. "Field of Dreams" is on TV. Carmela enters with buttered popcorn.

FATHER PHIL
Darn but these laser disks are incredible.

CARMELA
Tony watches "Godfather 2" all the time. He says the camera work looks just as good as in the movie theater.

FATHER PHIL
(stuffing his face with popcorn)
Gordon Willis. Tony prefers '2', not '1'?

>CARMELA

He likes the part where Vito goes back to Sicily. '3', he was like, "what happened...?"

>FATHER PHIL

Where does Tony rank 'Goodfellas'?

They hear a SOUND on the roof.

>FATHER PHIL

You have raccoons?

>CARMELA

Too heavy. Someone's walking!

She looks out the window. The lawn is empty and iridescent green in the mercury lamps. The NOISE happens again. Carmela reaches up into a closet, comes out with an AK-47. Loads and locks.

>FATHER PHIL

Jeez Louise...

42: INT. GARAGE – NIGHT

Carmela comes downstairs into garage. Father pads behind in Birkenstocks. Carmela, gun ready, sees back door ajar. She tiptoes warily, edges along. Rounds corner and aims up at an intruder.

43: EXT. SOPRANO HOUSE – BACKYARD – NIGHT

>CARMELA

Hold it!

Someone trying to jimmy a window – turns in fear.

>CARMELA

Meadow...?

A glaring security lamp behind Meadow makes Carmela shield her eyes.

>CARMELA

What are you doing?

Meadow is also squinting into a bright light.

>MEADOW

I noticed this glass rattles every time I walk to the laundry room. Do we have any...what do you call, putty?

>CARMELA
>*(to Meadow)*

Don't give me that. You snuck out.

>ANTHONY JR.
>*(appears, casual)*

What's going on?

>MEADOW

You locked my bedroom window on purpose so I'd get caught!

>CARMELA

Normal people thought you were upstairs doing your homework. You're becoming a master of lying and conniving.

>ANTHONY JR.

Right in front of Father.

She lunges for Anthony Jr.

>FATHER PHIL

Guys. Let's dial down the casting stones a few notches.

> **MEADOW**
> *(to Carmela)*
> You're so strict about curfew I have to sneak out.

> **CARMELA**
> Don't start with me with what other parents allow. You're in the Soprano household.

> **MEADOW**
> I know I'm grounded. But Patrick's swim meet is tomorrow and he needed me.

> **CARMELA**
> For this? Grounded. Oh, no. You're not going to Aspen with Hunter Scangarelo – that's where you're not going.

Meadow's whole face falls in disbelief. She glares.

> **MEADOW**
> Okay, mom.
> *(sobs; runs inside)*
> If this is the way you want it...

44: INT. DR. MELFI'S OFFICE – DAY

> **TONY**
> But, look, this shit I'm telling you, it'll all blow over.

> **MELFI**
> Didn't you admit to Dr. Cusamano you were feeling depressed?

He doesn't want to answer.

> **Tony**
> Melfi. What part of The Boot, hon?

> **MELFI**
> My father's people were from Caserta.

> **TONY**
> *(points to self)*
> Avellino. My mother would have loved it if you and I had hooked up.

He wonders why he said that. Clams up.

> **MELFI**
> Anxiety attacks are a legitimate psychiatric emergency. Suppose you were driving and passed out.

> **TONY**
> Let me tell you something – today everybody goes to shrinks and counselors. Everybody goes on Sally Jesse Raphael and talks about their problems.
> *(building anger)*
> Whatever happened to Gary Cooper? The strong silent type. That was an American. He wasn't in touch with his feelings. He did what he had to do!
> *(almost yelling)*
> Unfortunately, what they didn't know was once they got Gary Cooper in touch with his feelings, they wouldn't be able to shut him up!
> Dysfunction this! Dysfunction that! Dysfunction va fan cul'!

> **MELFI**
> You have strong feelings about this.

> **TONY**
> Let me tell you something – I understand Freud. I had a semester and a half of college. So, sure, I get therapy as a concept. But in my world it doesn't go down.

He stares at her.

TONY
Could I be a little happier? Sure. Who couldn't?

MELFI
Do you feel depressed?

He averts his eyes. Admits.

TONY
Since the ducks left, I guess.

MELFI
The ducks that preceded your losing consciousness. Let's talk about them.

He simply gets up and leaves.

45: INT. AIRPORT AREA TOPLESS BAR – DAY

Two NAKED DANCERS grind away on small stage/riser to the beat of En Vogue. Men hunch over draft beers watching the women with expressionless eyes. Tony and Christopher are at a back booth having drinks with HERMAN "HESH" RABKIN, 70, whose bulk is swaddled in Filawear.

HERMAN
Mahaffey does not have the money.

CHRISTOPHER
What do you mean Mahaffey does not have the money?

HERMAN
Mahaffey does not have the money.

CHRISTOPHER
How could he not have the money?

HERMAN
The man does not have the money.

CHRISTOPHER
We ran over him with the car. T. himself —

HERMAN
(shrugs)
The man has no wiggle room. He is bled dry.

A waitress sets down a round of drinks.

HERMAN
So I hear Junior wants to whack Pussy Bonpensiero?

TONY
Pussy Malanga.

HERMAN
Oh, Little Pussy...

TONY
Yeah, Little Pussy. You think he's going to fuck with Big Pussy? My Pussy?

Silvio Dante appears.

SILVIO
Sandrine, this table, drinks on the house, all night.

HERMAN
Your uncle resents that you are boss.

33

SILVIO
The sadness accrues.

HERMAN
Junior's had a hard-on all his life – first, that your father, his younger brother, was a made guy before him? Now you? So, sure, he can't stomach you telling him what to do.

TONY
Yet I love him.

HERMAN
The man is driven in toto by his insecurities. He register the beef with New York?

TONY
He's got their okay on the hit.

SILVIO
(moving off)
I feel bad I was the messenger.

HERMAN
Your friend with the restaurant – send his sinuses to Arizona.
(off Tony's look)
Get him out of town for three weeks. This way the restaurant closes. The hit has to go down somewhere else.

TONY
No wonder my old man relied on you, you fuckin' Jew.

HERMAN
What about the fuckin' Jew's two fifty on Mahaffey's hundred?

TONY
Mahaffey now has a business partner. You. Every day these HMOs pay out millions in claims. Doctors, hospitals...a fuckin' MRI costs a grand a pop. We give Mahaffey a choice – he either has his company start paying out on phoney claims – to fake clinics we set up – or he pays Hesh the two hundred and fifty thousand he owes – which we know he cannot do – or it's a fuckin' rainy night in Lyndhurst.

HERMAN
That's very smart. This could be major.

Tony
Could be as good as garbage.

CHRISTOPHER
(emotional)
Garbage is our bread and butter.

TONY
Was.

46: INT. GREEN GROVE RETIREMENT COMMUNITY – DAY

Tony, Carmela, the kids and Livia tour the facility. It resembles a hotel on Cap Ferrat. Well-dressed seniors read or hurry to various activities. Livia keeps knotting her hands.

TONY
Wow, look at this, mom.

DIRECTOR
(indicates library)
Our lecture series in action – today it's someone from the university, they're discussing the novels of – I believe – Zora Neale Hurston.

> **CARMELA**
> Didn't you just read her in school, Med'?

Nothing. Cold freezeout.

> **ANTHONY JR.**
> This place is neat, Grandma. You should really think about this.

> **LIVIA**
> What's going on behind there?

> **DIRECTOR**
> Those doors lead to our nursing unit.

> **LIVIA**
> This is a nursing home!

> **DIRECTOR**
> This is a residence, but just in case -

> **LIVIA**
> You're not putting me in a nursing home! I've seen these women in these nursing homes, babbling like idiots!

Residents look up. Tony turns crimson.

> **TONY**
> You're not listening – what the lady said was –

> **LIVIA**
> *(to director)*
> You think you're pretty high and mighty here, don't you, with your fancy authors!

Tony squints... blinks... can't breathe... steadies himself on a table.

> **LIVIA**
> *(to Tony)*
> People come here to die. If your father saw what you're doing...

Then, crash, down he goes –

47: EXT. CONSTRUCTION SITE – NIGHT

The street is dark. A forty foot roll-away trash container is labelled KOLAR SANITATION. Christopher's Lexus drives up, lights off. Christopher and Big Pussy get out and go to the trunk. Christopher pops the lid.

They muscle Emil Kolar's body out. It's wrapped in a plastic tarp. They carry Kolar toward the roll-away container.

> **BIG PUSSY**
> You can't blame T. for being pissed you whacked this kid. You should have waited for me, Christopher.

> **CHRISTOPHER**
> Last time I show any fuckin' initiative. And then – can you imagine, Pussy, how I felt when T. runs down the garbage business. And I just fuckin' wet a guy to help hold on to one of our stops.

> **BIG PUSSY**
> He's not running it down. It's just gettin' harder in New York. Sure T. wants to keep any contracts we got.

> **CHRISTOPHER**
> So. Kolar Sanitation'll finally get the message. Ready?

> **BIG PUSSY**
> *(stops, holds heart)*
> Out of breath.

> **CHRISTOPHER**
> One... two...

They start to swing the corpse by its hands and feet.

> **CHRISTOPHER**
> ...three!

They let the body go, but it doesn't achieve the twelve vertical feet needed to go into the open-topped container.

Instead it goes CONK against the metal sidewall and flops to the street.

> **BIG PUSSY**
> Fuck.

They pick it up again.

> **CHRISTOPHER**
> One... two... three!

Up, up... CLONG. The head hits. It falls back into the street.

> **BIG PUSSY**
> Let's just sit him up against it.

> **CHRISTOPHER**
> It's better if he's in it.

> **BIG PUSSY**
> What are you, fuckin' Michelangelo? Sit him up against it or I'm gonna get really pissed off here now.

As they haul Kolar upright and try to prop him up –

> **BIG PUSSY**
> Wait a minute – this is fucked up.

> **CHRISTOPHER**
> (pissed)
> What, Pussy?

> **BIG PUSSY**
> The uncle's gonna find the kid dead on one of his bins and get out of our fuckin' business?

> **CHRISTOPHER**
> 'Louis Brassi sleeps with the fishes.'

> **BIG PUSSY**
> Luca Brassi. Luca.

> **CHRISTOPHER**
> Whatever.

> **BIG PUSSY**
> There's differences, Christopher, okay? From situation to situation. The Kolars know the kid is dead, it hardens their position. Plus, now the cops are looking for a fuckin' murderer.

> **CHRISTOPHER**
> (bored)
> Whatever.

> **BIG PUSSY**
> The kid disappears, never comes home, they know but they don't know. They hope maybe he'll turn up. IF.

They start lugging the body back to the car.

CHRISTOPHER
Pussy, T. with these mental seizures or whatever. If he kept getting worse, what would you do?

BIG PUSSY
I'm gonna tell you?

Christopher shrugs it off.

48: INT. DR. MELFI'S OFFICE – DAY

Tony sits with his face in his hands, unable to speak.

MELFI
So you've come back for help. Don't look at that as a defeat.

TONY
You can't imagine the humiliation. Beautiful retirement center I'm gonna spend five thousand a month on and she's yelling and screaming like a cafone.

MELFI
For us baby boomers, dealing with our parents' aging is extremely painful.

TONY
She's part of that generation raised in the Depression. But for her the Depression was a trip to Six Flags.

MELFI
There's that 'D' word again.

He slumps back in his chair.

MELFI
Eighteen million Americans are clinically depressed.

TONY
What's happened to society? Everything's broken down.

MELFI
We're not here to talk about society. We're here to talk about you. Stay with your mother.

TONY
Now that my father's dead? He's a saint. When he was alive?
    (scoffs)
My dad was tough. Ran his own crew. Guy like that and my mother wore him down a little nub. He was a squeaking gerbil when he died.

MELFI
Quite a formidable maternal presence.

TONY
I might as well be honest – I'm finding much of the satisfaction gone from my work, too.

MELFI
Why?

TONY
Probably because of RICO.

MELFI
Is he your brother?

TONY
The RICO statutes.

37

MELFI
Oh...of course...right.

TONY
You read the papers. How the Justice Department is using RICO and these legal strategies and electronic technology to squeeze our business.

MELFI
(sadly)
Do you ever have any qualms about how you actually make your living?

TONY
I find I have to be the sad clown – upbeat on the outside, crying on the inside.
(beat)
See, things are trending downward. Used to be, guy got pinched, he took his prison jolt no matter what. Everybody upheld the code of silence.
(shakes head)
Nowadays? No values. Guys today have no room in their life for the penal experience. So you get all this turning government witness.

MELFI
(stymied)
I see.

TONY
I feel exhausted just talking about it.

MELFI
Well –
(picks up prescription pad)
– with today's pharmacology, no one needs to suffer with feelings of exhaustion or depression.

TONY
Here we go...here comes the Prozac.

49: INT. SOPRANO HOUSE – PANTRY – DAY

Carmela, in gold and diamond bracelets and white gloves, opens the door, goes to a row of B&B Baked Beans cans. She unscrews the bottom of one – removes a wad of cash five inches thick, peels off what she needs.

50: INT. SOPRANOS HOUSE – HALLWAY/MEADOW'S ROOM – DAY

Carmela goes to a bedroom door and knocks.

CARMELA
Miss Meadow.

No response. Carmela pokes her head in, revealing Meadow on her bed.

MEADOW
I'm not going.

CARMELA
Every year on this date since you were itty-bitty, Mom and Meadow get all dolled up and drive to the Plaza for tea under Eloise's portrait. Look –
(waves white gloves)
Where's yours?

MEADOW
I have too much homework.

CARMELA
(smile faltering)
Med', it's our little tradition. We always have so much fun.

> **MEADOW**
> Tell you the truth, I've felt it was dumb since I was eight. I just go because you like it.

She goes to desk, pecks at computer keys.

> **CARMELA**
> *(hiding hurt)*
> And here I thought it was something we'd do long after you were married. With girls of your own.

> **MEADOW**
> Hopefully, I won't be living anywhere around here by then.

A silence. Broken by a merry computer voice.

> **COMPUTER VOICE**
> Check your mailbox!

> **CARMELA**
> Meadow, you can't lie and cheat and just break the rules you don't like.

Meadow shoots her an amused cynical look.

> **CARMELA**
> What? Is there something you want to say?

> **MEADOW**
> Look, mom, do you have any idea how much it means to actually go skiing in Aspen? You think that's going to happen every year? Like lame tea and scones at the Plaza Hotel?

> **CARMELA**
> Good-bye.

> **MEADOW**
> Close my door, please.

51: INTO. BUCCO'S VESUVIO – KITCHEN – DAY

Kitchen staff sweating over vats of pasta at the boil. Toiling hardest is Arthur Bucco. Tony enters. Christopher follows.

> **TONY**
> Listen, Artie, I wonder if you could help me out.

> **ARTHUR**
> *(nervous smile)*
> What?

Tony takes a packet from his pocket. Christopher has helped himself to two meatballs and now sits eating daintily off a small plate.

> **TONY**
> Cruise – Caribbean – S.S. Sagafjord, 11th through the 29th. Pair of tickets... I can't use them. Can you take them off my hands?

> **ARTHUR**
> *(apprehensive)*
> Where are they from?

> **CHRISTOPHER**
> Comps.

> **ARTHUR**
> What does that mean, 'comps?'

> **TONY**
> In my position as business agent for the Kitchen and Restaurant Workers Union, it's my responsibility to administer the dental plan. The

dentists awarded us these in appreciation. Problem is, I can't get away those dates.

Arthur looks longingly at the tickets.

> **TONY**
> When's the last time you closed up and got away for a couple weeks?

52: INT. DR. MELFI'S OFFICE – DAY

Melfi sits in her chair, waiting, in slatted light. The door to the waiting room is open. There's nobody there. The clock says 1:20. Melfi stares grimly out the window.

53: INT. BUCCO'S VESUVIO – NIGHT

Arthur and Charmaine, bone weary, are closing up.

> **CHARMAINE**
> You can't accept a gift like that from Tony Soprano.

> **ARTHUR**
> Don't you tell me what I can and cannot do.

> **CHARMAINE**
> Go ahead. Wind up in jail.

> **ARTHUR**
> Charmaine, don't talk like an idiot.
> *(pleading)*
> Three weeks... all expense paid. I'm telling you, if I have to put my hand up the ass of one more chicken without a break, I'm gonna go post office.

> **CHARMAINE**
> I don't wish to talk about it, Arthur.

She goes to a booth where their two kids have fallen asleep over their homework.

> **CHARMAINE**
> Art... Melissa... time to go home.

> **ARTHUR**
> Honey, you have to get away – we have to. For our marriage.

> **CHARMAINE**
> No. It's bad enough these mobsters still patronize the place.

> **ARTHUR**
> Yeah, but so what? We're not connected.

> **CHARMAINE**
> Right. Because we just turned down those tickets.

> **ARTHUR**
> *(whining)*
> Tony's a labor leader. The tickets were comps.

> **CHARMAINE**
> Oh, Arthur, grow up. Does not the mind rebel at any possible scenario under which dentists send the don of New Jersey first class on a Norwegian steamship?

He rubs his face.

> **CHARMAINE**
> Somebody donated some kneecaps for those tickets.

54: EXT. STATE PARK – DAY

A haggard, miserable Alex Mahaffey labors to crutch his way up concrete steps. His leg is in a full hip-to-toe cast. Flanking Mahaffey are Herman Rabkin and Big Pussy. They stroll (at least the two able-bodied ones stroll) away from an ice cream stand toward a picturesque roaring waterfall. It's a fine day.

> **MAHAFFEY**
> Herman. There is no way I can subvert my fucking company... Have them pay claims for MRI's that never happened.

> **BIG PUSSY**
> We'll set up MRI clinics that are just shells. The paperwork will look fantastic.

> **MAHAFFEY**
> How do I not get caught?!

> **HERMAN**
> *(sharply)*
> Alex, I don't like to see you knocking yourself like that. You're a smart guy.

> **MAHAFFEY**
> I'm depressed... I'm so fucking depressed... I can't eat, sleep...

> **HERMAN**
> You on Prozac?

> **MAHAFFEY**
> Zoloft. Similar. It's supposed to help with the gambling, too.

> **BIG PUSSY**
> No shit?

> **MAHAFFEY**
> These new serotonin reuptake inhibitor anti-depressants are useful against compulsive behaviors.

> **BIG PUSSY**
> That's a shame. A medication comes along after your gambling gets your fucking hip busted to shit.

> **MAHAFFEY**
> I'm trying not to be cynical.

They're out over the falls now on a pedestrian bridge.

> **HERMAN**
> You're going to have a chance to make good. Because, Alex, your debt and the feelings accompanying it are the source of all these problems. You know it, I know it.

> **MAHAFFEY**
> *(tears come)*
> I'm sorry I haven't paid you, Herman.

> **HERMAN**
> *(consoling)*
> I know you are.

> **MAHAFFEY**
> And I certainly never meant to denigrate Tony Soprano.

> **HERMAN**
> Want to walk out on the rocks.

> **MAHAFFEY**
> The – the crutches –

> **HERMAN**
> We'll help you... it's beautiful out there. I go there to think.

Mahaffey looks behind him. The ice cream stand and humanity are a long way off. Big Pussy tosses his cone into the abyss.

> **MAHAFFEY**
> *(scared)*
> It's okay... no, look... let's... let's try it... what you were saying before.

55: EXT. PITCH 'N' PUTT – DAY

In the Meadowlands, under the Turnpike. Tony practices his wedge. Looks at his watch, remembering something.

He takes Prozac bottle from his pocket. He makes sure no one is watching, takes two capsules.

> **PAULIE WALNUTS (O.S.)**
> T.?

Tony looks up. Paulie Walnuts is waving and calling to him.

> **PAULIE WALNUTS**
> Dick's looking for you.

56: EXT. BARONE SANITATION – DAY

Tony and Paulie walk back from the Pitch 'n' Putt next door. Dick Barone drives up in his car.

> **DICK BARONE**
> I just heard from Triboro Towers. Kolar withdrew the bid.

> **TONY**
> Hey, that's good anyway.

> **DICK BARONE**
> *(driving off)*
> Artie Bucco's here to see you.

57: EXT. PLASTIC MOUND – DAY

Arthur waits nervously. Tony approaches.

> **TONY**
> You all right, Artie?

Arthur takes the tickets, holds them out to Tony.

> **TONY**
> What are you talking about? You need to leave town. We discussed this.

> **ARTHUR**
> Melissa's in a dance recital.

Tony just stares at him.

> **ARTHUR**
> I'm sorry.

> **TONY**
> Hey, you can't go, you can't go. You're making a big mistake.

Arthur averts his eyes.

> **ARTHUR**
> Thank you. I mean that.

He skulks off. Christopher has been watching sullenly. Tony stares at the tickets in frustration.

> **TONY**
> This fuckin' thing again. How do I help my friend? Huh?

Christopher shrugs listlessly.

> **TONY**
> The fuck you sulking about?

Tears fill Christopher's eyes. He storms out, kicking stuff.

> **TONY**
> The fuck's with him?

> **PAULIE WALNUTS**
> Probably shooting fuckin' crank again.

> **TONY**
> Where's the maturity? That's what I want to know.

Paulie shrugs.

58: OMITTED

59: EXT. IL GRANAIO – NIGHT.

A smallish, discreet restaurant, hardly recognizable as a restaurant. On a side street in the Village, curtained storefront window, no sign.

60: INT. IL GRANAIO – NIGHT.

Total zoo. Toney patrons jammed five deep at the bar waiting for tables. Waiters slither through with hundred dollar lobsters. Crushed in the crowd of hopefuls is Dr. Melfi. She watched her date, NILS, whimper to the hostess.

> **NILS**
> This is outrageous. I had an eight o'clock reservation I made a month ago.

> **HOSTESS**
> *(Roman shrug)*
> Sir, as I explained, people are not leaving their tables and there's five parties ahead of you.

He folds up meekly, struggles back to Melfi.

> **NILS**
> I tore her a new one.

The front door, barely visible in the crush, has opened and Tony has entered with an attractive, if blowsy, young woman, IRINA, on his arm.

> **OWNER**
> *(rushes to him.)*
> Mr. Soprano, how you doing tonight?

Melfi's head snaps over. The owner snow-plows for Tony, the crowd squeezing to let him by.

Melfi is uncomfortable. Their eyes meet. Tony is all charm.

> **TONY**
> Hello, how are you?

> **MELFI**
> *(coolly)*
> Hello.

> **TONY**
> Come here a lot?

> **MELFI**
> *(terse)*
> When possible.

> **TONY**
> Nice to see you.

He moves off, then comes back.

> **TONY**
> I owe you an apology for not showing up the other day. Turned out not to be so urgent. Those decorating tips you gave me worked.

> **MELFI**
> Good.

He waves and goes with the hostess and is seated immediately. Melfi meets Nil's gaze, flustered.

> **NILS**
> Do you know who that was!? Well, obviously, you do. Is he a patient?

> **MELFI**
> You know I can't say.

> **NILS**
> 'Decorating tips.' Yeah, right.

> **MELFI**
> *(sharply)*
> Nils, shut the fuck up.

Tony is seen speaking briefly with the owner and hostess. The hostess comes right up to Nils and Melfi.

> **HOSTESS**
> Mr. Borglund, they're setting up your table right now.

Nils stares at Melfi, blown away.

> **NILS**
> Whoa.

Melfi looks to where Tony is in conversation with the Woman. She nods a 'thank you.' He winks.

61: EXT. MARINA – NIGHT

In the Hackensack River. A 35-foot cabin cruiser, The Stugots.

62: INT. CABIN CRUISER – BELOW DECKS – NIGHT

Tony and Irina laugh and kiss.

> **IRINA**
> Who was that woman tonight?

> **TONY**
> My decorator.

> **IRINA**
> What, you are redoing the garbage dump?

She runs off with a skipper's hat.

> **TONY**
> *(following)*
> You mess that hat up...

63: EXT. CABIN CRUISER – TOP DECK – NIGHT

She scurries up into open air, uses the hat to cover between her pubic area.

> **TONY**
> Irina... Jesus...

> IRINA
>
> I know there's something intimate with you and her.

> TONY
>
> Intimate? No, we talk.

As they kiss, we PAN to the water.

64: INT. IL GRANAIO – NIGHT

Different crowd, different night, but the same crush. Door opens. Tony enters. With Carmela. Owner runs over.

> OWNER
>
> Mr. Soprano, bona sera. Months we don't see you. Where you been?
> *(busses Carmela)*
> Signora.

65: OMITTED

66: INT. IL GRANAIO – NIGHT – LATER

Carmela and Tony in the afterglow of a superb meal.

> TONY
>
> Sometimes life is good.

> CARMELA
>
> Life is often good.

> TONY
>
> This Regaliali for example.

> CARMELA
>
> You've been in good spirits the last couple days.

He smiles, mulls this.

> TONY
>
> Carmela...
> *(with difficulty)*
> ...there's something I should confess.

Her smile fades, she fingers her glass.

> TONY
>
> What are you doing?

> CARMELA
>
> Getting my wine in position to throw in your damn face.

> TONY
>
> Always with the drama.

> CARMELA
>
> *(upset)*
> Confess will you, please? Get it over with.

> TONY
>
> I'm on Prozac.

She almost spit-takes.

> CARMELA
>
> Oh, my God...

> TONY
>
> I'm seeing a therapist.

She almost jumps in his lap, clutches his hand.

CARMELA
I think that's great! I think that's so wonderful. I think that's so gutsy.

TONY
(taken aback)
Take it easy, will you?

CARMELA
I just think that's very wonderful –

TONY
You'd think I was Hannibal Lecture.

CARMELA
Psychology doesn't address the soul, but it's something, it's a start – okay, I'll shut up.

She shuts up, but is glowing. He drops his voice.

TONY
Let me tell you something – you're the only person who knows. I'm telling you because you're my wife, you're the only person in my life I'm completely honest with.

She rolls her eyes. He grabs her wrist – hard.

TONY
Hey, I'm serious. The wrong people knew about this I'd get the steeljacket anti-depressant right in the back of the head.

It gets quiet.

CARMELA
I didn't realize you were that unhappy.

TONY
I dunno...my mother... dunno...

CARMELA
You told him about your father?

TONY
Told who? My therapist? Yeah, I told him.

CARMELA
Good. But your mother's the one.

TONY
(scared)
Lately, I feel like my life is out of balance. I feel disconnected...It's...

CARMELA
Our existence on earth is a puzzle. My own daughter hates me.

TONY
She doesn't hate you, Carm.

CARMELA
She broke my heart, Tony. We were best friends.

TONY
Girls and their mothers. She'll come back to you.

CARMELA
But who knows if she'll ever get to go to Aspen again.

TONY
(hard)
She should have thought about that before she stiffed us on the money –

> (shakes cobwebs)
> — I mean before she broke curfew.
> (beat)
> See? What's happening to my mind?

67: OMITTED

68: INT. SOPRANO HOUSE — KITCHEN — NIGHT

Meadow eats cereal and milk. Phone rings.

> **MEADOW**
> Hello?

> **CHRISTOPHER (V.O.)**
> Jesus, I got through! No social life?

> **MEADOW**
> Blow me. Dad — !

Tony and Carmela enter, Meadow holds out the phone.

> **CARMELA**
> Here, I brought you my primavera. Your favorite.

Meadow coldly walks out.

> **TONY**
> (into phone)
> Yeah?

> **CHRISTOPHER (V.O.)**
> A friend of ours just got back in town.

69: INTERCUT — INT. APARTMENT BEDROOM — NIGHT

The Young Secretary who witnessed Alex Mahaffey's beating and Christopher are post-coital and looking at the TV, where aged PUSSY MALANGA is taken away by wheelchair, jacket pulled over his head.

> **ANNOUNCER VOICE**
> Malanga... also known as Little Pussy, was released after questioning, but not before an ugly scene at Newark Airport...

> **YOUNG WOMAN**
> (whispering)
> Are you gonna break somebody's leg?

> **CHRISTOPHER**
> (shushing her)
> So it's gonna go down soon.

> **TONY**
> I think I figured a way to put this to bed.

70: INT. DR. MELFI'S OFFICE — DAY

Tony is in the patient chair, she in her chair.

> **MELFI**
> It's not the Prozac.

> **TONY**
> Why not?

> **MELFI**
> You said you're thinking clearer and your wife told you you seemed better. It's not the medication. Prozac takes several weeks to build up effective levels in the blood.

          TONY
        (disappointed)
What then?

          MELFI
Coming here – talking. Hope comes in many forms.

          TONY
Who's got the time for it?!

She maintains that maddening shrink stare.

          MELFI
What is it you really want to say to me?

          TONY
I had a dream last night. My belly button was a Philips-head screw. And I was working unscrewing it. And when I got it all the way unscrewed my... my penis fell off. And I'm running around with it yelling, trying to find this mechanic used to work on my Lincoln when I drove Lincolns and he was supposed to screw it back on, only this bird swooped down and took it in its beak and flew off with it and I woke up.

          MELFI
What kind of bird?

          TONY
Seagull or something.

          MELFI
A water bird.

          TONY
I saw 'The Birds' last week on cable. You think maybe that planted the idea?

          MELFI
What else is a water bird?

          TONY
        (thinks)
Pelican... flamingo – my father used to say, 'I'll do the flamingo on your head...'...but he meant flamenco – the dance.

          MELFI
What about ducks?

He stares in amazement, feeling a little chill.

          TONY
The ducks. Those damn ducks.

          MELFI
What was it about those ducks that meant so much to you?

          TONY
Did you know the word for duck in Italian is 'anatra'? So Sinatra probably means 'without ducks.'

          MELFI
Is that why you blacked out? Ducks and Sinatra?

          TONY
        (sheepish)
No.
        (stares off)
I don't know, it was just a trip having those wild creatures come to my pool to have their babies.
        (voice breaks)
I was sad to see them go.

He hides his face behind his hand. Reaches for a Kleenex. Dabs tears.

TONY
Look at this. Oh, fuck. Now he's crying.

MELFI
Once those ducks had their babies, they became a family.

TONY
So?

But then he stares at her in recognition.

TONY
You're right – that's what I'm full of dread about, that I'm going to lose my family. Just like I lost the ducks. It's always with me –

MELFI
What are you afraid's going to happen?

TONY
(completely rattled)
I don't know! But something. I don't know!

71: EXT. PAROCHIAL SCHOOL BALL COURT – DAY

A heated girl's volleyball game in progress. Meadow makes a save. Tony, in the stands with other parents, claps. The home team is African-American. Meadow's team is Visitors. With Tony is Silvio Dante. They cheer.

TONY AND SILVIO
Way to go, Falcons! [Etc.]

SILVIO
So when would you need this by?

TONY
Right away. Go Meadow, yes!!!

SILVIO
I think I can get a party like that together. Side-out! Side-out!

TONY
(furious at ref)
Hey. Ref! Oh-oo!

72: EXT. INNER CITY PAROCHIAL SCHOOL – DAY

Tony waits. Meadow comes out, changed into street clothes.

MEADOW
Mom didn't come?
(sees Silvio with daughter)
Hi, Mr. Dante!

Silvio gives a friendly wave.

TONY
Mom didn't think you wanted her to. Car's this way.

Meadow tries not to have a reaction. They walk.

TONY
You guys played a good game. That Heather Dante – where'd she get that spike?

MEADOW
Dad, don't you think it's totally unfair what mom is doing? And now, like, making this little movie scene out of it – the sad mom who, like, can't even come to her daughter's sports event?

49

Tony is staring off. The cathedral has caught his attention.

MEADOW
Dad...?

73: INT. CATHEDRAL – DAY

Vast. Empty. Candles flicker. Built a hundred years ago, it now slumbers in the heart of a ghetto. Tony and Meadow enter.

MEADOW
Don't you think it's totally out there? I mean, my Aspen trip? What is she thinking?

TONY
It's been years since I been here.

MEADOW
Dad, please talk to her, please! This is so stupid.
(realizes)
Why are we sitting here?

They are sitting in the pews. The vaulted ceiling soars above. Shafts of light pierce the gloom.

TONY
Your mother feels you have the capacity to be a top student. That you're special. I agree.

MEADOW
(tears)
What do you guys want? Perfection?
(notes his distraction)
What are you looking at?

TONY
Your great-grandfather and his brother Frank? They built this place.

MEADOW
(cares less)
Big whoop.

TONY
Stone and marble workers. Came over from Italy. They built this.

MEADOW
Yeah, right – two guys.

TONY
(patiently)
No, they were just two guys on a crew of... I don't know. Laborers. They didn't design it. But they knew how to build it.

She follows his look up and around to the faded somnolent beauty and burnished gold. She feels it.

TONY
Go out now and find me two guys who can even put decent grout around your bathtub.

Meadow takes in the cathedral with new eyes, her mind racing.

74: INT. DR. MELFI'S OFFICE – DAY

Tony in therapy, seated in the chair, facing Melfi.

TONY
– like during Gotti's trial a couple years ago, I said to my mother –

> MELFI
> Could I interrupt you a second?
> *(shifts weight nervously)*
> Am I, y'know, 'okay'? Hearing this?

> TONY
> What? Oh – Gotti? It worries you?

> MELFI
> Yes, but I'm a doctor. It's my job to treat.

> TONY
> Us being compare.

> MELFI
> Being Italian is irrelevant. I run a psychiatric practice, not a zeppola
> stand at the feast of San Gennaro.

He shrugs.

> MELFI (cont'd)
> You were telling me how when John Gotti was sent to prison you went into a
> profound feeling of despair and you said something to your mother.

> TONY
> I don't think so. I don't think I was talking about my mother. I was
> talking about that cock-suck motherfucker Rudy Giuliani and how he's
> ruined things for lots of people.

> MELFI
> Is there someone in your early life who raises the same fear and control
> issues as Mayor Giuliani?

He doesn't want to answer.

> TONY
> Well, look at the clock. Hour's up.

> MELFI
> You can answer the question.

Suddenly he stands. He goes to her, leans down, moves her hair aside and softly kisses
her neck.

> MELFI (cont'd)
> That's outside the boundaries of what we do here.

> TONY
> You're the most fantastic woman I've ever seen.

> MELFI
> I'm not going to kick you out of therapy, so stop trying.

Tony studies her, impressed.

75: EXT. BUCCO'S VESUVIO – NIGHT

The street is deserted. Silvio Dante, newspaper under his arm, calmly walks from the
direction of the restaurant and away. There's a BLINDING FLASH and ROAR as the
restaurant blows out in the rear.

HOLD on the flames of the burning restaurant.

CUT TO:

76: EXT. SOPRANO BACKYARD – DAY

BARBECUE GRILL

Steaks and sausages HISS and SIZZLE. Tony sips a beer, tends steaks. He looks toward
the house where guests are starting to arrive. The fire belches smoke and –

77: EXT. CATHEDRAL – DAY – SKEWED LOW ANGLE

More smoke. The church's twin spires jab at a lowering sky. Meadow is being burned at the stake, hooded medieval figures toss wood on the fire. She shouts at the leaden sky with a crazed smile, the wind and flames lashing her face.

> **MEADOW**
> Yes! Yes!

78: INT. SOPRANO HOUSE – MEADOW'S ROOM – DAY

Meadow's face aglow with fantasy. She swigs coffee, writes furiously in her journal. KNOCK. Carmela peeks in.

> **CARMELA**
> Guests are arriving and the table isn't set.
> *(notes)*
> How many cups of coffee have you had?

> **MEADOW**
> *(writing)*
> Be right there.

Carmela hesitates a second, then holds out new ski boots.

> **MEADOW**
> You mean I can go to Aspen?

> **CARMELA**
> Christmas break is just that. A break. When you get back to school, you'll really apply yourself.

> **MEADOW**
> *(speeding)*
> I was just thinking I probably shouldn't go. So close to finals.

> **CARMELA**
> *(thrown)*
> Excuse me?

> **MEADOW**
> *(urgent)*
> I was just writing in my journal – how somebody in this family has to do something.

> **CARMELA**
> Well...
> *(beat)*
> About what?

> **MEADOW**
> Perfection. Earthly perfection. It's a Soprano tradition.

> **CARMELA**
> *(beat)*
> It is?

> **MEADOW**
> I may become a nun. I have to look up our family motto... I think the Web has a genealogy bulletin board.

She starts scribbling again. Carmela stares, pole-axed. She leaves the room in a fog.

79: EXT. SOPRANO BACKYARD – DAY

Father Phil munches appetizers and chats with Mrs. Dante. The sun sets; family and friends chat. Christopher, Paulie Walnuts, Big Pussy, Silvio and a dazed and haggard Arthur Bucco stand around the brand new Weber with beers in hand as Tony cooks.

ARTHUR
You work and work so damn hard and then to have your life's dream burn down.

TONY
Look at it this way – at least you collect the insurance.

PAULIE WALNUTS
You got to say to yourself, "It could have been worse."

ARTHUR
How? How could it be worse? Fucking faulty stove!

CHRISTOPHER
Suppose people stopped coming to the restaurant. Suppose... I dunno.

TONY
There's no insurance for that.

ARTHUR
Why would people stop coming to the restaurant? It's just starting to catch on.

Tony puts a hand on Arthur's shoulder.

TONY
Know what I'm figuring out lately? Talking helps.
(beat)
Hope comes in many forms.

Arthur breaks down sobbing. Everybody consoles him. Except Christopher. Tony hugs Artie.

TONY
I'll always help you, Artie.

Tony notes Christopher off by himself brooding. He crosses.

TONY (cont'd)
Someday I'll tell him we torched the restaurant as the best solution.
(off Christopher's sullenness)
Enough of this shit. What's the matter?

CHRISTOPHER
A simple, "Way to go, Chris" on the Triboro Towers contract would have been nice.

Tony stares silently. We don't know what's going to happen.

TONY
You're right. I have no defense. It's from how I was parented. Never complimented or supported.

CHRISTOPHER
(still angry)
My cousin Gregory's girlfriend is what they call a development girl out in Hollywood. She said I could sell my life story for fuckin' millions. But I didn't. I stuck with you.

TONY
Hey.
(smacks his face)
I'll fuckin' kill you. You gonna go Henry Hill on me now? Too many wiseguys are making book deals and causing all kinds of shit.

CHRISTOPHER
She said maybe I could even play myself.

>   **TONY**
>   *(grabs and shakes him)*
> Forget Hollywood screenplays. Forget those distractions. You think I
> haven't had offers?
>   *(beat)*
> Hear me? We got work to do. New avenues.
>   *(calming down)*
> Everything's gonna be fine from here on. If we don't lose who we are.
> Look. It's a beautiful day.

80: INT. JUNIOR'S LINCOLN – DAY

Junior drives. Livia breaks the silence.

>   **LIVIA**
> It was nice of you to pick me up for the party, Junior. At least somebody
> cares about me.

>   **JUNIOR**
> These kids today.

>   **LIVIA**
> I suppose he thinks once he's got me locked away in a nursing home I'll
> die faster, then he won't have to drive me anywhere.

Junior shakes his head in sympathy.

>   **LIVIA (cont'd)**
> If his father was still around you can bet your boots he'd show decency
> and respect for his mother.

>   **JUNIOR**
> Well, my brother John was a man among men.

>   **LIVIA**
>   *(dabbing tears)*
> He was a saint.

>   **JUNIOR**
>   *(winks)*
> Hey, if he could steal you away from me he musta been something.
>   *(somberly)*
> ...anyway, lots of things are different now from Johnny's and my day.

>   **LIVIA**
>   *(looks over)*
> What do you mean?

>   **JUNIOR**
> I'm not free to run my business like I want.

>   **LIVIA**
> Isn't that awful.

>   **JUNIOR**
> ...just this week your son stuck his hand in – 'course, I can't prove it was
> him – made it a hundred times more difficult for me. Plus, he thumbs his
> nose at New York.

She looks over, horrified. He nods.

>   **JUNIOR (cont'd)**
> What are you gonna do? He's part of a whole generation. Remember the
> crazy hair? And the dope? Now it's fags in the military.

>   **LIVIA**
>   *(could go off)*
> Stop it, Junior, you're making me very upset!

JUNIOR
I don't like to, Livia, but I'm all agita all the time. And I'll tell you something else. Things are down. All across the board.

She looks at him.

JUNIOR (cont'd)
A lot of friends of ours are complaining. We used to be recession-proof? No more. You can't blame it all on the Justice Department.
("casually")
Our friends say to me, "Junior, why don't you take a larger hand in things?"

Livia gazes out the side like maybe he isn't even saying anything. He sizes her up, emboldened.

JUNIOR (cont'd)
Something may have to be done, Livia, about Tony. I don't know.

She says nothing! Junior smiles ever so slightly to himself. He has her blessing. He steers the car through the open gate into Tony's driveway.

81: EXT. SOPRANO HOUSE – BACKYARD – DAY

Tony waves in his BBQ apron. Junior and Livia get out of the car.

TONY
There they are! Hi, Ma!

LIVIA
What, you're using that mesquite? It makes the sausage taste peculiar.

ANTHONY JR.
Hi, Grandma!

LIVIA
(painfully pinches Jr.'s cheek)
Hello, my big boy.

TONY
Carmela, my mother's here.

CARMELA
Okay, let's eat everybody!

Tony Sr. and Jr. carry platters of meat to the house. The Soprano family and friends drift pleasantly toward the house.

PAN to the still and silent pool.

THE END

FADE OUT.

"College"

S105

Written by
James Manos, Jr. and David Chase

Directed by
Allen Coulter

Soprano Productions, Inc.

Production Draft   6/31/98
Full Blue   7/16/98
Full Pink   7/22/98
Reshoot pages 10/30/98
Reshoot pages   11/3/98
FINAL SHOOTING SCRIPT

CHARACTER LIST

TONY SOPRANO
CARMELA SOPRANO
DR. JENNIFER MELFI
CHRIS MOLTISANTI
MEADOW SOPRANO
ANTHONY SOPRANO JR.
IRINA
FATHER PHIL

Fred Peters
Peters' Wife
Peters' Daughter
Lucinda
Dean
Bowdoin Student
Bates Student Worker
Bartender

SETS

INTERIORS

Odenoki Motel – Tony's Room	N
Odenoki Motel – Meadow's Room	N
Peters Travel – Front Room/Porch	D
Soprano Living Room	D/N
Soprano Kitchen	D/N
Soprano Master Bedroom	D
Soprano Family Room	N
Soprano Back Door	D
Soprano Hallway	N
Soprano Master Bathroom	N
Soprano Vestibule	N
Restaurant w/Bar (Waterville)	N
Peters' Car	D/N
Admissions Office (Bowdoin)	D
Melfi's House	N
Bada Bing – Back Room	D
Tony's Rental Car (Crown Vic)	D
Irina's Apartment	D

EXTERIORS

Odenoki Motel	D/N
Peters Travel	D/N
Colby Campus	D
Roads (Waterville)	D
Payphone – Odenoki Motel	D/N
Rural Road (Waterville)	N
Road (Waterville)	D
Main Drag/Main Street (Waterville)	N
Peters' House	N
Colby Campus	D
Road (Colby)	D
Highway Gas Station/Mini Mart	D
Admissions Building (Bates)	D
Admissions Office (Bates)	D
Phone Booth – Street	N
Gas Station/Convenience Store	N

1: INT. ADMISSIONS OFFICE – BATES COLLEGE, MAINE – DAY

Fidgety, Tony flips through the BATES CATALOG. He steals a glance at the student worker talking silently on the phone, picks up the student newspaper:

FRONT PAGE

Headline: GAY-LESBIAN STUDENTS' UNION – MONDO WEEKEND.

TONY

Quizzical. Puts the paper aside.

> **TONY**
> 'Scuse me. How much longer you think my daughter'll be in there?

> **STUDENT WORKER**
> Probably another ten minutes...

2: EXT. ADMISSIONS BUILDING – BATES – DAY

Tony comes out, fires up a cigar. He takes in the campus – old money, green leaves, The Enlightenment. Not his natural habitat. He exhales cigar smoke. He eyes –

STUDENTS

backpack-toting, earring-wearing, lacrosse-playing, vegan, chain-smoking, fiscal conservatives.

MEADOW

comes out of the Admissions Office.

> **TONY**
> How'd it go?

> **MEADOW**
> They've got a 48 to 52 male-female ratio which is great – strong liberal arts program, and this cool Olin Arts Center for music. Usual programs abroad – China, India –

> **TONY**
> You're just applying here and you're already leaving?

> **MEADOW**
> It's an option, dad. Junior year.

> **TONY**
> What do you study in India? How to avoid diarrhea?

> **MEADOW**
> They don't require SAT scores but mine'll help 'cause they're high. Socially – I don't know. This one girl told me there's this saying, 'Bates is the world's most expensive form of contraception.'

> **TONY**
> What the hell kind of talk is that? You mean the girls at the other colleges we been to just put out?

> **MEADOW**
> Oh, my God.

> **TONY**
> And another thing – every school we visit there's the gay/lesbian this and that – the teachers know this is going on?

> **MEADOW**
> Oh, my God.
> *(stops, admires campus)*
> Pretty, huh?

> **TONY**
> *(agrees, then –)*
> Two to go. Colby up.

They walk through the leafiness.

> **MEADOW**
> Dad... how come you didn't finish college?

> **TONY**
> I had that semester and a half at Seton Hall.

> **MEADOW**
> Yeah? And?

> **TONY**
> *(chooses words)*
> Grandma and Grandpa didn't stress college. They were working class
> people.

> **MEADOW**
> Even Grandma? With her whole 'tude?

> **TONY**
> What 'tude?

> **MEADOW**
> 'The D'Agostino's are from Providence and we're a couple notches above
> the Sopranos. The Sopranos are...' what is it? – 'car phones'.

> **TONY**
> *(laughs)*
> Cafone.

> **MEADOW**
> What does that even mean?

> **TONY**
> Peasants. Low class mutaints.

> **MEADOW**
> How come your parents were anti-education?

> **TONY**
> *(uncomfortable)*
> Not anti. Look, I can't lay it all on them. I got in trouble as a kid.

She looks at him, then away. They continue walking. That seems to be it.

3: INT. RENTED CROWN VIC – DAY

*Tony and Meadow drive the rural Maine roads. She fiddles with the radio. Sits back and
rides. Finally breaks the silence.*

> **MEADOW**
> Grandma said you stole cars.

> **TONY**
> Thank you, grandma.

> **MEADOW**
> No, it's kind of cool.

> **TONY**
> No, it's not cool.

> **MEADOW**
> *(snaps)*
> Dad, don't turn this into a lecture, okay? I'm just trying to make
> conversation. In case you haven't noticed, you don't need to motivate me.

Long silence. Meadow works herself up to something.

> **MEADOW (cont'd)**
> Are you in the mafia?

> **TONY**
> Am I in the <u>what</u>?

> **MEADOW**
> Whatever you want to call it. Organized crime.

> **TONY**
> *(angrily)*
> That's total crap. Who said that?

> **MEADOW**
> Dad, c'mon. I've lived in the house all my life. I've seen the police come with warrants. I've seen you going out at three in the morning –

> **TONY**
> You never seen Doc Cusamano going out in the middle of the night? On call?

> **MEADOW**
> Did the Cusamano kids ever find fifty thousand dollars in Krugerrands and a .45 automatic while they were hunting for Easter eggs?

> **TONY**
> *(hard-line)*
> I'm in the waste management business. Everybody immediately assumes you're mobbed up. It's a stereotype. And it's offensive. And you're the last person I would want to perpetuate it.

> **MEADOW**
> Fine.

She turns away from him to the passing scenery. He watches her, troubled.

> **TONY**
> There is no mafia.

Meadow shrugs, fine. But then turns and looks at him. It's that face – direct and questioning.

> **TONY (cont'd)**
> Look, Mead' – you're right, you're almost a grown woman – some of my money, yeah, comes from illegal gambling. And whatnot.

She watches him.

> **TONY (cont'd)**
> How's it make you feel?

> **MEADOW**
> Well... at least you didn't keep denying it, like Mom.
> *(beat)*
> And kids in school think it's actually kinda neat.

> **TONY**
> *(sighs)*
> They seen *The Godfather*, right?

> **MEADOW**
> *(askance)*
> Not really. *Casino*, we liked. Sharon Stone – the '70's clothes, pills –

> **TONY**
> I'm not asking about those bums. I'm asking about you.

> **MEADOW**
> Sometimes I wish you were like other dads.

He looks away.

> **MEADOW (cont'd)**
> But then, like... Mr. Scangarelo for example? An advertising executive. Working for big tobacco.
> *(beat)*
> Or lawyers? Yuch. So many dads are full of shit.

> **TONY**
> Oh, and I'm not?

> **MEADOW**
> You finally told the truth about this.
> *(lighter)*
> And anyway, you're my sexy dad.

> **TONY**
> Meadow, part of my income is from legitimate business – stock market –

> **MEADOW**
> Dad. Please, okay? Don't start mealy-mouthing.

He goes quiet. She turns the radio way up.

4: EXT. HIGHWAY GAS STATION/MINI MART – LATER

CARS scream past on the highway. We pull back off the highway. Tony talking on the pay phone. Meadow is walking into the mart.

> **TONY**
> How's my sweetheart?

5: INT. IRINA'S APARTMENT – INTERCUT

Sexy Irina sprawls in bed on the phone.

> **IRINA**
> I'm so pissed I can hardly see.

> **TONY**
> Getting the flu?

> **IRINA**
> No. My cousin Svetlana.

> **TONY**
> The amputee?

> **IRINA**
> Two months only she is in America and she is already getting married.

> **TONY**
> Look, you knew what the deal was. I have two kids high-school age –

> **IRINA**
> Yes, and a wife whenever you want. What do I have in my life?

> **TONY**
> Boy, am I glad I called.

> **IRINA**
> Well, fuck you, then. Hang up.

> **TONY**
> *(cheery)*
> How's the whirlpool bath? They finally get the jets aimed right?

> **IRINA**
> Don't throw up to me in my face the <u>things</u> you buy me, okay? Her prosthetic leg fall off in Gap store? And he carries her out like knight in white satin armor.

> **TONY**
> I gotta go. My daughter's coming.

He clicks off, jams more quarters in phone.

> **TONY (cont'd)**
> AJ, how's it going pal?

6: INT. SOPRANO HOUSE – KITCHEN – DAY

It's POURING RAIN outside. Anthony is glum.

> **ANTHONY JR.**
> Mom's got the heat turned up to like a thousand degrees. I was on the toilet and I almost passed out.

> **TONY**
> But you're taking care of her like we said, right? Put her on.

> **ANTHONY JR.**
> Ma!

Tony yanks the phone away from his ear. Sees Meadow walking out of the Mini-mart talking to some young good looking COLLEGE KID. Tony waves her over. She pays no attention.

7: INT. SOPRANO HOUSE – MASTER BEDROOM – DAY

> **CARMELA (O.S.)**
> Ton'?

> **TONY**
> Yeah hi. How you feeling?

Carmela lies in her rumpled bed, in an oversize T-shirt, watery-eyed, nasal. Blows her nose.

> **CARMELA**
> I think better, actually. Fever just broke. I miss you two. Maybe I'll fly up tomorrow.

> **TONY**
> Nah, it's good you stayed home. You'd croak in a car.

> **CARMELA**
> So how's the interviews going?

Something catches Tony's eye – a goateed middle aged MAN filling his Lincoln Navigator at the pumps.

> **TONY**
> (distracted)
> Good, real good.

> **CARMELA**
> Did she like Colby...?

Tony doesn't respond. His attention is on the man.

> **CARMELA (cont'd)**
> 'Cause anything to get her off this Berkeley kick.
> (silence)
> Tony? Did she like Colby?

> **TONY**
> *(muttering to himself)*
> What the fuck...

> **CARMELA**
> Tony!

> **TONY**
> *(quickly)*
> Yeah, yeah, I'm sorry. Everything's good. I'll call you later from the hotel.

He SLAMS the phone down. Pissed, Carmela slams the phone down.

BACK TO TONY

He takes a few steps sideways for an unobstructed view.

MAN

He feels something – someone watching him. They catch each other's eyes. The man casually turns away, unhooks the pump and gets into his car.

TONY

He walks quickly toward his rented Crown Vic.

> **TONY (cont'd)**
> Meadow. Let's go.

Still flirting, she sees her father WILDLY WAVING at her. The Man's Lincoln Navigator drives off the lot. Tony jumps in his car.

> **TONY (cont'd)**
> Meadow, we got to go right now!

Meadow saunters towards the car. Tony lurches forward.

> **MEADOW**
> *(getting in)*
> Ok, what's the rush?

He floors it – while her door is still open.

> **MEADOW (cont'd)**
> Jesus, dad!

8: INT. CROWN VIC – DAY

Tony speeds onto a two-lane road.

> **MEADOW**
> What's going on?

The car hauls ass in search of the Navigator. He floors it.

> **TONY**
> I think I saw an old friend, that's all.

> **MEADOW**
> You know that guy at the gas station?

> **TONY**
> Maybe not. Probably not.

> **MEADOW**
> Then what – ? Dad, slow down!

Tony suddenly passes cars, veering over the white line. An oncoming car almost hits them.

> **MEADOW (cont'd)**
> Dad!

He sees the Lincoln Navigator, slips in, keeping a car between them for cover.

> **MEADOW (cont'd)**
> Jesus. What's with you?

And up ahead we see signs for "WATERVILLE" one way and "COLBY" another.

> **MEADOW (cont'd)**
> Dad – Colby! Turn!

Tony says nothing. The Navigator turns for "Waterville." Tony follows toward "Waterville."

> **MEADOW (cont'd)**
> Dad!

> **TONY**
> See? 'Cause you're talking to me so much!

He continues on, eyes on the Navigator.

9: EXT. WATERVILLE ROADS – DAY

They come to an intersection. To the Left is the Odenoki Motel. To the Right is another road to Colby. The Nav bears right.

> **MEADOW**
> Hey, this gets you toward Colby anyhow –
>   *(then)*
> Dad, there's our hotel.

But Tony keeps following the Navigator. He passes the motel.

> **MEADOW (cont'd)**
> Dad, hello! Our hotel's right there.

Frustrated, Tony quickly takes a second road into the motel.

> **MEADOW (cont'd)**
> <u>Did</u> you know that guy?

> **TONY**
> Nah, wasn't him.

10: OMITTED

11: INT. SOPRANO HOUSE – MASTER BEDROOM – DAY

Anthony Jr. enters with a food tray. Carmela comes out of the bathroom, thermometer in mouth.

> **CARMELA**
> Mon dyoor, room serveece et arrivee.

She gets into bed, reads thermometer. He places tray.

> **CARMELA (cont'd)**
> Why thank you, kind sir.

He plops in a chair. She picks up a fork, tests the food.

> **ANTHONY JR.**
> What? You said poached eggs.

She maintains a smile, cuts with fork – a yolk, hard as a ball bearing, rolls out from the white.

> **CARMELA**
> Nothing, no problem.

> **ANTHONY JR.**
> You're not gonna eat them now? After all that work?

CARMELA

I just finished throwing up. Guess my eyes were bigger than my stomach.

Anthony, bored, stares "bravely" at the floor.

CARMELA (cont'd)

Anth', why don't you go over to Jason's, play Nintendo.

ANTHONY JR.
(perked way up)
Really? You don't mind?
(jumps up)
I'll probably be back in like an hour.

CARMELA
(he comes to kiss her)
Eh-eh. No kiss. Cooties.

She blows kisses. He's out of there.

12: EXT. ODENOKI MOTEL – DAY

Tony comes to pay phone. Somebody's on it. He champs.

13: INT. BADA BING – BACK ROOM – DAY

CHRISTOPHER plays pool with himself. Phone RINGS.

CHRISTOPHER
(answers phone)
The Bada Bing.

INTERCUT – Tony on same pay phone.

TONY

Take this number down, call me back on the outside line.

CHRISTOPHER

Now? It's pouring down here.

TONY

207-555-0185.

Tony's HANG UP says 'Now'.

14: EXT. PHONE BOOTH – ROUTE 4/STRIP MALL – NEW JERSEY – DAY

Chris's car jerks to a stop. Jacket over his head, Chris runs to a pay phone, jams his body under the shell, inserts quarters while rain pelts his back.

CHRISTOPHER

Motherfuck.

INTERCUT WITH –

14A: EXT. ODENOKI MOTEL – PAY PHONE – DAY

Tony paces, PAY PHONE rings. Tony answers.

TONY

Hey. I'm not sure, but I think I just saw Fabian Petrulio.

CHRISTOPHER
No shit?
(beat)
Refresh my memory.

TONY

Febby Petrulio. Maybe he was before your time. Made guy, he flipped about ten years ago when he got busted for peddling H. Fucker ratted

out a lot of people. Some in our outfit. My old man was sick at the time –
he never really recovered after the news hit.

> **CHRISTOPHER**
> Mingye, you saw this guy?

> **TONY**
> That's what I'm saying. I think, but I'm not sure.

> **CHRISTOPHER**
> Up in Maine? What the fuck?

> **TONY**
> He went in the program. Then they kicked him out. Till last year this
> cocksucker was still flown to trials to testify about historical
> relationships. And he picks up speaking fees at colleges talking about
> when he was a big bad mafiusu.

> **CHRISTOPHER**
> Piece of shit.

> **TONY**
> Febbie and me met a couple times but Jackie Aprile knew him good.
> They did overlapping counts in Lewisburg. Matter of fact – ever see that
> carved wooden bust of Sinatra Jackie had in his rec room? Febby made
> that in the prison woodshop.

> **CHRISTOPHER**
> That was Frank, that bust? I always thought it was Shaquille. Fucker
> needs to practice a little on lips.

> **TONY**
> Get these plates run...

Tony takes out note, sees Meadow walking out of their room – toward him.

> **TONY (cont'd)**
> *(quickly)*
> Maine plates. T-X-6-6-9-2. Call you back tonight at 10.

Tony hangs up.

> **MEADOW**
> What's wrong with the phone in your room?

> **TONY**
> What's wrong? Nothing. I was stretching my legs, saw the phone,
> thought I'd give Christopher a call.

> **MEADOW**
> Oh yeah? Everything okay?

> **TONY**
> Yeah – well, they got a leak in the roof.

15: INT. SOPRANO HOUSE – VESTIBULE – NIGHT

Doorbell is RINGING. Wrapped in a throw, Carmela goes to the door.

> **CARMELA**
> Who is it?

> **FATHER PHIL (V.O.)**
> Father Phil.

> **CARMELA**
> *(panicked)*
> Just a second.

67

16: INT. SOPRANO HOUSE – MASTER BATHROOM – NIGHT

Carmela dashes in, quickly splashes water on her face, frantically brushes her hair. Throws on a robe.

17: INT. SOPRANO HOUSE – HALLWAY – NIGHT

Carmela races back down, opens the front door.

> **FATHER PHIL**
> Oi.
> *(sopping wet; enters)*
> Hope I'm not barging in –

> **CARMELA**
> No, no. Just watching TV.

> **FATHER PHIL**
> I was at the clothing drive and I thought you were up in Maine – by the way, your Moschino pedal-pusher suit? <u>Flew</u> outta there.

> **CARMELA**
> Oh, good.

> **FATHER PHIL**
> – anyway Jean Cusamano said you were ill –

> **CARMELA**
> Ecch – was. That flu that's been going around?

> **FATHER PHIL**
> Yipes.

> **CARMELA**
> I still have a little fever but –

> **FATHER PHIL**
> I also have a confession to make.
> *(beat)*
> I have a jones for your baked ziti.

> **CARMELA**
> Sure, anytime. Think I got some in the freezer. I can reheat it.

> **FATHER PHIL**
> Ooh, it's better like that, eh? The moozadel' gets nice and chewy.

> **CARMELA**
> I love that too. I was having a little Fernet. Settles the system. Would you like something?

> **FATHER PHIL**
> Some wine if it's open? So how's Mead and Tony's trip going?

> **CARMELA**
> I should know? He doesn't have time to talk to me for two lousy minutes.

18: INT. RESTAURANT – WATERVILLE – NIGHT

A candle-lit place built in the 1750's. Off to the side is a large bar that's alive with Colby students. Tony and Meadow are at a table. Tony wears a suit and tie. Meadow looks pretty. He reads the menu.

> **TONY**
> Man, never thought I'd be lobstered out.

> **MEADOW**
> Dad... what happened before?

TONY
Hey, that was fancy footwork on the pedals, huh? Sorry. Stupid wild goose chase.

WAITRESS brings diet coke for Meadow and bottle of Bolla Soave. Pours glass for Tony.

MEADOW
(troubled)
I don't know dad.

TONY
Jesus, what's to know? I thought I saw a guy I recognized. Is it my fault he turns out to be Mr. Pepperidge of Pepperidge Farm?

Waitress leaves. Tony and Meadow clink glasses. Tony smiles long and hard.

MEADOW
Dad, stop staring. Why are you doing that?

TONY
It's an exciting time. I can't tell you how proud I am to have a real student at casa Soprano. And she looks like those models on the cover of Italian Vogue.

MEADOW
Italian, Italian, Italian.
(smiles)
Thank you.
(points)
You're definitely up to something.

TONY
Oof. How'd you get so cynical? Just like your mother.

She grins. Then looks toward student LAUGHTER from the bar.

TONY (cont'd)
What we talked about before. How's that sitting with you?

MEADOW
It's not like I wasn't ninety per cent sure already.

TONY
What about your brother. You think he knows?

MEADOW
I think so. But if it's not on a screen it's not real to him.

TONY
There was a time, Meadow, when the Italian people didn't have a lot of options.

MEADOW
You mean like Mario Cuomo?
(beat)
Sorry.

TONY
(sharp)
Look, I put food on the table.
(beat)
My father was in it. My uncle. Maybe I was too lazy to think for myself. I considered myself a rebel. But maybe being a rebel in my family would have been selling patio furniture on Route 22.

MEADOW
In college nothing interested you?

TONY
I barely got in. Actually, wait – history I kinda got off on.

MEADOW
(smiles)
Yeah?

TONY
Napoleon. Roman empire. The Potsdam Conference. That kinda stuff.

MEADOW
What's the Potsdam Conference?

TONY
Potsdamned if I know now.

MEADOW
(rolls eyes)
Oh, my God.
(smile fades)
Dad, I got something to tell you.

TONY
Yeah?
(she hesitates)
You're not...

MEADOW
No. Jesus!
(beat)
A couple of weeks ago, me and some of my friends, we were doing speed. We did...kind of a lot of it for awhile.

TONY
What?!

MEADOW
It was like between homework and SAT's and just the general...pressure of life, we needed something to keep going.

TONY
That crap'll kill you!

MEADOW
I know –

TONY
I oughta slap hell outta you! Where'd you get it?!

MEADOW
(teeth gritted)
If I thought it was gonna be a lecture I would never have told you.

TONY
Take a reality check. I'm gonna shut up about it? Where'd you get it?!

MEADOW
No way I'd tell you. Especially after this reaction.

TONY
What did you tell me for?

MEADOW
You were honest with me today.
(beat)
I won't be doing it again. It got too scary.

TONY
Right under my nose. Christ. And you always think you'll know.

> **MEADOW**
> No, dad. You won't.

A sobering reality. He lifts his glass to drink, puts it down.

> **TONY**
> (beat)
> Meadow, I'm glad you told me. In spite of everything.

> **MEADOW**
> I'm glad I did too. I'm glad we have that kind of relationship.

He takes her hand across the table.

19: INT. SOPRANO HOUSE – LIVING ROOM – NIGHT – SAME

Father Phil lights kindling under three logs. Carmela is on the couch drinking Fernet-Branca.

> **CARMELA**
> Tony hates building fires. Those same three logs have been there since Lincoln split them.

Getting up, wine in hand –

> **FATHER PHIL**
> That could be positive. Fear of fire is a good deterrent to keep out of hell.

> **CARMELA**
> Then maybe there's hope for him.

She coughs. The fire is crackling. He sits next to Carmela.

> **FATHER PHIL**
> I have something for you.

Hands her a book – "The Religions of Man" by Houston Smith.

> **FATHER PHIL (cont'd)**
> It's what we were talking about. The chapter on Buddhism is spectacular.
> (wags finger)
> But I don't want you going over to those zany zennies.

> **CARMELA**
> Fat chance. I can never just sit on the floor and think of nothing.

> **FATHER PHIL**
> You'll see how Islam has gotten a bad rap in the current culture.
> (sips, savors)
> This Chianti, though, is beyond reproach. Word up.

Carmela smiles and refills his glass. She coughs.

20: INT. RESTAURANT – WATERVILLE – NIGHT

Tony's plate shows remains of steak dinner. His crumpled napkin is on the table. Tony alone at the table, antsy. Checking his watch. 9:55. He looks up and sees Meadow with two COLLEGE GIRLS. They approach the table.

> **TONY**
> Thought you fell in.

> **MEADOW**
> This is Carrie... Lucinda. They go to Colby –

> **TONY**
> (quickly)
> So why don't you hang out with them?

MEADOW
(mortified)
Dad!

TONY
What? Great way to learn about the college.

MEADOW
Yeah, maybe. But you don't just... God!

LUCINDA
No, that'd be cool.

MEADOW
Please excuse him.

LUCINDA
No, really. We love to dish the school.

MEADOW
Well...

TONY
Go 'head.

MEADOW
All right. Geez. See you later.

The girls head toward the bar. He stops Meadow.

TONY
But no drinking, okay? Stick to Cokes?

MEADOW
Okay.

TONY
I'll pick you up in an hour and a half.

He kisses her on the cheek and Meadow joins the group.

21: EXT. PHONE BOOTH – STREET – NIGHT – SAME

Through the pouring rain, we see a PAIR OF HEADLIGHTS coming right at us. Christopher's Lexus screeches to a halt in front of the phone booth. He jumps out of the car and LUNGES for the RINGING phone. INTERCUT – Tony at restaurant pay phone.

CHRISTOPHER
Yo.

TONY
What do you got?

CHRISTOPHER
Wet shoes.

TONY
You chose this life. You don't want to work in the rain, try out for the fuckin' Yankees.

CHRISTOPHER
(off note)
The car is registered to Frederic Peters, 38 Washington Street, Waterville, Maine. It's off route 201, I looked it up.

TONY
Frederick Peters, Fabian Petrulio...good match, huh?

CHRISTOPHER
I guess. I don't know. T., what are you going to do?

As Tony twists around talking on the phone, he notices Meadow looking at him from the bar area. He gives a little finger wave. This embarrasses her into turning back around.

> **TONY**
> I don't know. I got Meadow here. Jesus.

> **CHRISTOPHER**
> Fuckin' nightmare. You want I'll fly up, take care of it?

> **TONY**
> You're a good kid. Sit tight for now. Maybe call Pussy or Paulie.

> **CHRISTOPHER**
> Oh, what, they can do it but I can't?

> **TONY**
> Don't be so sensitive. This boochiachiada is of their generation. Their friend Jimmy died in prison on account of him.

> **CHRISTOPHER**
> I'll let them know.

> **TONY**
> Fuck! I gotta go do my homework to positively ID this guy.

> **CHRISTOPHER**
> Thought you said it was him.

> **TONY**
> I haven't seen the man in twelve years, for crissake. I don't want to be wrong. Call you around midnight.

Tony hangs up. Christopher stands in the downpour.

22: INT. SOPRANO HOUSE – KITCHEN – NIGHT

Carmela is reheating the baked ziti, Father Phil's tossing a salad. The Chianti bottle is down two thirds.

> **FATHER PHIL**
> You think I'm a schnorrer, don't you?

> **CARMELA**
> A who?

> **FATHER PHIL**
> Yiddish. Somebody who always shows up in time for free grub.

> **CARMELA**
> You're here a lot. But you're a man. You like to eat. I can't get over you with that Yiddish.

> **FATHER PHIL**
> My neighborhood in Yonkers was mixed Jewish and Italian. I hung out with guys of all stripes.

> **CARMELA**
> *(flash of worry)*
> Really? Were there Jewish girls there too?

> **FATHER PHIL**
> Sure. In fact, I never did date a Shiksa before I went into Seminary.

> **CARMELA**
> So you dated. Jewish girls.

Phone RINGS.

> **FATHER PHIL**
> *(peering in fridge)*
> Cajun stuffed olives.

> **CARMELA**
> Hello.

> **WOMAN'S VOICE (O.S.)**
> Yes, hi, I'm calling for Tony Soprano.

> **CARMELA**
> *(suspicious)*
> Who can I say is calling?

23: INT. MELFI'S HOUSE – NIGHT – INTERCUT

Melfi is in bed with Filofax and phone.

> **MELFI**
> This is Dr. Melfi.

> **CARMELA**
> His nurse?

> **MELFI**
> No. Is this Mrs. Soprano?

> **CARMELA**
> *(with an edge)*
> That's right and you are again?

> **MELFI**
> Jennifer Melfi, Dr. Melfi.

> **CARMELA**
> Jennifer... lovely name. He's not here.

> **MELFI**
> Could I impose on you to let him know I have to reschedule Monday's appointment? I'm down with the flu.

> **CARMELA**
> *(sharp)*
> I had it too.

> **MELFI**
> Oh. Well. Sorry to hear that.

> **CARMELA**
> There's worse things. Does he have your number, Jennifer?

> **MELFI**
> Let me give it to you just in case.

> **CARMELA**
> I lost my pencil. Up his ass. I'll tell him you called.

She SLAMS the phone down. Melfi ponders, then gently puts it back on the cradle.

> **CARMELA (cont'd)**
> *(fighting tears)*
> WHY DOES HE HAVE TO LIE? Why couldn't he have just told me his therapist is a woman. What is he hiding?

Father Phil wraps his arms around her shoulders.

> **FATHER PHIL**
> Maybe he did tell you and you didn't hear him clearly.

CARMELA
(pulling away)
Oh, come on! I mean, why wouldn't he tell me his therapist is a woman, unless he's screwing her?

FATHER PHIL
Carmela, please...

CARMELA
(pours herself wine)
And I thought he was changing. I thought this therapy was going to help clear up that fucking freak show in his head.

FATHER PHIL
Carmela, I'm sure you're wrong about them. Therapy's a start, a good start. But yes, it doesn't fix the soul. He's going to need help from other sources to repair that.

CARMELA
Then you talk to him. You help him.

FATHER PHIL
But there ya go. Will he listen?
(beat)
He must be a very unhappy man.

CARMELA
He's unhappy? Sleep is my number one – oh, shit, why go into it?

A deathly silence. Tears well up in her eyes. Father Phil gives her a hug. She lets him.

24: EXT. PETERS' HOUSE – NIGHT

Tony walks carefully along the house, hunching over. The back yard is gated and fenced. He moves quietly along the plank fencing. Peers through a crack.

POV

The Man from the gas station (Peters) and his young wife are in a steaming spa, cuddling, whispering and smoking a joint. He does something that makes her jump and giggle.

WIFE
Fred!

He buries his face in her breasts. Suddenly –

DAUGHTER
Mommy...?

Peters bitches sotto voce. Shifting position, Tony can make out an 8 yr. old girl backlit in a doorway of the house.

WIFE
Yes, Bear?

DAUGHTER
Would you put me to bed? I'm scared.

Peters and Wife hold a murmured argument. Wife gets out, wrapping herself in a towel. She's long-legged and chesty – tip-toes across the yard into the doorway.

WIFE
Daddy's going to come too. We'll both put you to bed.

DAUGHTER
Hurry, daddy.

PETERS
(irritated)
Yeah, yeah.

75

Watching Peters luxuriate in the steam, Tony tries to figure his next move. Peters stands. He's naked. He steps out of the spa and strolls unhurriedly toward the house, sandals slapping. He towel-wraps himself, his belly protruding over the knot. He goes in.

TONY

Tony scopes out the situation. Suddenly he hears BARKING and exterior lights on the house next door hit him.

VOICE NEXT DOOR
Is someone out there?

The barking intensifies. Tony backs away toward the street.

PETERS' BACK DOOR

Peters returns, switches on outside lights, peers into the night – listens to the barking.

25: EXT. STREET – NIGHT

Tony hurries to his car, jumps in.

PETERS' FRONT DOOR

The door opens. Peters looks out in time to see tail-lights fading. He stares pensively.

26: INT. SOPRANO LIVING ROOM – NIGHT

Both pleasantly buzzed, Father Phil and Carmela eat by firelight. He eats. Packs it away, actually. She barely nibbles toast.

CARMELA
Good as Willem Dafoe was, I cannot picture that Jesus looked like him.

FATHER PHIL
Could you pass the cheese?

CARMELA
Not that he didn't do a good job, Willem Dafoe. But the story's confusing. He gets down off the cross?

FATHER PHIL
(shows critical response; then)
Originally Bobby D. was supposed to have the role.

CARMELA
Really? Oof. Different picture.

FATHER PHIL
Totally. 'You talking to me, Pilate'?
'Cause I don't see nobody else here.'
(beat)
'Except Barrabas over there.'
You know what's remarkable? Is if you add up everything Jesus ever said, it amounts to only two hours of talk.

CARMELA
(shocked)
Nooo. But wait, I heard the same thing about the Beatles except if you put all their songs together it only comes to ten hours.

FATHER PHIL
Yes. Except it wasn't just what Christ said, it was his deeds.

CARMELA
But that's my question. I understand what he did, but a lot of what he said, I don't get. Like, the sun rises on the just and the unjust alike. Why?

FATHER PHIL
Because Christ was saying...

CARMELA
(overlapping)
...or that whores will go to heaven before a lot of the righteous?

FATHER PHIL
(refilling wine glasses)
Uh-huh.

CARMELA
But that's not right. I mean let's face it Father, we got some major contradictions here.

FATHER PHIL
It's about love. Think about it that way.

CARMELA
I don't know...

FATHER PHIL
Unfortunately Carm, our hearts are just too small to understand everything He was saying.

CARMELA
What does that mean?

FATHER PHIL
It means, hopefully someday, we will learn to tolerate, accept and forgive those that are different. Change through love.

Carmela reaches for the plates on the coffee table. Father Phil wipes his mouth with his napkin.

FATHER PHIL (cont'd)
I should be heading home.

CARMELA
Where you going? You just got here.

FATHER PHIL
(fishing)
It's getting late.

CARMELA
Come on, it's pouring rain out and I know you love that DVD player. Just got "Remains of The Day."

He wiggles his eyebrows excitedly.

CARMELA (cont'd)
See? Do I know you?

FATHER PHIL
Anything with Emma Thompson, I'm there. The thinking man's Jennifer Lopez.

CARMELA
(blank stare)
Ohhhh-kay.

FATHER PHIL
Hey, there's no accounting for these notions.

CARMELA
Father Phil, I didn't know you looked.

> **FATHER PHIL**
> To take in with the eyes a beautiful woman is that so different than a sunset, a Douglas fir or any of God's handiwork?

Their eyes meet. Father Phil smiles. Carmela quickly walks out with the plates.

27: EXT. GAS STATION/CONVENIENCE STORE – NIGHT

The attendant is taking a cig break outside. Peters walks to him.

> **ATTENDANT**
> Hey, Fred.

> **PETERS**
> Tanky.

> **ATTENDANT**
> Gonna be handing out that homemade cheese this year?

> **PETERS**
> With what they get for cream? Listen, Tank – anybody been in looking for me? Or asking questions about me? Big guy. New York-sounding.

Attendant thinks, shakes his head.

> **ATTENDANT**
> Problem?

> **PETERS**
> Dipshit hit me with his boat when I was tubing on Caribou Lake. Now he claims it's my fault.

> **ATTENDANT**
> Want me to call you if he shows?

> **PETERS**
> Wouldn't mind.

Peters sees a customer at the service island walking near his car and he hurries toward it. TRACK Peters back to his car as he gets in and puts a newspaper over what he was so concerned about – a .22 target pistol on the front seat.

The druggist shakes his head. Peters waves, drives off.

28: EXT. MAIN STREET – WATERVILLE – NIGHT

Tony parks, gets out, walks pensively, mulling things over. The bell in the ancient colonial church starts to RING. Tony looks up at the spire. He lights a cigar.

29: SCENE OMITTED

30: EXT. MAIN DRAG – WATERVILLE – NIGHT

Tony walks the deserted streets. He stops – looking into the window of a store – PETE'S HARDWARE. He mulls this, tries to see inside. A Waterville Police Car drives by. He sees it. They don't stop. He turns back to Pete's Hardware. Gets an idea. He hurries off.

31: EXT. MOTEL PAYPHONE – NIGHT

Tony skids to a stop, jumps out, goes to the payphones. He opens the phone book, flips to the Yellow Pages. Quickly rifles until he hits the heading "HARDWARE". His fingers slide down the page bringing us to: PETE'S HARDWARE – SINCE 1957." There's a Yellow Pages-type photo of Pete – a gaunt Yankee.

TONY

Thinks. Then flips to the white pages. His comes to the PETERS listed. Frederic Peters is not there. Tony sees PETERS, BETTYE – YARN SHOP. The only other Peters business is PETERS TRAVEL. Tony returns to the Yellow Pages – "TRAVEL". Looks at –

'PETERS TRAVEL'

A Tuscan scene and "Ask for Fred." Also, "CHEEPSEETS@EARTHLINK.COM" Tony tears out the page, exits the phone booth.

32: EXT. RURAL ROAD – NIGHT

Tony navigates a dark two-lane – slides to a halt where a gravel driveway meets the road. A lit sign: PETERS TRAVEL – DISCOUNT AIRFARES. Tony coasts down the gravel drive to a closed, silent salt box. He gets out.

33: INT. RESTAURANT – WATERVILLE – NIGHT

In a corner, the collegiates are boozing. Peters enters, looks around.

34: EXT. PETERS TRAVEL – NIGHT

Tony climbs the stairs of the porch and peers inside. Two desks, computers, posters – neat, bland, offering nothing. Tony moves around to another window, peers in. He wipes the glass with his hand, peers.

SHELF

books, knick-knacks. There is a carved wooden bust of Ronald Reagan. Decent likeness – except for the lips. They are larger than Reagan's, vaguely negroid. Tony smiles.

35: INT. BAR AT THE RESTAURANT – SAME – NIGHT

Peters is with the BARTENDER.

> **BARTENDER**
> Nobody's asked, Fred.

> **PETERS**
> All right, Vitus. Thanks.

He taps the bar with his knuckles and walks toward the exit – then stops. He remembers something.

WHAT HIS MIND SEES

Through the rear view mirror of his truck, he sees Tony's car make that right turn. He exits.

36: EXT. ODENOKI MOTEL – NIGHT

Peters walks from his car along the row of rooms facing the parking lot. He sees the light in the motel office go out. Looking the other direction, he sees a CHAMBERMAID push a housekeeping cart along the sidewalk. She unlocks a guestroom door, goes in.

PETERS

crosses to the cart, quietly picks up the guest manifest. Scans. Sees SOPRANO – 112/114. He looks chilled.

37: INT. SOPRANO HOUSE – CLOSE ON TV – NIGHT

Anthony Hopkins' and Emma Thompson's characters, clearly in love, are having a tortuous indirect conversation.

CARMELA AND FATHER PHIL

Sitting close to each other on the couch. Wine glasses in their hands. Carmela dabs her eyes with a tissue.

> **CARMELA**
> This just breaks my heart.

THE TV

The key moment where they almost touch... but then he retreats into his notion of "reading for education." She is silently devastated.

Tears streak Carmela's cheek. He smiles sadly. Makes no move to take her hand. But they are both well aware how physically close they are. SUDDENLY, Carmela is sobbing.

CARMELA (cont'd)
Oh, Father, turn it off, I can't handle it.

FATHER PHIL
What? What is it?

CARMELA
Oh, Father, I'm a terrible person.

FATHER PHIL
(takes her hand)
No... you're a wonderful woman.

CARMELA
(pulls her hand away)
Father, I need to get it out. It's been building in me, there's so much in me... I want... I want to...

FATHER PHIL
(helping her, gently)
Carmela, if I can help. Please.

CARMELA
How...?

FATHER PHIL
How long has it been since you last confessed?

CARMELA
(hesitates)
I... well...

FATHER PHIL
If you like, I can do this with you.

CARMELA
(unsure)
But... you mean, right here, Father? Now?

FATHER PHIL
The whole world is God's church. He hears and sees everything.

Carmela stares at him and then slowly, unsteadily, sits back down on the couch. Father Phil sits next to her. He turns his back to her. She follows suit. They are back to back.

CARMELA
This feels strange.

FATHER PHIL
It shouldn't.

CARMELA
(slowly)
Forgive me, Father, for I have sinned. It's been four weeks since my last confession.
(stops, defeated)
Oh, what am I saying? That's a lie. I haven't truly confessed in twenty years.

FATHER PHIL
Go on.

CARMELA
I have forsook... I have forsaken...
(stops; takes breath)
...what is right for what is easy. For a life of comforts I have turned a deaf ear and blind eye, allowing what I know is evil in my house, allowing my children, oh my God, my sweet children to be part of it.

(with difficulty)
I have committed the sin of omission, because I wanted things for them, a better life, good schools... I wanted this house, money in my hands, money to buy anything I ever wanted... I'm so ashamed.

FATHER PHIL
(she cries quietly)
It's all right, Carmela, go on.

CARMELA
My husband... I think he has committed horrible acts. I think he has...
(getting angry)
You know all about him, Father Phil, you know! AND I'M THE SAME! And I have said nothing, done nothing about it...
(wipes tears)
I can't pretend anymore. The pain is unbearable. I got a bad feeling. That it's just a matter of time before God compensates me with outrage for my sins.
(beat)
Please forgive me...

38: EXT. ODENOKI MOTEL – NIGHT

Tony's Vic pulls into the parking lot. He gets out, walks over to the passenger door – opens it and helps a sick, drunk Meadow out of the car. She is crying, slurring words.

MEADOW
Sorry, Dad.

TONY
Whoa, tequila breath! It's ok, kiddo, hold on to me.

39: INT. PETERS' CAR – NIGHT

He has the Ruger .22 target pistol, feeding the clip from a box of longs. He slams the clip home, gets out.

ON PETERS

Picking up pace as he walks behind a line of parked cars. He darts in between two vans and STOPS. He watches Tony and Meadow. She trips and teeters. Peters grips the Ruger.

ON TONY AND MEADOW

Approaching their motel door, Tony fumbles for keys.

PETERS

Stands, brings the pistol over his head and down to an expert level firing position. The sights cover Tony's head. Faint voices reach him.

MEADOW
You're not mad, are you, Daddy?

TONY
Little bit. I'm supposed to be. Come on riot girl, we're almost in.

MEADOW
I love you, Dad.

TONY
I know.

PETERS

His finger tightens. But Peters doesn't fire. He glances around, never relaxing his firing stance. There's activity in the office. And a guest room gives off LAUGHTER. Tony's motel door swings open. Tony and Meadow enter. Peters lowers the gun, starts toward his car.

40: INT. SOPRANO FAMILY ROOM – SAME

With her head buried in a pillow, Carmela cries softly. Father Phil is still on the couch with his back to her.

> **FATHER PHIL**
> You must truly repent, honestly and genuinely. And in the future, you must renounce all these actions and then God will absolve you.

> **CARMELA**
> I don't know Father. I'll try but I still love him. I still believe he can be a good man.

> **FATHER PHIL**
> Then you help him change into a better man and then you will have done good in God's eyes.

She hangs her head, exhausted. Gently –

> **FATHER PHIL (cont'd)**
> I think that you should take communion.
> *(off her look)*
> I carry a kit for just that purpose. It's out in my car.

She smiles wearily. Then realizes he's not kidding.

41: SCENE OMITTED

42: INT. ODENOKI MOTEL – NIGHT

Illuminated by the small bedside lamp, Tony tucks Meadow into her bed, kisses her forehead. He exits.

43: INT. SOPRANO LIVING ROOM – NIGHT

The fire is waning as they enter.

> **CARMELA**
> Why do you have that with you?

> **FATHER PHIL**
> *(gently)*
> Unfortunately, I had to say mass for someone in intensive care.

Carmela drops to her knees facing Father Phil – his clothes sopping wet, his hair matted to his head. He takes the bottle of red wine, pulls a small gold chalice out of his bag and pours wine into it. He whispers a prayer and raises his hand and makes the sign of the cross over the goblet. He reaches into the bag and retrieves a Eucharist wrapped in trace paper. He exposes it, raises it high in the air.

> **FATHER PHIL (cont'd)**
> This is the body of Christ that was broken for you.

Carmela takes it on her tongue.

> **FATHER PHIL (cont'd)**
> This is the blood of Christ that was shed for you.

She drinks.

> **FATHER PHIL (cont'd)**
> Accept the spirit of Christ, our Lord, our Savior.

Carmela crosses herself. Father Phil wipes the rim of the chalice and slowly raises the goblet to his lips, and with some difficulty, drinks the remaining liquid. He gets down on his knees, faces Carmela, holds her.

44: EXT. PAY PHONE – ODENOKI MOTEL – NIGHT

> **TONY**
> You find the two P's?

> **CHRISTOPHER**
> Pussy's kid says Pussy and Paulie took the girls to the Vegas Luxor on a special package.

> **TONY**
> Fuck.

45; INT. ODENOKI MOTEL – MEADOW'S ROOM – SAME

Sweating and sick, Meadow kicks the blankets off. Calls out:

> **MEADOW**
> Dad...?

No answer. She gets out of bed.

46: EXT. PAY PHONE – NIGHT

> **CHRISTOPHER**
> I booked a seat on a Boston flight tomorrow, four o'clock. Best I could get. Roanne, the dancer with the cross-eyed nipples? She's from Maine – says it's three hours from Beantown.

> **TONY**
> *(beat)*
> Don't come.

> **CHRISTOPHER**
> Oogots 'don't come'. I'll make sure you and Meadow have cleared the state before anything happens. We don't ever meet face to face.

> **TONY**
> No, this is my thing.

> **CHRISTOPHER**
> I'm your soldier, Antonio. This is my duty. Like we're always talking about.

> **TONY**
> The way this went down. This is my call. I got to vouch for this myself.

> **CHRISTOPHER**
> Clipping a famous rat would put me a cunt hair away from being made.

> **TONY**
> If he recognized me at the gas station he could lam any time.

> **MEADOW (O.S.)**
> DAD!

Tony turns and sees Meadow standing at the door.

> **TONY**
> *(into the phone)*
> Stay put. End of discussion.

He hangs up and walks toward Meadow.

> **MEADOW**
> Why are you using the pay phone again?

> **TONY**
> Those walls are like paper. I didn't want to wake you.

> **MEADOW**
> Dad, please don't lie to me.

> **TONY**
> Come on, let's get back to bed.

She rebuffs his arm.

MEADOW
Lying down made me throw up!

Reels back into her room. Tony follows.

47: INT. SOPRANO HOUSE – LIVING ROOM – SAME

Spent, tired, Carmela and Father Phil are silently watching the fire.

CARMELA
I want to thank you. I feel much better.

FATHER PHIL
(eyes closed)
Carmela.

She lets herself be held.

CARMELA
Such a feeling of peace.

She drifts with it. Phone RINGS. They laugh sadly at the timing. Carmela crawls over on hands and knees, answers.

CARMELA (cont'd)
Hello?
(listens; then softly)
Oh, hi honey... Oh yeah? Was it fun? Good.
(listens)
Oh. You want to sleep over there?
(glances at Phil)
Okay. Love you.

She rejoins Phil, sits near him on the floor.

CARMELA (cont'd)
That was AJ. He's sleeping over.

FATHER PHIL
I see.

CARMELA
At a friend's house.

FATHER PHIL
(hushed)
Ah.

CARMELA
(eyes on his lips)
The Pucillos. I don't know if you know them.

He runs his fingers through her hair. She raises her lips to his. SUDDENLY, Father Phil leans back, wipes the sweat off his brow...

FATHER PHIL
(wobbling)
I...

CARMELA
Are you all right?

He gets to his feet, leaves the living room. Into the guest bathroom. Carmela walks over and knocks on the door.

CARMELA (cont'd)
Father Phil. Are you ok?

We HEAR him VOMIT. Carmela pulls out a chair from the dining room table, sits alone in the dimness, enfolds herself in her arms.

48: INT. ODENOKI MOTEL – TONY'S BEDROOM – NIGHT

High angle on Tony lying on his bed, fully clothed, eyes wide open.

49: INT. SOPRANO HOUSE – FAMILY ROOM – NIGHT

Carmela drapes a comforter over Father Phil, who has passed out on the couch. She walks out of the living room and into –

50: INT. SOPRANO HOUSE – KITCHEN – NIGHT

Nervous, Carmela picks up the phone and dials. We hear the phone ring –

51: INT. ODENOKI MOTEL – TONY'S BEDROOM – NIGHT

Phone RINGS. Once. Twice. He leans over, answers. No one's there... DIAL TONE.

52: INT. SOPRANO KITCHEN – NIGHT

Carmela quickly hangs up.

53: INT. PETERS' CAR – DAY

He is folded on the seat, asleep in a sleeping bag, <u>having spent the night</u>. He jolts awake, wide-eyed. Unshaven, tousled. It has not been a bad dream – he is, in fact, parked within view of the Odenoki Motel Motor Lodge. He takes a pair of mini sports binocs from the console.

BINOCULARS POV

Tony's room door is open. Tony appears with suitcase, crosses to Crown Vic, tosses bag in. Meadow comes out, shielding her eyes from the light, walks zombie-footed to the car, puts bag in. Tony playfully grabs the back of her neck, shakes.

> **MEADOW**
> *(slapping at him)*
> Ow! Don't!

Tony chuckles.

PETERS

watches as they get in the car and drive off. He slides behind the wheel, starts up.

54: EXT. ROAD – DAY

Peters follows them until he sees Tony's car headed safely off toward Colby College. Peters slows to a stop, slumps in relief. His head falls to his chest.

55: EXT. COLBY CAMPUS – DAY

Tony pulls up before the Admissions Office.

> **TONY**
> I'll pick you up in a little while. Knock 'em dead.

> **MEADOW**
> *(shocked)*
> Aren't you coming in?

> **TONY**
> *(shows wrist)*
> Left my watch at the motel. I'll try and join up with you. Grab me a student paper.

She eyes him curiously, slams the door of the car and walks into the building. Tony peels out.

56: INT. SOPRANO HOUSE – KITCHEN – MORNING

Carmela, hung over, is at the kitchen counter having a difficult time making the coffee. The sink is full of last night's dishes. Father Phil enters. He is dishevelled, wearing pants, T-shirt, no socks or shoes. He doesn't know what to say.

CARMELA
(not looking at him)
You should have some coffee.

FATHER PHIL
Last night...

CARMELA
(still not looking)
Yeah?

FATHER PHIL
(partly a question)
We didn't do anything out of line.

CARMELA
(quick)
There's nothing to apologize about.

FATHER PHIL
(beat)
Right.

CARMELA
That's right.

FATHER PHIL
I should get dressed, get going.

CARMELA
Anthony Jr.'ll be home soon.

FATHER PHIL
(realizes)
My car's been out there all night. In plain sight.

CARMELA
If we didn't do anything wrong we didn't do anything wrong. There a commandment against eating ziti?

He catches the edge in her voice. He says nothing.

CARMELA (cont'd)
It's ok. Take a shower, get dressed. Don't forget your sacrament kit, whatever.

ANTHONY JR. (O.S.)
I'M HOME!

They freeze. Jr's FOOTSTEPS clomp upstairs. They relax.

FATHER PHIL
Carmela – I just – I don't know where to begin – it's not that I don't... desire you in my heart –

CARMELA
Madonn'. Father, please.

FATHER PHIL
Last night was one of the most difficult tests from God, ever, for me.

CARMELA
Then you've had a charmed life.
(beat)
What are you talking about? We're friends.

FATHER PHIL
What's that look about?

> **CARMELA**
> Me? I look some way?
> *(attempt at lightness)*
> I was just thinking about when we watched *Casablanca* last week.

> **FATHER PHIL**
> The new print was so great.

> **CARMELA**
> When Bogie says, 'Of all the lousy gin joints in the world, why did she have to pick mine?' Of all the finook priests in the world, why did I have to get the one who's straight?

> **FATHER PHIL**
> *(gently admonishing)*
> Carmela.

> **CARMELA**
> C'mon! It's a joke.

He touches her face. Leaves the kitchen. Carmela stares wistfully out the window.

57: INT. PETERS TRAVEL – DAY

Peters paces. Sitting facing Peters' empty desk chair is LON LE DOYENNE, local junkie, an inbred. Lon's 20 year old girlfriend, TIFF, glares and smokes. She is not one of Narcotics Anonymous' success stories.

> **PETERS**
> I would have done him myself last night but some people came along.

Lon stares at him balefully.

> **PETERS**
> Gray Town Car. New model. You pick him up on the Colby campus, stay on him.

> **LE DOYENNNE**
> *(dour)*
> Where on the Colby campus?

> **PETERS**
> What'd I just say? His kid's applying. The fuckin' admissions office!

Le Doyenne scowls at Tiff.

> **PETERS**
> You follow them an hour outta town, pull alongside, twelve gauge.

> **LE DOYENNNE**
> Fuck that!

> **PETERS**
> Lon, do what I'm asking or you'll never get another bag off me.

> **LE DOYENNNE**
> Ten grand.

> **PETERS**
> My ass! You take the thousand and be happy.

Lon looks at Tiff. Gets up. She follows.

> **LE DOYENNNE**
> Fuck that!

> **PETERS**
> You want the cops to find out who burned down the historical house?

Tiff, last out the door, gives Peters the finger.

87

PETERS
We were volunteer firemen together, asshole! I know!

A big ass motorcycle is heard STARTING, then LEAVING. Peters bites his lip in frustration.

TIME LAPSE CUT TO:

58: INT. PETER'S TRAVEL – DAY

Peters is on the phone, somewhat frantic.

PETERS
Yeah, is Dougie there?

He waits. HEARS something. He listens. Another SOUND. He quietly hangs up phone, takes a target pistol from the door.

59: INT. FRONT ROOM – DAY

Peters walks silently to the front door, peers cautiously through a glass pane.

HIS POV

the empty gravel driveway, silent woods. No cars, nobody.

PETERS

stays flattened against the wall. Listens. Silence. He carefully, silently, unlocks the door, peers out. He goes out onto –

59A: EXT. PORCH – DAY

He edges out, pistol ready. He walks – silently – to the edge of the porch. Studies the woods. He comes down the steps. Moves past his Lincoln Navigator. Stops. Studies the surrounding woods. Suddenly sees –

DEER

A young two point buck staring at him.

PETERS

registers this, stares back. Suddenly the deer bolts – but just before Peters realizes it's not he who spooked it, there are crashing footsteps – only two or three – and as Peters tries to turn a wire loops over his head and tightens around his neck. Tony, pressed against his back, pants in his ear.

TONY
Leggo the fuckin' piece! Let it drop!

Tightens the wire. Peters' eyes bug, he gags, his face bright red. The Ruger falls. In Peters' ear –

TONY
Good morning, rat!

PETERS
(gagging)
Who are you? What is this?

TONY
Don't fuckin' make me laugh.

Peters closes his eyes, tries to think.

PETERS
Look, Teddy – there must be something I can do to –

TONY
It's Tony, you fuck! You know how much trouble you're in now?

PETERS
I got a little girl!

TONY
Guys with little girls went to prison.

PETERS
I could have killed you last night. Outside the motel. Your daughter was drunk. Remember? I was there in the parking lot.
                    (Tony reacts)
I had a gun. But I didn't do it. Because of her. I said to myself, 'He's just a dad this time. It's just a coincidence. He's taking his little girl to college.'

TONY
One thing about us wiseguys – the hustle never ends. Fuckin' shooting at the motel would have flushed your life down the pisciadood.

PETERS
                    (weeps)
I'm begging you.

Tony releases some tension on the wire, then Peters pulls.

TONY
Jimmy says hello from Hell.

Peters' eyes pop. They totter, stumble... fall to the ground. Tony is on Peters' back, pulling the wire.

DEER

stares impassively, chewing a leaf.

TONY

teeth gritted. The wire cuts his hand. Peters finally lays still. Tony gets to his feet. He stares down at Peters. Takes his pulse. He turns abruptly and crosses toward the woods, wrapping his cut in his handkerchief. There's a beating, honking overhead. Tony looks up.

HIS POV

a few wild ducks in a V winging toward somewhere.

TONY

lowers his head, keeps walking.

60: EXT. COLBY CAMPUS – LATER

Tony drives up to the Admissions Office. Meadow is waiting at the curb.

TONY
How'd it go?

MEADOW
Where have you been?

TONY
Watch wasn't there. I had to go back to the restaurant, wait for them to open.

MEADOW
The restaurant had your watch?

He shows her the watch on his wrist.

TONY
I took it off in the men's room to wash my hands. Better get going, we're going to be late for Bowdoin.

89

Tony takes off. They drive along. Meadow leans over to turn on the radio and sees MUD all over Tony's shoes.

> **MEADOW**
> Dad, what's up with that?

> **TONY**
> The restaurant. I tried the back door. There were puddles, I guess.
> *(off her askance look)*
> I know, it was dumb.

She stares at him a long time. Turns away. Just the sound of the road. Tony turns the wheel, showing his cut hand.

> **MEADOW**
> Your hand is bleeding.
> *(beat)*
> Dad, where'd you go? You saw that man, didn't you?

> **TONY**
> Cut my hand on a screen door. What man?

> **MEADOW**
> The man you said you didn't know.

> **TONY**
> A va napola – what is it you think happened?

> **MEADOW**
> I don't know! You got in a fight?

> **TONY**
> You don't know? You makes this big deal and you don't know?

> **MEADOW**
> You were on the pay phone again last night. At one o'clock in the morning.

> **TONY**
> Last night at one in the morning I was talking on a pay phone? Sorry to inform you – Miss Cuervo Anejo – but you can't be trusted on what you saw because you were seeing pink elephants.

This blunts her. She stares off, trying to think. They drive along silently.

> **MEADOW**
> Dad... you're being honest with me, right?

> **TONY**
> Pretty soon here you're gonna hurt my feelings.

> **MEADOW**
> We have that kind of relationship, you said.

> **TONY**
> Well, we do or we don't. It takes two to tango.

> **MEADOW**
> Dad...?

> **TONY**
> What?

She studies him.

> **MEADOW**
> Nothing.
> *(beat)*
> I love you.

TONY
I love you too.
(beat)
Where's my student paper?

MEADOW
I forgot.

TONY
She forgot.

He shakes his head. Meadow stares out at the road ahead.

61: INT. ADMISSIONS OFFICE – BOWDOIN COLLEGE – DAY

Tony and Meadow sit waiting. Each in their own world. An ADMISSIONS DEAN emerges.

DEAN
Miss Soprano, come on in. Shall we talk about your future?

Meadow follows the Dean. The door clicks shut softly. An ancient clock ticks. Tony sits.

CLOSE – TONY

Drained of expression. Tired. He slumps back – sees an inscription above the lintel of a door: "NO MAN CAN WEAR ONE FACE TO HIMSELF AND ANOTHER TO THE MULTITUDE WITHOUT FINALLY GETTING BEWILDERED AS TO WHICH MAY BE TRUE" – Nathaniel Hawthorne. A STUDENT WORKER sees Tony looking.

BOWDOIN STUDENT
He's our most famous alum.

Tony continues staring at the inscription.

62: SCENE OMITTED

63: INT. SOPRANO BACK DOOR – DAY

They enter. Carmela greets them. Evidence of the recent flu is the Kleenex in hand.

CARMELA
Well, there they are. The two Ivy Leaguers.
(warm kisses all around)
Youse want something to eat? How was it?

MEADOW
(subdued)
It was good. I gotta call Hunter.

Tony studies Meadow as she leaves the room.

CARMELA
Gee, she spared me no boring detail.

MEADOW (O.S.)
I'll be back!

TONY
(distracted)
What a trip. I'm beat.

CARMELA
What? New England? It's so gorgeous.

He rouses himself from his sober mood, puts on a smile.

TONY
You still sound a little nasal but you look good.
(smooches her)
Got any cold past'?

CARMELA
There was some ziti but it all got eaten.

She realizes what she just said but doesn't waver. Tony rummages the fridge.

TONY
From last Sunday? That whole tray? Monsignor Jughead must have been here.

CARMELA
If you're referring to Father Intintola, yes he was.

He glances at her, eating cappacola direct from the butcher paper.

CARMELA
He spent the night here.

TONY
(beat)
Yeah, right.

CARMELA
(shrugs)
Okay.

TONY
Wait – the priest spent the night here? What happened?

CARMELA
Nothing.

TONY
Where was Anthony?

CARMELA
Sleeping over. At Jason's.

Silence. Tony stops chewing, tries to clear the cobwebs.

TONY
The priest slept over here. Nothing happened. And you're telling me this because...?

CARMELA
You might hear something, take it the wrong way. His car was out front all night.

TONY
(smolder)
Know what? This is too fucked up for me. What'd the two of you do for twelve hours, play 'Name That Pope'?

CARMELA
He gave me communion.

TONY
I'll bet he gave you communion.

CARMELA
Excuse me?

TONY
(dry laugh)
Well, c'mon, Carmela – guy spends the night here with you and all he slips you is a wafer?

CARMELA
(tight smile)
That's verging on sacrilege.

> **TONY**
> *(mock apologetic)*
> I didn't mean to verge.

> **CARMELA**
> You think I'm lying?

> **TONY**
> I don't know...just sounds to me...

> **CARMELA**
> Would I tell you about it voluntarily if there'd been anything to be ashamed of? Do I look like the friggin' Thornbird over here?

Tony is quiet a long time, ham in his cheek.

> **TONY**
> He's a fag. That's it.

She laughs delightedly, goes out shaking her head, laughing.

> **TONY**
> What? Or else I gotta question what I'm hearing here.

> **CARMELA**
> Oh, Tony... you're a sketch.
> *(stops)*
> By the way, your therapist called. Jennifer?

Her eyes locked on his, she leaves. Tony pales, goes after her.

> **TONY**
> Carm', I just thought you'd think it was weird me seeing a woman psychiatrist.

No answer. He is gone after her.

> **TONY (O.S)**
> Carm? It's just therapy. Pure and simple. Carm'?

THE END

"The Legend of Tennessee Moltisanti"

S109

Written by
Frank Renzulli and David Chase

Directed by
Tim Van Patten

Soprano Productions, Inc.

Production Draft	7/29/98
Blue Pages	8/4/98
Full Pink	8/27/98
TV New Script	9/3/98
Full Yellow	9/4/98
Green pages	9/4/98
Goldenrod pages	9/10/98

FINAL SHOOTING SCRIPT

CHARACTER LIST

TONY SOPRANO	Richard La Penna
CARMELA SOPRANO	Jason La Penna
DR. JENNIFER MELFI	Aida Melfi
CHRIS MOLTISANTI	Joseph Melfi
MEADOW SOPRANO	Counter Boy
ANTHONY SOPRANO JR.	Georgie
LIVIA SOPRANO	Adriana
UNCLE "JUNIOR" SOPRANO	Dr. Reis
PAULIE WALNUTS	Agent Harris
SILVIO DANTE	Agent Grasso
PUSSY BONPENSIERO	Larry Boy Barese
MIKEY PALMICE	News Anchor
	Jeffrey Wernick
	Patient
	Emil Kolar
	Raymond Curto
	Bride
	Bakery Customer (Gino)
	Jimmy Altieri
	Comedian

SETS

INTERIORS		**EXTERIORS**	
Melfi's Office	D	Green Grove	D
Soprano House	D	Street	D
Soprano Kitchen	D/N	Vacant Lot	D
Soprano House Stairwell	D	Meadowlands Marsh	D
Soprano House – Family Room	D	Pussy's Back Yard	D
Soprano House – Hallway	D	Trucking Yard	D
Anthony Jr's Bedroom	D		
Green Grove/Livia's Room	D		
Green Grove – Auditorium	D		
Christopher's Apartment	D/N		
Christopher's Bedroom	D/N		
Christopher's Kitchen	D		
Bada Bing/Front Room/Back Room	D		
Bada Bing – Men's Room	D		
Christopher's Car (Lexus)	D		
Dr. Reis's Office	D		
Russo's Bakery	D		
Casa Di Roma – Wedding Reception	D		
Melfi's Parents House – Dining Room	N		
Melfi's Parents House – Kitchen	N		
Pork Store – Butcher Area/Front Room	D		
Pork Store – Espresso/Pastry Area	D		
Melfi's House – Bedroom	D		

1: INT. PORK STORE – ESPRESSO/PASTRY AREA – DAY

Christopher sips a single in front of the piggies mural. He hears a voice.

> **VOICE (O.S.)**
> In the Czech republic too we love pork. Ever had our sausages?

Chris looks around. He gets up, stoned, goes into –

2: INT. PORK STORE – FRONT OF STORE – DAY

JUMP CUT TO:

Christopher slowly floats behind the meat cases. Getting behind the case, he sees Adriana on her knees in a white dress. A human hand protrudes from the cold case feeding knockwurst into her mouth. She is finishing one and the hand extends another and she starts to nibble that sausage.

> **CHRISTOPHER**
> Adriana?

When she looks up, it's Carmela. A horn <u>toots</u> out in the street. Chris peers over the counter top. He sees –

EMIL KOLAR

Out in the street, <u>night</u>. He is wrapped in plastic as on the night Chris and Pussy buried him. His left eye is shot out.

CHRIS

Is now wearing a butcher's smock.

> **CHRISTOPHER (cont'd)**
> Help you?

Suddenly, Emil is inside standing right across the counter. Carmela is gone. A wind begins to blow, neither Chris nor Emil noticing it, not having to speak over it, though it blows every piece of paper.

> **EMIL**
> Salami sub, hold the mayo.

> **CHRISTOPHER**
> We're out of mayo.

> **EMIL**
> *(female voice)*
> Change my meat to black forest.

Chris works on the sandwich. The disembodied, severed hand in the case giving him ham slices, bread, etc.

> **EMIL (cont'd)**
> You killed me.

> **CHRISTOPHER**
> What do you want me to do about it now?

> **EMIL**
> I want to tell you.

> **CHRISTOPHER**
> Tell me what? You come here every night.

> **EMIL**
> You fucked up.

> **CHRISTOPHER**
> What do you mean?

> **EMIL**
> Here's these.

He lets four flattened 9mm slugs clatter onto the cold case.

> **CHRISTOPHER**
> Where did you find them?

> **EMIL**
> One in the table, three in my skull.

Chris's eyes widen in fear.

> **EMIL (cont'd)**
> You will have our sausages.

Chris picks up the slugs, hands them to the hand.

> **CHRISTOPHER**
> Get rid of these.

But the hand grabs his wrist.

3: INT. CHRISTOPHER'S APARTMENT/BEDROOM – NIGHT

CHRIS – REAL TIME

jolts awake. Heart pounding. ADRIANA snores softly.

4: INT. CASA DI ROMA RESTAURANT/WEDDING RECEPTION – DAY

LARRY BOY and wife MARIE, parents of the bride, are greeting people as they enter the reception through a DECORATED ARCHWAY that reads: "CONGRATULATIONS HUGH AND MELISSA". Each guest is greeted as if the party wouldn't be the same without them. Tony and Carmela and Livia enter.

> **LARRY BOY**
> Carm' you look gorgeous.
> *(he kisses her)*
> Who's your date?

> **TONY**
> I'll give you 'who's your date'.

Larry and Tony embrace that manly embrace. Tony kisses Marie.

> **TONY (cont'd)**
> Melissa was beautiful up there.

> **LARRY BOY**
> Mamma Livia, come sta, darling?

> **LIVIA**
> *(takes embrace stiffly)*
> Listen to him with that darling. I'm nobody's darling.

> **LARRY BOY**
> *(tickled)*
> Never disappoints, this one.

> **LIVIA**
> *(reproving)*
> You still seeing your other women, Lorenzo?

> **CARMELA**
> C'mon, Ma, let's mingle.

> **LARRY BOY**
> *(as they go, sotto)*
> Ton' –

TONY
I'm sorry, Larry, it's getting worse as she gets older.

LARRY BOY
Nah, I heard some disturbing shit last night. But with the rehearsal dinner and all –

Before Larry can go further, GUESTS enter and he turns his attention to them.

5: INT. WEDDING RECEPTION – CLOSE ON WINE GLASS

A FORK is TAPPING it gently. As the sound SWELLS we PULL BACK and see that virtually every guest is seated and doing the same. The BRIDE and GROOM answer the call with A KISS.

5A: A TABLE

Seated together are Tony, Carmela, Junior, Livia, Pussy and his WIFE.

PUSSY
– I said to her, 'I'm gonna send you to It'ly all summer while you goof off from college? You need a psychiatrist.'

LIVIA
Maybe somebody at the table could give her a name to go to.

Those who heard glance curiously. Tony, looking elsewhere, isn't sure he heard right.

PUSSY
She goes, 'Dad, all these girls are going to meet up at Piazza Navonna.' I said, 'Guess what, You'll be meeting people at Barone's Pizza.'

Laughter. In b.g., Meadow and Anthony Jr. are having too much fun with their cousins.

5B: RECEIVING LINE

Guests congratulating the Bride and Groom then handing the BOOST to the BEST MAN who then unceremoniously stuffs it into the SILK SATCHEL. Standing in the line are Christopher and ADRIANA. He is carrying a computer in its box.

CHRISTOPHER
I would of wrapped it but...

BRIDE
(delighted)
That's ok.

CHRISTOPHER
This model got such a good write-up I got one for myself.

ADRIANA
(quickly)
Okay, let's move on, okay?

They take us to –

PAULIE
Federal indictments? Where the fuck'd you get this?

LARRY BOY
I got the goomar of a guy who owes me working word processing at FBI headquarters.

PAULIE
When's it comin' down?

LARRY BOY
We don't know. She's on it.

5C: PAULIE AND TONY AND LARRY BOY AND PUSSY

TONY
Indictments. Fuck.

PUSSY
You sure about this?

LARRY BOY
It's not just my source and it's not just Jersey. Half of New York's in Lauderdale already.

5D: JIMMY ALTIERI AND CHRISTOPHER.

CHRISTOPHER
Fuck. They're gonna want my ass.

JIMMY
Why?

CHRISTOPHER
Whatiya mean, why? I'm O.C.

JIMMY
When the fuck did you get your wings?

CHRISTOPHER
I didn't. Not yet, anyway.

5E: THE CHAMPAGNE FOUNTAIN – LATER

Tony, Pussy, Silvio, Ray Curto, Jimmy, Junior, Mikey, and Paulie.

PUSSY
Fuck. I just gave a G-note to Larry Boy's kid for the gift. If I knew I may have to lam it in a hurry I would have duked her another time.

TONY
Unc'? You want to say anything about this?

JUNIOR
You guys see indictments under your bed at night. Right away everyone is ready to lam it. As far as I'm concerned it's just speculation.

MIKEY
Rumor.

RAYMOND
(to Tony)
Better be safe than sorry, no? I say we all duck for a while.

JUNIOR
And what're we gonna do? Close shop? We can't do that.

MIKEY
Absolutely not.

RAYMOND
Tony?

JUNIOR
(nasty)
What the fuck are you asking him for? I just gave you the answer.

The others are uncomfortable by this exchange. They too could care less what Junior thinks. As far as anyone is concerned Tony is the real boss.

TONY
Junior's right. We lam it and it becomes open season. Fuckin' Albanians will be living in our houses.

5F: RECEPTION LINE

Pussy goes straight to the Groom who is with the Bride and Best Man and the satchel of 'Boost' (gifts). Pussy whispers something to the groom. The Groom looks confused. Pussy whispers something else to him. The Groom embarrassedly starts digging into the satchel. Gives Pussy back his envelope. The bride looks curiously to her new husband...

5G: CHAMPAGNE FOUNTAIN

> **JUNIOR**
> I say don't draw any unnecessary attention and everybody'll be fine.

Seems like so-so advice – all eyes glance to Tony.

> **TONY**
> I agree with my uncle. He calls the shots. We do it.
> (beat)
> But for right now, today, Uncle Jun'? Maybe you were thinking everybody do some spring cleaning?

> **JUNIOR**
> That was my next comment.

The group discreetly breaks up.

5H: SERIES OF SHOTS

Men talk urgently to their wives who look either confused, annoyed, or freaked as they get their coats or round up their children to leave. The groom is bewildered, the bride is crying. Carmela holds and comforts her.

6: INT. SOPRANO HALLWAY – DAY

Hurriedly taking off his wedding suit jacket, Tony slides a chair under an A.C. duct and stands on it. Carmela steadies the chair.

> **CARMELA**
> Think they'll come over the weekend?

> **TONY**
> They're coming some day.

He takes off the grate and removes a SAWED OFF SHOTGUN AND A 9 MILLIMETER W/SILENCER. He puts it in a black plastic bag.

> **TONY (cont'd)**
> Where's the money?

> **CARMELA**
> Everywhere.

> **TONY**
> Gather it. What else?

> **CARMELA**
> The guns. The money. What about your phone numbers?

> **TONY**
> Anyone who's anyone is in my head.
> (sees her cloud over)
> What's the matter?

> **CARMELA**
> Nothing. Here we go.

> **TONY**
> Why now? Why the fuck now? Just as things are looking good.
> (takes jewelry off)
> Better give me yours too.

Carmela removes pieces of jewelry.

TONY (cont'd)
I don't want them stealing shit from us. 'Cause they know we can't produce receipts.

Tony waits for more.

CARMELA
I'm not taking off my engagement ring. It's not stolen.
(beat, looks at Tony)
Is it?

TONY
What do you think I am?

7: INT. SOPRANO HOUSE – STAIRWELL – DAY

Meadow is eavesdropping. She's heard enough.

8: INT. ANTHONY JR.'S ROOM – DAY

Anthony Jr. is swatting at a mosquito with a swatter.

MEADOW
Boot your computer. The cops are coming.

ANTHONY JR.
So?

MEADOW
So, you want them to see all that porno you downloaded?

Anthony Jr.'s eyes pop and he's down off the bed. Meadow rushes out.

9: EXT. PUSSY'S BACK YARD – DAY

Pussy's got a fire going in his barbecue, burning shit. His wife comes out with another load.

10: INT. CHRISTOPHER'S APARTMENT – DAY

Christopher is hunched over his computer, hunting and pecking.

ANGLE – SCREEN

ROCCO
I thought I was daed but I manuged to get the drip on him.

CHRISTOPHER
Motherfuck.

Christopher corrects 'drip' to 'drop'. He picks up a copy of Viki King's, "How to Write a Movie in 21 Days." He reads awhile.

CHRISTOPHER (cont'd)
1) Writing is not hard. 2) Good writing is so easy it's accidental. 3) It's no accident that good writing is personal.
(mulls this)
Personal...

Goes back to the keyboard. Suddenly the text vanishes.

CHRISTOPHER (cont'd)
ADRIANA!

She comes out in wedding attire and bare feet.

CHRISTOPHER (cont'd)
It ate my whole script now!

ADRIANA
You're still in the file. You must have deleted the text.

CHRISTOPHER
The fuck! Whatever!
(throttles computer)
You fucking asshole!

ADRIANA
All right – stop with the hysteria would you please! If you're gonna keep behaving like a baby, fuck it, I'm not gonna help you, Christopher. I mean it.

CHRISTOPHER
Least you work that Squirrel program at the restaurant –

ADRIANA
This is my first time with script writing software too, Christopher! Jesus!
(presses keys)
There. The text came back. You put it in buffer memory. You click on the little paste jar to reattach it.

CHRISTOPHER
Little paste jar.
(beat)
What do you think?

ADRIANA
Of the script? Babe, I can't like, give an opinion every time you add a sentence. I gotta have the whole story flow.

CHRISTOPHER
I'm starting with the dialogue.

To appease him she reads some. Beat.

ADRIANA
'I manuged to get the drop on him.' Do you mean to say 'managed to get the drop' or is he saying 'manuge' like 'manugia l'amerigan'?

He shoots her a look, types fixes. She smooches him –

ADRIANA
My Tennessee William.

He hunts and pecks. But as she's leaving he gets panicky with the prospect of writing and grabs her and hugs her.

CHRISTOPHER
Where you going?

ADRIANA
I've never seen you apply yourself like this.

CHRISTOPHER
I love movies. You know that. That smell in Blockbuster? That candy and carpet smell? I get high off it. I'm gonna let all that love and knowledge go to waste? My cousin Gregory's girlfriend, Amy, that works for Tarantino? She said mob stories are <u>always</u> hot. I could make my mark.

ADRIANA
Babe, with these indictments shouldn't you put the script away for awhile and get rid of evidence.

CHRISTOPHER
(indicates apartment)
Travel light. Free bird.

ADRIANA
You stole this computer plus the one you gave Melissa at ten o'clock this morning.

Phone RINGS. Chris answers.

CHRISTOPHER
I'm writing.

Intercut GEORGIE in the Bing back room.

GEORGIE
Turn on Channel 6.

CHRISTOPHER
Turn on Channel 6.

She does.

NEWS ANCHOR
– New Jersey Attorney General James D. Ricci stated at a fund raiser that a grand jury has been empaneled to look into mob activities in the Garden State with indictments to follow...

11: INT. MELFI'S HOUSE – DAY

MELFI at home, watching newscast, transfixed (intercut as needed).

NEWS ANCHOR
With us is syndicated columnist and author of "Mafia: America's Longest Running Soap Opera," Jeffrey Wernick. First of all, welcome.

JEFFREY WERNICK
Thank you. Pleasure to be here.

NEWS ANCHOR
For years now the F.B.I. has told us that the Mafia is all but dead...

12: INT. SOPRANO HOUSE – FAMILY ROOM – DAY

Tony and Carmela watching the newscast (intercut as needed).

JEFFREY WERNICK
Let me interject. While it is true that the mob is getting a standing eight count I wouldn't call the fight. The government knows that better than anyone. If you've ever had termites in your house you know that one fumigation is never enough.

NEWS ANCHOR
Murder, truck hijacking as well as money laundering are expected to be amongst the inquiries. Do we know yet the names of those who'll be indicted?

JEFFREY WERNICK
The indictments are sealed. But with the recent death of acting Di Meo family boss Jackie Aprile, it's almost a foregone conclusion authorities will focus on developments within that group.

NEWS ANCHOR
Di Meo?

JEFFREY WERNICK
A North Jersey group. Sources tell me Corrado "Junior" Soprano was made new boss after the death of Aprile. The Di Meos – or now the Sopranos – have long historic ties to the New York families.

13: INT. CHRISTOPHER'S APARTMENT – DAY – SAME

Christopher is glued by newscast. Ade plays footsies with his stomach.

NEWS ANCHOR
What about these possible murder charges?

JEFFREY WERNICK
There will undoubtedly be focus on the as yet unsolved execution style

slaying of Soprano family associate Brendan Filone. Was it part of a power struggle?

> **NEWS ANCHOR**
> Interesting.

> **CHRISTOPHER**
> No one would <u>ever</u> have ranked him as associate!

> **JEFFREY WERNICK**
> Here's a loyal soldier, if you will, and he winds up dead for no as-yet apparent reason.

> **NEWS ANCHOR**
> Thank you, Jeffrey.

> **CHRISTOPHER**
> (shuts it off)
> Brendan Filone? Associate? Soldier? Fuck you!

He throws the REMOTE across the room.

> **ADRIANA**
> Je-sus!

> **CHRISTOPHER**
> (dials phone)
> Georgie, you see it from the beginning? Did they mention my name?
>
> (vast disappointment)
> Stop the fuckin' chit-chat. I gotta go.

14: INT. MELFI'S PARENTS' HOUSE – KITCHEN – NIGHT

Melfi, her father JOSEPH, her mother AIDA, as well as her ex-husband, RICHARD LA PENNA, are pitching in to ready dinner. Melfi's home-from-college son, JASON LA PENNA, slacks around stealing bits of food.

> **JASON**
> Nobody makes ginzo gravy like you, Nana. I'm up at Bard waiting on my care package.

> **MELFI**
> I don't like that word, Jason.

> **JASON**
> What? Ginzo?

> **MELFI**
> Jason, that word is offensive.

> **AIDA**
> She's right, Jason. It's not a nice word.

> **JASON**
> Sorry. What's it mean?

> **RICHARD**
> It's derived from the word guinea.

> **JASON**
> What's that mean?

No one knows. Beat. Somehow this nettles Richard even more.

> **RICHARD**
> It's a derogation.

> **MELFI**
> I have a patient, you wouldn't want to say 'guinea' around him.

> **RICHARD**
> An Italian male seeing a shrink. Let me guess – mother issues.

He's half-joking but the fact that he's right annoys Melfi.

> **JASON**
> Why wouldn't you say it, mom?

> **MELFI**
> You just wouldn't.

> **AIDA**
> *(joking)*
> What's he in the mafia?

Melfi laughs a little but she let something show and now has everyone's attention. It makes her uncomfortable.

> **MELFI**
> No. I shouldn't have mentioned it. Let's change the subject.

> **JASON**
> No way. What's he do, mom? Is he in the mob?

> **RICHARD**
> Oh, God, he's not a mobster, is he Jen?

> **MELFI**
> You know better than anyone I can't discuss my patients.

> **AIDA**
> I just hope he's not one of those crumbs they were talking about on the news.

> **RICHARD**
> *(off her silence)*
> Jesus, Jen.

> **JOSEPH**
> Refer him to another doctor. You can do that, can't you?

> **MELFI**
> Grate the cheese, dad.

> **RICHARD**
> Of course she can.

> **MELFI**
> That might be what you'd do Richard – if you were still in practice and not consulting to hospital corporations.

> **AIDA**
> Jenny...

> **RICHARD**
> No problem, Aida. During our marriage I developed the same carapace used by thousand pound sea turtles.

TIME LAPSE CUT TO:

14A: INT. MELFI DINING ROOM – NIGHT

The family is eating.

> **MELFI**
> Why should I refer him to someone else? He's my patient.

> **RICHARD**
> You say that like you're proud of it.

MELFI
What the hell does that mean?

RICHARD
You know you can't treat sociopaths. The man is scum and you shouldn't be helping him with his bed wetting.

MELFI
You don't have any idea who this man is yet you call him scum.

RICHARD
People like him are the reason Italian Americans have such a bad image.

AIDA
I agree.

RICHARD
Ask any American to describe an Italian American and they will invariably reference the *Godfather* or *Goodfellas*.

JASON
Good movies.

RICHARD
And the rest will mention pizza.

JASON
Good movies to eat pizza by.

MELFI
Stop it, Jason.
(*pissy*)
I never said he was in the mafia.

JOSEPH
(*of food; annoyed*)
It's all mooshadd'?

RICHARD
Why do you think we'll never see an Italian president?

MELFI
And that's my patient's fault? I realize you're in the anti-defamation lobby – so go after Hollywood if you feel you absolutely have to but leave my patient alone.

RICHARD
It's a synergy. News items and the constant portrayal of Italian-Americans as gangsters. What about Enrico Fermi? Why can't we see a movie about him?

This gets polite enthusiasm.

JASON
Wasn't that Italian anti-def dealie started by Joe Columbo? A mobster?

RICHARD
(*ignores him*)
Italians Against Discrimination did a study, and at its height, the mafia in this country had less than five thousand members. Yet that tiny insignificant fraction casts a dark shadow over more than twenty million hard-working people.

JASON
Dad, at this point in our cultural history mob movies are classic American cinema. Like westerns.

JOSEPH

I kinda agree there, Rich. You never saw the Scotch-Irish pissing and moaning 'cause they were always portrayed as rustlers and gunslingers who held contests to see who could shoot who first.

JASON

See what you started with your gravy, Nana.

JOSEPH

(holds up wine glass)
To we... the twenty million. Cent ann'.

15: INT. CHRISTOPHER'S APARTMENT – COMPUTER SCREEN – DAY

Words dribble onto the screen, as follows.

BEAUTIFUL GIRL

Thank you!!!

CHIP

I must be loyel to my capo.

CHRISTOPHER

That's as far as he can get. He stares off thinking. The seconds fall like huge stones. Phone RINGS.

CHRISTOPHER

What?!

16: INT. BADA BING – BACK ROOM – DAY

Tony on the phone(intercut as needed).

TONY

Get down here right away. We're exterminating.

CHRISTOPHER

I'm kinda busy –

TONY

And stop and get some shfooyadell and cannolis and shit for the guys.

Tony hangs up. Christopher angrily chafes.

17: INT. RUSSO'S BAKERY – DAY

It has that look of an "Old Neighborhood Bakery". Large round Neapolitan bread loaves of all shapes and sizes. A COUNTER BOY, maybe 20, in a sleeveless tee shirt, is working the counter. He has bleached BLONDE hair, wears an earring and has a tattoo on side of his neck.

DOOR

The little bell rings, Christopher enters. He sees five CUSTOMERS waiting to be served. He chafes, takes a number.

COUNTER BOY

Number 26!

An old woman takes five minutes to get to the counter.

LATER

The crowd has thinned. Chris is waiting with a housewife. As the Counter Boy is taking care of her we hear the little BELL. Another CUSTOMER enters. The Counter Boy finishes up with the woman then immediately turns his attention to the customer who just walked in.

COUNTER BOY

What can I get you, Gino?

BAKERY CUSTOMER
Gimme some...

CHRISTOPHER
Whoa, whoa. Number 34 right here.

COUNTER BOY
(sneers)
He was in line. He just went out to get gas in his car.

CHRISTOPHER
I could go out and fuck your sister, come back Saturday. I could go to the front of the line?

COUNTER BOY
(attitude)
I said he could.

CHRISTOPHER
Hey, Pop 'n' Fresh. I'm in no fuckin' mood today. I'm next. Now get a fuckin' pastry box.

COUNTER BOY
(defiant; to customer)
What can I get you?

CHRISTOPHER
(can't believe this)
Ho!

BAKERY CUSTOMER
That's all right, Dougie, let him go first.

COUNTER BOY
He don't make the rules here!

BAKERY CUSTOMER
(shrugs)
Two Neapolitan loaves, a –

CHRISTOPHER
You touch a single fuckin' crust and you'll wish you took that job in McDonald's.

COUNTER BOY
Fuck you.

CHRISTOPHER
(to Customer)
Alright, take a walk.

Christopher opens the door.

BAKERY CUSTOMER
What about my bread?

CHRISTOPHER
Come back in ten minutes.

COUNTER BOY
What the fuck do you think you're doing?

CHRISTOPHER
(to Customer)
Come on.

Intimidated, the Customer leaves. Christopher flips the OPEN sign around to "CLOSED".
He pulls out his GUN. The Counter Boy ducks behind the counter.

CHRISTOPHER
Get up. I'm not gonna hurt you.

The Counter Boy gets up. Chris goes around the counter.

CHRISTOPHER
What is it? Do I look like a pussy to you?

COUNTER BOY
No.

CHRISTOPHER
I'm serious. Be honest. I won't get mad.

COUNTER BOY
No.

CHRISTOPHER
Then why the fuck would you give me a hard time and talk to me like I'm nothing to worry about?

COUNTER BOY
I... I'm sorry.

CHRISTOPHER
Get the pastry box.

He doesn't move. Christopher SHOOTS down at his feet. The Counter Boy moves quickly and grabs a box.

CHRISTOPHER
That's better. Now fill it with cannoli, shfooyadell and Napoleons.

Once again he doesn't move quick enough for Christopher who lets another shot fly into the floor near his feet. The Counter Boy fills the box.

CHRISTOPHER
Good. Give me the box.

The Counter Boy gives him the box.

CHRISTOPHER
Next time you see my face... show some respect.

COUNTER BOY
I will.

On that Christopher SHOOTS the Counter Boy in the FOOT. The Counter Boy goes down... screaming and clutching at his foot.

COUNTER BOY
My foot! You motherfucker, you shot my foot.

CHRISTOPHER
It happens.

Chris exits... his arm reaches back in and flips the sign back to "OPEN".

18: INT. BADA BING – BACK ROOM – DAY

Tony, Pussy, Paulie and Silvio. Georgie is sweeping the room with a de-bugger for any signs of listening devices.

PUSSY
If I'm getting an invitation to the dance, I wish the Feds'd hurry the fuck up about it.

TONY
You heard what they're saying on the news. The way things are working it's gonna be Junior's party.

                    SILVIO
          That was a far-thinking plan you had.

Christopher enters carrying the box of pastry. He clearly has a hair up his ass. Tony, good-naturedly teasing –

                    TONY
          I called you on Christmas.

                    CHRISTOPHER
               (drops box too hard)
          Fuck this.

                    PAULIE
          Hey, the shfooyadell!

                    SILVIO
          Were you brought up in a barn?

                    TONY
          What the fuck's your problem? Now is not the time to go on the rag with
          this indictment shit.
               (like a forgiving father)
          Go'head now. Keep an eye on Georgie while he sweeps for bugs.

19: INT. BADA BING – MEN'S ROOM – SAME – DAY

Christopher stands over Georgie like a foreman while Georgie lifts up the TOILET BOWL SEAT and practically sticks his head into the bowl. Christopher opens the HAND TOWEL DISPENSER and checks inside.

                    GEORGIE
          I hope they'll be alright.

                    CHRISTOPHER
          Who?

                    GEORGIE
          The guys.

                    CHRISTOPHER
          What about me?

                    GEORGIE
          You'll be ok. They didn't mention your name.
               (beat)
          Fucking amazing, huh? I heard the news guy say 'Brendan Filone' and
          the hairs on the back of my neck stood up. I knew the guy. One time me
          and him ate off the same sangwich.

                    CHRISTOPHER
          They made him look like John fuckin' Gotti. I brought him around here.
          Tony wouldn't even have known him if it wasn't for me.

                    GEORGIE
          I had no idea.

20: EXT. GREEN GROVE – DAY

Tony pulls up in his car and parks. A few beats later another car pulls in a few spaces away. Carmela gets out, looks over to Tony. He nods and she enters the building.

21: INT. GREEN GROVE – LIVIA'S ROOM – DAY

Livia is reading the obituaries. A knock at the door.

                    LIVIA
          Who is it? I'm sleeping.

CARMELA (O.S.)

Carmela.

A lock unlocks and the door opens.

LIVIA

I just said that in case you were that snooty-ass Mrs. Ryan down the hall. She's just shanty Irish with all her airs – she doesn't fool me for a second.

CARMELA

Come on, get dressed. I'm taking you to brunch.

LIVIA

What?

CARMELA

You heard me. Get dressed.

LIVIA
(wringing white Kleenex)

What's wrong? Tell me.

CARMELA

Nothing's wrong. Why does something have to be wrong?

LIVIA
(clutching Kleenex)

Is it Anthony? Those indictments? His father could take it in his stride but he can't.

CARMELA

I don't believe you.

LIVIA

Is Meadow all right, she eats like a bird?

CARMELA

Everybody's fine, Ma, relax. There's nothing wrong.

LIVIA

You come by unannounced and I shouldn't think something's wrong?

CARMELA

Well, gee, I'm sorry. It's a beautiful day. I thought I'd take you out.

LIVIA

I don't want to go out.

22: EXT. GREEN GROVE – DAY

Tony waits in his car, antsy, checking his watch.

23: INT. LIVIA'S ROOM – DAY

Carmela is trying to hide her urgency. Livia is plumping pillows. Carmela steals a glance at her watch. Coaxing –

CARMELA

Oh, c'mon. Get dressed.

LIVIA

We just went to a wedding.

CARMELA

That's a big to do. This way you and me'll get to have some quality time.

LIVIA

Why spend money? They've got food here.

112

> **CARMELA**
> *(finality)*
> Ma, The Manor is going to stop serving brunch soon.

> **LIVIA**
> *(studies Carm; fights tears)*
> Did he cheat on you again?

> **CARMELA**
> You know, I try to do something nice... I come here to take you out and right away you think I have some other agenda, that I got to talk to <u>you</u> about? Don't flatter yourself.

> **LIVIA**
> I'll throw something on.

24: EXT. GREEN GROVE – MOMENTS LATER – DAY

Carmela is in her car with Livia. They pull out. PAN to Tony, slouched so he can't be spotted by Livia. When they're gone he gets out, pops the trunk, takes out a sports duffel, heads toward the building.

25: INT. LIVIA'S ROOM

We hear Tony unlocking the door. He enters and quickly puts the lights on. He scans the room as if he's looking for something.

TONY'S POV

The lamp... No. The ceiling... No.

BEDROOM – ALCOVE

Tony enters. Again he scans.

THE CLOSET

He opens it. In there, amongst the obvious, are FIVE LARGE HAT BOXES. He takes one down and opens it. It's one of those days gone by hats that old ladies like to keep. Too big to wear but too expensive to throw away. Tony smirks then TOSSES the hat on the floor. He plops the duffel bag down and opens it. In there is a small fortune. STACKS of BILLS bound with rubber bands. Mostly hundreds. Tony loads as much as he can into the Hat Box. He then PULLS another HAT BOX down and again tosses the hat. He puts in the REMAINING MONEY along with the TWO GUNS we saw him take out of his dropped ceiling at home. He puts the Two Boxes in their original spots careful not to disturb the closet. He EXITS the room and quickly returns with a GREEN GARBAGE BAG. He stuffs the two Hats into the Bag and leaves.

26: INT. MELFI'S OFFICE – DAY

A man. He is dejected.

> **PATIENT**
> – I mean, what a sense of shame.

> **MELFI**
> Among the sexual paraphilias, diapers is fairly common.

> **PATIENT**
> My sexuality is fucked up. I'm from Passaic. Oh, I present just great.

We can tell Melfi is bored.

> **MELFI**
> Remember? What we said recently? You use your shame itself as a shield, a wall?

> **PATIENT**
> I said that?

> **MELFI**
> *(dispirited)*
> It was a significant breakthrough.

He shrugs uncaringly. She glances at the clock.

> **MELFI**
> We'll have to continue next time.

> **PATIENT**
> *(as they walk to door)*
> You know, in Japan, they have special nightclubs for executives who want to wear diapers. They can shit in them and everything and geisha-types change and powder them.

> **MELFI**
> See?

He leaves and she closes the door, blinks her eyes and tries to wake up. She sits at her desk and sorts papers then hears a noise. Goes to the waiting room door and opens it. Tony is settling in with a magazine.

> **MELFI**
> *(pleasant surprise)*
> Mr. Soprano...

> **TONY**
> I'm early. I'll read.

> **MELFI**
> Let's get a leg up.

He's not enthused. She waves impatiently, smiling. He reluctantly enters.

> **MELFI**
> So what's been going on in your life?

27: INT. MELFI'S OFFICE – LATER – TIME LAPSE – DAY

They've been talking awhile.

> **TONY**
> It's not definite but I thought I'd tell you. You know, in case I don't show for an appointment.

> **MELFI**
> So you're telling me that you are planning a vacation but you don't know when exactly it will be.

> **TONY**
> That's right. I mean I may never go. But put it this way, there's a strong possibility that it could happen.

> **MELFI**
> Does this have anything to do with what's been on the news lately?

He merely looks at her. She nods.

> **MELFI**
> So. If suddenly you stop coming to your appointments...I will assume you are on "vacation" and I will further assume that you will not be contacting me?

> **TONY**
> *(smiles)*
> That would be a good assumption.

Melfi is somewhere between concerned and intrigued.

28: INT. CHRISTOPHER'S APARTMENT – NIGHT

The room is dimly lit. Clothes on the floor, an ash tray overflowing with butts and roaches. The tossed Viki King book on screenwriting. Finally, we see Christopher in his underwear and T-shirt smoking a cig and staring at the ceiling. KNOCK on the door. Chris doesn't move. More and more KNOCKS.

> **CHRISTOPHER**
> Who is it?

> **PAULIE (O.S.)**
> Paulie. Open the door.

Christopher drags himself off the couch and opens it. He immediately heads back to the couch and sits.

> **PAULIE**
> I thought we were steppin' out. I got two broads in the car. You said Ade went to stay at her mother's.

> **CHRISTOPHER**
> I was trying to write, she was not supportive.

> **PAULIE**
> No wonder. This place is a fuckin' sty. What's wrong with you?

Paulie throws a light on. Christopher squints.

> **PAULIE**
> Talk to me. This ain't like you, kid.

Chris shrugs.

> **PAULIE**
> I ran into Billy Cracchiolo.

> **CHRISTOPHER**
> The meter maid? What about him?

> **PAULIE**
> Told me the regular cops in Nutley are looking for a guy, blew off a kid's toe for no good reason in Russo's bakery. Drove a Lexus.

> **CHRISTOPHER**
> Does Tony know about this?

> **PAULIE**
> What's goin' on, Chrissy?

> **CHRISTOPHER**
> I don't know what it is. I'm tired all the time.
> *(beat)*
> I been working my ass off on this movie script. Know how many pages I got? Nineteen.

> **PAULIE**
> Is that a lot or a little?

> **CHRISTOPHER**
> Says in the books a movie's supposed to be about a hundred and twenty pages.
> *(Paulie whistles)*
> I got this fuckin' computer, I thought it would do a lot of it.

> **PAULIE**
> *(warning)*
> If you're being frank about the business kid...

> **CHRISTOPHER**
> I would never do that. It's 'suggested by'.

PAULIE
That one writer. With the bullfights? Blew his own fuckin' head off.

CHRISTOPHER
I bought a script writing program and everything.

PAULIE
My advice? Put the thing down awhile – we go get our joints copped –
and tomorrow the words'll come blowing out your ass.

CHRISTOPHER
Did you ever feel like nothing good was ever gonna happen to you?

PAULIE
Yeh, and nothing did. So what? I'm alive. I'm surviving. Fuck it.

CHRISTOPHER
That's just it. I don't want to just survive.
  (beat)
These movie writing books say every character has an arc.
Y'understand?

Paulie shrugs, shakes his head.

CHRISTOPHER
Everybody starts out somewheres. But then they do something or
something gets done to them that changes their life. That's called their
arc. Where's my arc?

Paulie shrugs, trying to mull it.

CHRISTOPHER
Okay, take Richard Kimble – no, that's no good, his arc is just run, run,
jump off a dam, run.
  (beat)
Keanu Reeves – *Devil's Advocate*. You see that?

PAULIE
  (approving)
Al.

CHRISTOPHER
Right. Keanu is a lawyer, gets all turned on by money and power and the
devil, then his wife says, 'You're not the man I married' and leaves him.
You see the arc?
  (shows with hand)
He starts down here –
  (goes higher with his hand)
And he ends up here. Where's my arc, Paulie?

Paulie stares at him.

PAULIE
Kid – Richard Kimble... the devil's whatever – those are make believe.
You're a real guy, born in St. Vincent's Hospital.

Chris has stopped listening and is playing a computer game on his laptop.

PAULIE
I got no arc either. I was born, grew up, spent a few years in the army, a
few more in the can and here I am, a half 'o wiseguy.

CHRISTOPHER
You're missing my point. I got no identity. Even Brendan Filone's got an
identity and he's dead.
  (beat)

I kill that fuckin' E-mail Kolar and nothing. I don't even move up a notch. All I got is nightmares. That Polish, Czechoslovak, whatever the fuck he was, haunting me in my dreams ev'ry night.

29: INT. BADA BING – BACK ROOM – DAY

Chris has been unburdening to Pussy.

PUSSY
That happens. The more of them you do the better you'll sleep. I had one prick chasing me for months in my dreams.

CHRISTOPHER
I feel like he's trying to tell me something. That we fucked up that night when we buried him –

PUSSY
We didn't fuck up.

CHRISTOPHER
That I'm in danger –

PUSSY
Can I ask you a question – why the fuck would he want to tell you you're in danger? Considering you put a fucking moonroof in the back of his head.

CHRISTOPHER
What did we do wrong that night? The gun was hot so the slugs in his head couldn't be traced back to me –

PUSSY
Know who had an arc? Noah.

Pussy chuckles. Chris leaves.

30: EXT. MEADOWLANDS MARSH – DAY

Georgie and Chris (wearing painters' face masks)are DIGGING. Christopher's shovel hits something. Christopher scrapes away the dirt exposing the plastic wrapped body that was buried FACE UP. Christopher and Georgie react immediately to the stench.

GEORGIE
Is that him?

CHRISTOPHER
Now that would be some fuckin' coincidence if it wasn't, wouldn't it?

Christopher turns E-Mail over. He gags and coughs. Georgie presses the mask against his face.

CHRISTOPHER
Holy shit. Look at that. Look through the plastic.

ANGLE – E-MAIL

Emil looks much like he did in Christopher's dream, only now he has a stubbly beard.

GEORGIE
What?

CHRISTOPHER
He was clean shaven. He's got a fuckin' beard!

GEORGIE
(creeped out)
That happens. I read it.

CHRISTOPHER
Jesus. I always thought it was bullshit.

> **GEORGIE**
> Look at his finger nails.

> **CHRISTOPHER**
> Oh, fuck, they're like a woman's.

> **GEORGIE**
> I'm gonna fuckin' puke.

He goes off into the weeds, not to be seen again.

> **CHRISTOPHER**
> Help me lift him, we'll take him down the Pine Barrens before they build a fuckin' condo here.
> > *(beat)*
> Georgie?

31: EXT. VACANT LOT – DAY

It's a pretty parcel. Melfi walks the property. A MERCEDES pulls up. It's Richard.

> **RICHARD**
> Sorry. Traffic.

> **MELFI**
> I don't know about selling this.

> **RICHARD**
> It hurts. But the way the market is makes it an excellent time to cash out.

> **MELFI**
> It's funny how, even during our marriage we usually saw things differently.

> **RICHARD**
> Such as...?

> **MELFI**
> I never thought of this lot as an investment. I thought we'd build a house. You know – when Jason was off to college.

> **RICHARD**
> I don't know about you but I could use an infusion if we're going to support Jas' after graduation. Till he gets on his feet. That's just the way it is with kids nowadays.

> **MELFI**
> With the kids of pyschiatrists.

> **RICHARD**
> > *(laughs)*
> You'll sell or what?

> **MELFI**
> For Jason. I don't want to hear you took one of your Colleens on a cruise.

> **RICHARD**
> What's that supposed to mean, Colleens?

> **MELFI**
> > *(smiles)*
> Come on Richard. You know you're a sucker for those Irish girls. Every Italian boy bows down to those freckles.

> **RICHARD**
> I married you.

> **MELFI**
> I was a mother figure.

(to his scoff)
How come whenever we got sexual, you called me 'mamma'?

RICHARD
Don't bust my balls, huh, with the Freud-by-numbers?

MELFI
'Bust my balls'. Watch it, Rich, your Calabrese is showing.

He levels a look at her.

RICHARD
Are you somehow implying by all this I'm ashamed to be Italian-American?

MELFI
(laughs)
Well – with all the poverty, starvation, ethnic cleansing and generally horrible shit in the world, to devote your energies to protecting the dignity of Connie Francis –

He walks away.

MELFI
You're so worked up about my patient – a man who has no bearing on who you are or where you are in the world.

RICHARD
Call him a patient. This man's a criminal, Jennifer – after awhile it finally gets beyond psychotherapy and its cheesy moral relativism. Finally, you get to good and evil. And he's evil.

This stalls her – she has thought this herself.

MELFI
If I was treating Mussolini would you say I should drop him? Or would you tell me he's important enough or fascism's important enough to warrant clinical understanding?

RICHARD
(gets in his car)
I'll call Coldwell-Banker.

32: EXT. TRUCKING YARD – DAY

On Tony, profile. Imposing, tough. We reveal what he's watching – Chris pulling up in his Lexus. Tony gets in. Chris looks like shit – unkempt, in shorts.

CHRISTOPHER
Sorry I'm late. The alarm –

TONY
(slaps him hard)
The fuck's the matter with you?

CHRISTOPHER
Didn't Paulie tell you I ain't been feeling good –?

TONY
Know what? I wipe my ass with your feelings.

CHRISTOPHER
(tears)
Thanks. Thanks a lot.

TONY
Drive, goddamnit.

Chris pulls out.

33: INT. LEXUS – DAY

They ride in cold silence on Rt.7. Then –

> **TONY**
> We're under a microscope and I gotta hear on the street you shot some civilian in the foot 'cause he made you wait for buns?!

> **CHRISTOPHER**
> Fuckin' Paulie –

> **TONY**
> Don't blame Paulie. Makazian says Nutley PD's got a description, a car. Why didn't you just leave a urine specimen?

> **CHRISTOPHER**
> If I –

> **TONY**
> Then – Georgie comes in the club, fuckin' vomit on his shirt, I ask him what the fuck, he tells me you're digging up a goddamn guy you clipped three months ago.

> **CHRISTOPHER**
> I was worried that –

> **TONY**
> Shut up. Person does something like that, he wants to get caught.

> **CHRISTOPHER**
> Oh, I want to get caught?

> **TONY**
> I seen it before. Fucking cowboy-itis. Gonna be a big bad guy, huh?

> **CHRISTOPHER**
> I was worried he –

> **TONY**
> Shut up!

They ride for awhile.

> **CHRISTOPHER**
> Can I try to explain here?
> *(of silence)*
> I don't know, Tony, it's like…like just the fuckin' regularness of life is… too fuckin' hard for me or something. I dunno.

Tony says nothing, stares ahead, full of contempt. Then –

> **TONY**
> Look at you. Bet you're fuckin' sleepin' all the time, too.

> **CHRISTOPHER**
> Only thing I still enjoy.

> **TONY**
> You getting laid?

> **CHRISTOPHER**
> *(hard to admit)*
> Last thing I fuckin' want.

Tony takes this in.

> **CHRISTOPHER**
> Know what I think, maybe? I have cancer. Remember? How Jackie got?

> **TONY**
> Cancer.

CHRISTOPHER
Something fuckin' horrible's going on inside my body. There's a physical change or something.

TONY
Does that word 'cancer' pop into your mind often? Sometimes? What?

CHRISTOPHER
Huh?

Tony shrugs. Looks away.

TONY
I don't know. I was thinkin' maybe...
(casually)
...you're depressed?

CHRISTOPHER
Me? I'm no fuckin' mental midget.

Tony nods, clams up. Sees Chris's cigarettes, takes one. He puts it in his mouth. Filter out. Is about to light it –

CHRISTOPHER
Watch the...

TONY
Huh? Oh.

He turns it around. Lights it.

TONY
I'm just saying. You might have a... a serotonin problem or whatever they call it.

CHRISTOPHER
You know about this shit?

TONY
I saw it last night on Dr. Dean Adel.

CHRISTOPHER
Take fuckin' Prozac? Not this skinny guinea.

TONY
Yeah. Good for you.

They both fall silent.

TONY
Let me ask you, though and you can be honest with me – you ever feel like...
(mimes gun in mouth)
...you know.

CHRISTOPHER
(obviously has)
Fuck no!

TONY
Good. Can you imagine fuckin' losers blowin' their skulls all over the bathroom?

CHRISTOPHER
Fuckin' pathetic.

Tony too snorts contemptuously. They pull up to a strange, deserted piece of roadway.

TONY
Everybody is tired of your crap. You hear me? Fix it.

Chris barely nods. Tony opens the door, gets half-way out. Without turning to face Chris –

> **TONY**
> But if you ever want to just... shoot the shit or whatever...

They glance at each other hesitantly. Tony gets out. Without looking back he walks off the road to where a man is waiting. On Chris –

34: INT. SOPRANO HOUSE – DAY

Anthony Jr. sits in front of the TV playing a fantasy shoot'em up on his Nintendo when the DOORBELL RINGS. He is too wrapped up in his game to hear it. It rings AGAIN. Still no reaction. Suddenly, Tony Sr. marches into the room.

> **TONY**
> Hey, stroonz! Don't you hear the goddamn doorbell?

> **ANTHONY JR.**
> I'm in the middle of a game.

> **TONY**
> *(heading for door)*
> You'll be in the middle of the fuckin' street if you don't wise up.

But then he notices two FBI AGENTS at the patio door. They tap. He crosses. One HOLDS up a BADGE.

> **AGENT HARRIS**
> Anthony Soprano?

> **TONY**
> What are you doing in my back yard?

> **AGENT HARRIS**
> Gate was open. I'm Agent Harris. This is Agent Driscol. May we come in?

> **TONY**
> If I say no?

> **AGENT HARRIS**
> If we were local we wouldn't have even knocked.

> **TONY**
> What's your point?

> **AGENT HARRIS**
> We have a search warrant.
> *(beat)*
> We know you have children in the house. That's why the team's waiting out front. We don't think it necessary to traumatize kids by kicking in doors. Why don't you take a minute to tell them you have visitors.

Tony just nods slightly.

35: INT. SOPRANO HOUSE – DAY

Carmela stands with her arms on Meadow and Anthony Jr. as the GROUP OF AGENTS are searching the house. Agent Harris is checking the cushions of the couch.

> **TONY**
> Any quarters you can keep.

> **AGENT HARRIS**
> *(chuckles)*
> You trying to bribe me?

> **TONY**
> Maybe if you tell me what you are looking for I can save you some time.

                    AGENT HARRIS
          Any incriminating evidence would be nice.

Just then Two Agents come down from upstairs carrying Meadow's and Anthony Jr.'s COMPUTERS.

                    MEADOW
          Dad?

                    TONY
                  (to Harris)
          You're shittin' me.

Agent Harris just shrugs as if to say "Sorry pal, but that's the way it goes".

                    ANTHONY JR.
          I better have all my programs on that when it comes back.

                    CARMELA
          Anthony.

A CRASH comes from the kitchen.

                    CARMELA
          What the hell are they doing?

36: INT. KITCHEN – DAY

An Agent, AGENT GRASSO, has the FRIDGE DOOR OPEN. A GLASS BOWL has fallen out and broken. Tony enters with Carmela and Agent Harris.

                    CARMELA
          What the hell are you doing in my refrigerator?

                    TONY
          Hey, pal, if you forgot your lunch box just ask.

Anthony Jr. laughs.

                    AGENT GRASSO
          I'm very sorry.

                    AGENT HARRIS
                  (produces pad & pen)
          Mrs. Soprano, how much would you say that bowl cost?

                    CARMELA
          I'm not cleaning that up.

                    AGENT HARRIS
          Grasso, get something to clean that.

                    TONY
          Grasso? Figures.

                    AGENT GRASSO
                  (smirk)
          You figure pretty good yourself.

                    TONY
          Fuck you.

                    AGENT HARRIS
          Hey, hey. Tony, take it easy. We'll be out of here in a few minutes.

Carmela holds Tony's arm.

                    CARMELA
          Let's wait in the living room.

She leads Tony away as he continues to stare at Grasso.

123

37: INT. MELFI'S OFFICE – DAY

Melfi sits at her desk writing when after a FEW MOMENTS she looks at her watch, gets up, and goes to the door. She opens it and scans the waiting room. No one. She's definitely disappointed.

38: INT. SOPRANO KITCHEN – NIGHT

Tony, Carmela, Meadow, and Anthony Jr. eat Chinese take-out. Tony is still pissed about earlier.

> **CARMELA**
> Anthony, don't open all the fortune cookies. That's so self-centered.

> **MEADOW**
> As if you have a future.

> **TONY**
> I know they're doin' their job, those Feds, but it still pisses me off the way they act.

> **CARMELA**
> That one guy wasn't too bad. Harris.

> **TONY**
> Trust me, he was the biggest sneak there. It's all part of the act.
> *(shakes head in disgust)*
> The guy who broke the bowl? He did that on purpose.

> **CARMELA**
> I don't think so. He was just a klutz.

> **TONY**
> What was his name? Rizzo?

> **CARMELA**
> Grasso.

> **TONY**
> You think it's by accident that they sent him. If he wasn't Italian he'd be back at the office sweeping up. The hard on. They prob'ly frisk him every night before he goes home.

> **ANTHONY JR.**
> Why?

> **TONY**
> Why? 'Cause he has a vowel on the end of his name. Grasso. What's he think he's gonna make it to the top by arresting his own people.

> **ANTHONY JR.**
> Pass the mu shu.

> **TONY**
> He'll find out. Forget it. You can only get so far with a vowel on the end of your name.

> **ANTHONY JR.**
> We have a vowel.

> **TONY**
> F'n right. And be proud of it. I swear to God you'd think there never was a Michelangelo?

> **CARMELA**
> Did you know that an Italian invented the telephone?

> **ANTHONY JR.**
> Alexander Graham Bell was Italian?

> **TONY**
> *(to Carmela)*
> You see?
> *(to Anthony Jr.)*
> Antonio Meucci invented the telephone but he got robbed. Everybody knew it, too.

> **MEADOW**
> Who invented the mafia?

> **TONY**
> What?

> **MEADOW**
> La Cosa Nostra. Who invented that?

> **ANTHONY JR.**
> Who cares?

He's uncomfortable with the subject. Tony's eyes flick to Anthony Jr. Then back to Meadow. A warning.

> **MEADOW**
> Wasn't it Salvatore Lucana better known as Charlie "Lucky" Luciano who organized the five families, Lucchese, Gambino, Bonnano, Profaci...

> **TONY**
> You got something you want to say to me?

> **MEADOW**
> I just like history, Dad. Like you.

> **ANTHONY JR.**
> Can't you just shut the fuck up about it?

> **CARMELA**
> Hey.

Tony stares at Meadow. Carmela interjects.

> **CARMELA**
> AJ, did you know that John Cabot was Italian?

> **ANTHONY JR.**
> Wow.

> **MEADOW**
> You can tell he doesn't know who that is.

> **CARMELA**
> The famous discoverer of Canada.

> **TONY**
> Did you ever hear of the Bank of America. One of the biggest banks in the world. Started by an Italian.

> **ANTHONY JR.**
> I know that the first American saint was an Italian American. Mother Cabrini.

> **CARMELA**
> That's right.

> **ANTHONY JR.**
> Is it true the Chinese invented spaghetti?

> **TONY**
> Think about it. Why would people who eat with sticks invent something you need a fork to eat.

Anthony Jr. ponders.

> **TONY**
> Here's something I bet you didn't know. More Italians fought for this country in World War II than any other ethnic group. And they'll never tell you about Sacco and Vanzetti either.

> **ANTHONY JR.**
> Two anti-christs who got the electric chair in Massachusetts.

> **MEADOW**
> Anarchists.

> **ANTHONY JR.**
> Isn't it anti-christs?

> **CARMELA**
> Two innocent men who got the chair because they were Italian.

> **MEADOW**
> There was more to it than that.

> **TONY**
> Not much.

> **MEADOW**
> How could there be two anti-christs? There was one Christ.

> **ANTHONY JR.**
> So?

> **TONY**
> And, of course – Francis Albert.

39: INT. MELFI'S OFFICE – DAY

Tony and Melfi.

> **MELFI**
> Will I see you next week?

> **TONY**
> Unless you know something I don't.

> **MELFI**
> I hate to have to talk business but we did have an agreement that if something came up and you had to cancel, you were to give me at least twenty four hours notice.

> **TONY**
> The problem with that is that they didn't give me twenty four hours notice.

> **MELFI**
> Just so you understand that I must charge you for the missed session.

> **TONY**
> What?

> **MELFI**
> We agreed on that from our very first meeting.

> **TONY**
> I explained to you my situation.

> **MELFI**
> I understand but it's important that we respect the agreement.

> **TONY**
> And what if I was hit by a car?

> **MELFI**
> But you weren't.

> **TONY**
> But what if?

> **MELFI**
> But you weren't.

> **TONY**
> I know that, but what if?

> **MELFI**
> You weren't.

> **TONY**
> (sudden rage)
> Answer my fuckin' question!

Melfi is stunned not to mention a bit scared.

> **MELFI**
> I will not.

> **TONY**
> You won't?

Tony stands and Melfi flinches. Tony pulls out a ROLL OF BILLS. He pulls a few off and tosses them in her direction.

> **TONY**
> Here. Here's your fuckin' money. That's all this about, right? Motherfuckin', cocksuckin', money.

> **MELFI**
> I don't really understand that comment but I don't appreciate being made to feel afraid.

> **TONY**
> Well, I don't appreciate being made to feel like I've been pouring my heart out to a fuckin' call girl.

> **MELFI**
> Is that how you see me?

> **TONY**
> As a call girl? Up until now? No. But it's clear to me that you don't give two fuckin' shits about my situation. If you did you wouldn't be shaking me down.

Not backing down –

> **MELFI**
> It'll show as paid on next month's bill.

> **TONY**
> Stick it up your ass.

On that he's out the door. Melfi looks down at the money.

40: INT. GREEN GROVE – AUDITORIUM – DAY

An OLD WOMAN walks by with the help of a WALKER. Junior and Livia are in the audience of seniors. A COMEDIAN with bad hairpiece is onstage.

> **COMEDIAN**
> And how about Dr. Goldman over here? Originally, he was gonna be a tree surgeon. But he fainted at the sight of sap.

Some laughter. Not Livia. And not Junior.

> **LIVIA**
> *(sotto voce)*
> What's the matter with you?

> **JUNIOR**
> Headaches that's all. And not the kind you take aspirin for.

> **LIVIA**
> *(bitter)*
> What're you gonna do? The whole world's gone crazy.

> **JUNIOR**
> Yeah, well...

> **LIVIA**
> *(off newspaper in lap)*
> Over in Metuchen they found a little baby at the city dump. The mother had thrown it there. What's wrong with people?

> **COMEDIAN**
> And movie night. Last week they showed the Polish version of *Rashomon*. Everybody remembers the rape exactly the same.

This one bombs bad. The crowd doesn't get it.

> **JUNIOR**
> I think we may have a bad apple.

> **LIVIA**
> Does Anthony know about this?

Junior nods "YES".

> **LIVIA**
> What're you going to do?

> **JUNIOR**
> There's not much to do. We just have to sit back and wait. And do me a favor, don't let Tony know you know. He's under enough pressure.

> **LIVIA**
> *(snide)*
> Oh, yes. And I'm sure he's telling that psychiatrist it's all his mother's doing.

> **JUNIOR**
> What're you talking about, psychiatrist?

> **LIVIA**
> A psychiatrist! He's been seeing one for awhile now.
> *(carefully watches Junior's reaction)*
> God only knows what he says. I've never deprived my children nothing.

> **JUNIOR**
> Tony??

> **LIVIA**
> Yes, Tony. Tony who had such a terrible mother.

> **JUNIOR**
> A psychiatrist?

> **LIVIA**
> Yes, Junior. For chrissake.

> **COMEDIAN**
> I said to the dietician, 'You call this Florida orange juice? I call it Agent orange juice'.

David Chase and James Gandolfini.

"College", Allen Coulter directs James Gandolfini
as a crew member wires him for sound.

Tony Soprano (Gandolfini) visits college campus with Meadow (Jamie-Lynn Sigler).

"The Legend of Tennessee Moltisanti", Carmela (Edie Falco) and Livia (Nancy Marchand) outside Green Grove Retirement Community.

"The Legend of Tennessee Moltisanti", director Tim Van Patten in the Sopranos house set with Gandolfini and producer Henry Bronchtein.

"The Happy Wanderer", Carmela (Falco) and Tony (Gandolfini)

"The Happy Wanderer", creator David Chase and Edie Falco
share a laugh in the high school auditorium.

"The Happy Wanderer", director John Patterson orchestrates the poker game.
Clockwise from Patterson: Tony Sirico, Steven Van Zandt, Robert Patrick,
Frank Sinatra, Jr.

"The Knight in White Satin Armor", Janice (Aida Turturro)
and Richie (David Proval) argue.

"Proshai, Livushka", Turturro and Gandolfini, and camera crew.

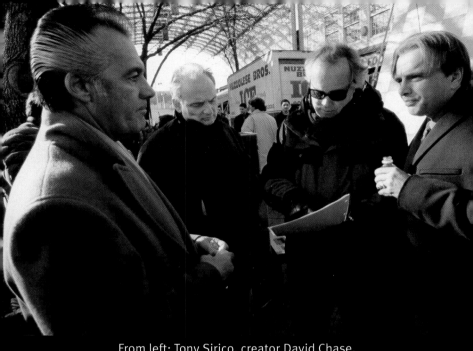

From left: Tony Sirico, creator David Chase,
director John Patterson and Joe Pantoliano.

Creator David Chase with Drea de Matteo.

"Proshai, Livushka", director Tim Van Patten directs the cast at Livia's funeral.

Actor/writer Michael Imperioli with creator David Chase

S109 "The Legend of Tennessee Moltisanti: FINAL SHOOTING SCRIPT

> **JUNIOR**
> Who? The psychiatrist, I mean?

> **LIVIA**
> You think I know?

> **JUNIOR**
> What'd you say to Tony about this?

> **LIVIA**
> Me? Nothing. I wouldn't give him the satisfaction.
> *(beat)*
> And Junior, I don't want there to be any repercussions.

> **JUNIOR**
> *(stunned)*
> A psychiatrist?

> **LIVIA**
> You're a broken record. Yes. Do I have to say it again?

Off Junior, wounded and still disbelieving.

41: INT. CHRISTOPHER'S APARTMENT/BEDROOM – MORNING

Christopher is sound asleep when he is awakened by the PHONE. He lets the machine answer it.

> **MOTHER (on machine)**
> Christopher? It's Mommy. I know you're there. Pick it up.

He rolls over and puts a PILLOW on his head.

> **MOTHER (on machine)**
> Are you alright? I'm worried about you. My God, they mentioned your name in the newspaper today, Christopher.
> *(weeping)*
> With all those scumbags.

Christopher whips the pillow off his head.

42: INT. DR. REIS' OFFICE – DAY

The La Penna's are there for family therapy with DR. SAMUEL REIS, 60. The wall behind Reis is evidence of a life of solidity and scholarly humanism – degrees, citations, genuine ancient art.

> **REIS**
> It's been awhile since we met for therapy. Jason, how's Bard?

> **JASON**
> I'm moving into a smoke-free dorm.

> **REIS**
> *(to parents)*
> And how do we feel about that?

They shrug... fine. Silence. To all –

> **REIS**
> Is that a subject we want to pursue in this hour?

> **RICHARD**
> I'm more interested in discussing what we mentioned before.
> *(to Melfi)*
> Married or not I still care about you and worry about you.

> **REIS**
> Jason, are you concerned that your mother is treating this 'patient X'?

JASON
(rather sullen)
I don't care.

REIS
As a colleague, Jen? I suggest you drop the patient. Given his lifestyle it seems he could hurt you more than you could ever help him.

MELFI
I'm here to talk about my family, not my workday.

RICHARD
After her last encounter with him she finally acknowledged she saw the different side of him. The sub-human.

REIS
I take it you were frightened.

MELFI
Frightened, revolted...

RICHARD
At long last, the appropriate emotions.

MELFI
For crissake, Richard. You too, Sam. When did we become so afraid to get our hands dirty?

JASON
That's what she gets paid for.

RICHARD
Would you like to see your mother... never mind, I'm not going to paint any graphic images.

JASON
See? He always does that.

REIS
Follow that up, Jas'. Dad does what?

JASON
He knows.

MELFI
Non sequitur accusation, Jason.

RICHARD
Sticking up for me? Don't change the subject. We were talking about your mobster patient.

MELFI
Richard knows I'm in no danger. His real issue is I should distance myself from this man on grounds of the stigma he brings us.

REIS
What does your therapist say? Would you share that?

MELFI
Elliot raised the notion that by retaining this patient I'm repudiating Richard. And, of course, the failed marriage.

RICHARD
Halle-fucking-lujah. I didn't think Elliot had it upstairs.

MELFI
Fuck you.

REIS
(chuckles)

I say refer this patient to a therapist that specializes in mafia depression.

> RICHARD
> Sam, this isn't funny.

> REIS
> (somberly)
> No, of course not. Jen has a real honest to goodness personal and professional dilemma.
> (concentration drifts; with a shit eating grin)
> You know on my mother's side we have a few dark sheep.

> RICHARD
> Excuse me?

> REIS
> Lepke.

Richard knows who it is but doesn't understand.

> JASON
> Who's Lepke?

> REIS
> Louis Lepke Buchalter. You know, Murder Incorporated. My mother's uncle was Lepke's wheelman. His driver.

> RICHARD
> (blank stare)
> Uh-huh.

> REIS
> Those were some tough Jews.

He smirks. He beams. Richard stares, pole-axed. Melfi tries not to smile, winds up laughing.

43: EXT. STREET – MORNING

Christopher's CAR pulls up to a NEWSPAPER VENDING MACHINE and Christopher jumps out leaving the door open. He puts a coin in and pulls out a NEWSPAPER. He quickly thumbs through it till he finds the page. He reads down until...

PAGE

A tiny mention in the midst of an article; "... Along with other reputed gangsters, Richard Catuso, Christopher Moltisanti, and Robert 'Quiet Bobby' Rufalo."

CHRISTOPHER

Excitedly puts in another coin and takes all the papers inside. The lid slams down. He heads for his car, wearing a smile. He breaks into a run, his smile widening.

FADE OUT.

THE END

"The Happy Wanderer"

S208

Written by
Frank Renzulli

Directed by
John Patterson

Soprano Productions, Inc.

Production Draft	8/24/99
1st Revision (Blue Pages)	8/27/99
2nd Revision (Full Pink)	8/30/99
3rd Revision (Full Yellow)	9/2/99
4th Revision (Green Pages)	9/9/99
5th Revision (Goldenrod Pages)	9/15/99
6th Revision (Buff Pages)	9/20/99

FINAL SHOOTING SCRIPT

CHARACTER LIST

TONY SOPRANO
CARMELA SOPRANO
DR. JENNIFER MELFI
CHRISTOPHER MOLTISANTI
ANTHONY SOPRANO, JR.
MEADOW SOPRANO
LIVIA SOPRANO
UNCLE "JUNIOR" SOPRANO
SILVIO DANTE
PAULIE WALNUTS
JANICE "PARVATI" SOPRANO
RICHIE APRILE

Artie Bucco
Johnny Sack
Matt Bevelaqua
Sean Gismonte
Furio
Barbara Giglione
Tom Giglione
Vito Spatafore
Hillel
David Scatino
Eric Scatino
Frank Sinatra, Jr.
Doctor Freid
Sunshine
Mrs. Scatino
Mrs. Gaetano
Cop
Fish Man (Formerly Fish Kid)
College Representative
Dealer
Hooker
Priest
Gudren

SETS

INTERIORS

High School "College Night"	N
Men's Room	N
Hallway	N
Melfi's Office	D
Richie's Social Club	N
School Auditorium	D/N
Backstage	N
Dr. Schreck's Office	D
Ramsey's Sports and Outdoor	D
Ramsey's Sports and Outdoor – Office	D
Fish Store	D
Flyaway Motel – Lobby	D
Flyaway Motel – Hallway	N
Flyaway Motel – Efficiency	N/D
Soprano House – Master Bedroom	D
Soprano House – Meadow's Room	D
Soprano House – Garage	N
Soprano House – Kitchen	N
Drago's Funeral Home – Tom Sr.'s Room	N
Drago's Funeral Home – Empty Viewing Room	N
Tony's Suburban	N
Richie's Car	N
Nuovo Vesuvio	D
Eric's SUV	D

EXTERIORS

Paulie's Car	N
Soprano House	D
Flyaway Motel	D
Scatino House	D

1: INT. HIGH SCHOOL "COLLEGE NIGHT" – NIGHT

A Brown University REPRESENTATIVE addresses a small group of STUDENTS and their PARENTS amongst whom WE SEE Carmela. Seated next to Carmela is Meadow, next to Meadow is student/friend ERIC SCATINO and next to Eric is his father DAVID SCATINO, owner of a local sports store, and his WIFE.

>   REP
> Our undergrad student body at Brown only numbers about six thousand
> people. That's from every state in this country and from more than sixty
> countries in the world. Admission is extremely selective.

ON AUDIENCE – David excuses himself as he slips by others.

>   REP (cont'd)
> So again, get all your academic and extra-curricular ducks in a row.
> Leave nothing to chance –

2: INT. MEN'S ROOM – NIGHT

Tony is at the urinal. David enters.

>   DAVID
> Hey, buddy!

>   TONY
> Ho, Davy... I spotted your wife alone, figured you for the trotters.

>   DAVID
> Not tonight. Had a customer I couldn't shake. Guy spends a half hour
> deciding between a twenty dollar soccer ball and a twenty two dollar
> soccer ball.

He sidles up to the next urinal.

>   DAVID (cont'd)
> So, who do you like?

>   TONY
> I don't know. The guy from Bowdoin is starting to make a little sense.

>   DAVID
> No, I mean in tonight's game.

The door opens and in pops Artie.

>   ARTIE
> Ho, what's this? You two want to be alone?

>   DAVID
> Boook. I saw that refreshment table out there, figured you were lurking
> somewhere.

>   ARTIE
> I don't know how I always get roped into this shit.

>   TONY
> Charmaine's no fool. One of your shfooyadell in the right mouth and
> your kid's a cinch wherever she wants to go.

>   ARTIE
> Yeah, so far the janitor is the only one going near them.

>   TONY
> Not a bad career for a young woman.

>   ARTIE
> Fuck you.

>   TONY
> I'm gonna grab one of those belly bombs.

135

ARTIE
Have I said "fuck you" yet?

3: INT. HIGH SCHOOL "COLLEGE NIGHT" – NIGHT

Tony, Artie, and David are at the food table.

DAVID
(mouth full)
Bon gusto, Artie. Glad I didn't eat tonight.

ARTIE
(directed at Tony)
Thanks Davy. It's nice to be appreciated by friends.

TONY
The sensitive chef.

Meadow, Eric, and a FEW other STUDENTS, come over.

DAVID
Hey, Eric, they all done in there?

ERIC
I guess. Dad, can I have twenty bucks?

DAVID
(to Tony)
You like this?

TONY
Why, did you think he was coming over to say thank you for taking the time to come to this important evening?

MEADOW
Ha, ha.

Tony gives Meadow a playful hug.

TONY
How you doin', Eric?

ERIC
Good, Mr. Soprano.

DAVID
(of table)
You guys want something to eat?

ERIC
Nah, we're going to Starbucks.

TONY
(laughs at Artie; then)
So, you thinking about goin' to Brown?

ERIC
(shrugs)
Really good school... lot of starfucking, though.

DAVID
Hey, latrine lip, let's uh...

MEADOW
(shrugs)
He's right.

DAVID
This jamoke'll go where his mother tells him. No different than his old man.

> **ARTIE**
> You too? What happened to us?

> **TONY**
> *(to Eric)*
> Listen to this shit. In high school these guys were
> Namath and Y.A. Tittle.

> **ERIC**
> *(bored)*
> I know, I've heard –

> **TONY**
> Now, they're Alan Alda and Phil Donahue.

The kids leave. Tony and David stroll.

4: INT. HALLWAY – CONTINUING

Posters, schedules, and other school type stuff hang on the hallway walls.

> **DAVID**
> Listen, I heard through the grapevine that you're taking over your
> uncle's game. You know the big one.

> **TONY**
> The grapevine. You know, if you listen to that song close, it says
> "believe none of what you hear and half of what you see."

> **DAVID**
> No, I was just... you know me. I like to play a little.

> **TONY**
> A "little"? Forget it. That game's not for you.

> **DAVID**
> Just I... you know. I just thought it would be a kick.

> **TONY**
> Davy, you're a good guy. I like you. Trust me, this isn't a game for you. I
> wouldn't want to see you get hurt. These guys play deep.

> **DAVID**
> *(playfully)*
> You know how many jock straps I sold last week?

> **TONY**
> *(chuckling)*
> Not enough for this game. Forget it. Let's go hear the walyo from
> Bucknell.

5: INT. MELFI'S OFFICE – DAY

Melfi and Tony sit in their usual seats. After a long silence...

> **MELFI**
> You want to tell me what you're thinking about?

> **TONY**
> Forget it. You don't want to know.

She just holds his look, waits...

> **TONY (cont'd)**
> You wanna know what I'm thinkin'? Seriously? I'm thinkin' how I'd like to
> take a brick and smash your fuckin' face into fuckin' hamburger.

Melfi can't cover being slightly taken aback.

MELFI
(trying to cover)
Ok.

TONY
I'm not... I mean... don't worry. I know I broke your coffee table. It's not gonna happen again. You asked, I told.

MELFI
But you would <u>like</u> to smash my face.

TONY
Not really, it was just a way of describing how I'm feeling.

MELFI
Do you think making hamburger out of me would make you feel better?

TONY
Mother of Christ. Is this a woman thing or what? You asked me what I was thinking, I told you. Now, you're gonna torture me with it. I don't know who the fuck I'm angry at. I'm just fuckin' angry, ok?

Long pause.

TONY (cont'd)
'Cause why the fuck am I here? And I even <u>asked</u> to come back. I got the world by the balls and yet I can't stop this feeling that I'm a loser.

MELFI
Who makes you feel like a loser? Your mother?

TONY
We wasted enough oxygen on her.

MELFI
Your father? <u>His</u> panic attacks?

TONY
I'm talkin' about everything and everybody. Sometimes, if I see a guy with a clear head, you know the type, always whistling like the Happy Fuckin' Wanderer. I see this and... I wanna walk up to him and rip his fuckin' throat open. For no reason at all. Just go up to him and fuckin' pummel him.

She waits.

TONY (cont'd)
Why should I give a shit if a guy's got a clear head? I should say, "a salut', good for him."

MELFI
Yes.
(beat)
Let's get back to smashing my face.

TONY
Ayyy.

MELFI
No, I think it all ties in.

TONY
Sometimes, I resent you making me feel like a victim, that's all.

MELFI
I make you feel like a <u>victim</u>?

TONY
First day I came here – first fuckin' day – I said how Gary Cooper was a

<u>man</u>. Strong. Silent. And how fuckin' Americans nowadays they're just pussys – crying, complaining, confessing – <u>fuck</u> 'em!
(beat)
But here I am – one of them. A patient.

MELFI
Your parents made it impossible for you to experience joy.

TONY
See? There you go again!

MELFI
You said yourself – you're not a happy wanderer.

TONY
(frustrated)
Yeah? Well, I'm more of one of those assholes than a fuckin' jerkoff. Like the other douchebags I see leaving this office.

6: INT. RICHIE'S SOCIAL CLUB – NIGHT

A POKER GAME in progress. Seated is Artie, David, VITO SPATAFORE, RICHIE, and of course the DEALER. They all turn over their cards and Artie is sitting pretty with a full house.

ARTIE
Santa Maria! Yes!

RICHIE
Santa Maria? More like fuckin' Santa Claus.

Artie starts grabbing the pot.

RICHIE
(to Dealer)
Did you cut the pot yet?

DEALER
Twice.

ARTIE
(throws the Dealer a chip)
Prick. Here. Make sure you spend it in my restaurant.

VITO
Ah va'napola. One chip? He can't buy a McDonald's with that.

Some chuckles. Richie pours Artie a refill.

ARTIE
Nah, I gotta get going.

DAVID
C'mon, Boook, another hour.

ARTIE
Nah, I can't. Charmaine will have my balls on the menu tomorrow.

Davy leans in to Richie.

DAVID
Rich, can I get another dime?

RICHIE
We only got three players.

DAVID
So, what? Vito's up for it, right?

139

> **VITO**
> Where the fuck do I gotta be? But let's up the ante.

> **RICHIE**
> *(sotto to David)*
> You sure? I mean, you're into me for seven G's now.

> **DAVID**
> That's all? I'll make that back from Vito in an hour.

> **RICHIE**
> *(to Dealer, smiling)*
> Count this crazy chooch out another dime.

7: INT. SCHOOL AUDITORIUM – DAY

Meadow and Eric wind up a piano accompanied duet rehearsal of "Sun/Moon" from "Miss Saigon."

> **ERIC/MEADOW**
> "– you are sunshine and I moon."

> **MRS. GAETANO**
> Okay. Well, we have our work cut out for us.
> *(to a student)*
> Gudren?

Another GIRL takes the stage as Meadow and Eric leave. The PIANO ACCOMPANIST starts and the girl begins her solo, a German lieder piece.

> **MRS. GAETANO**
> Meadow, can I talk to you a minute?

Eric has gone off to horse around with friends.

> **MRS. GAETANO (cont'd)**
> It's really sounding pretty good. I know you're disappointed...

> **MEADOW**
> It's just, when you try out for cabaret night the form asks what you want to do and I checked off solo –

> **MRS. GAETANO**
> You seniors, this is your last chance at cabaret. Gudren has never had a solo in four years here. I like to give everybody a shot.

> **MEADOW**
> Mrs. Gaetano, I was a sophomore when I did "Spider Woman." And now it's real important 'cause of college and all.

The teacher pats her back and goes off to listen. Meadow watches Gudren's German lieder ring out.

8: INT. DR. SCHRECK'S OFFICE – DAY

JUNIOR and Tony.

> **TONY**
> So, you ok with this?

> **JUNIOR**
> Do I have a choice?

> **TONY**
> Yeah, you have a choice. You can continue to run the game.

> **JUNIOR**
> You know I'm under fuckin' house arrest, you cute fuck.

TONY

So take the bite I give you and be happy. Either way I'm having the executive game.

Junior is quiet for a moment.

JUNIOR

You know your father an' me started that game over thirty years ago. It was our idea to have a game only once a month. We were talkin' one day about how the car credit card companies worked their angle. Y'know, how they only took people who could pay. How they didn't care what the fuck you bought as long as you didn't pay all at once. They juice you to death and you thank them for letting you have a card. You'd rather be juiced than pay all at once. Some people know the value of liquid. Smart money loves the juice. That's a certain kind of player. That's why we called it the executive game. My brother Johnny was one keen motherfucker.

TONY

Oh, yeah, how come he left us with ceci beans. You're not there, we're selling furniture.

JUNIOR

You don't know what you're talkin' about. Your father left Livia with a package that could choke a fuckin' elephant. I gotta tell you? She's like the woman with a Virginia Ham under her arm crying the blues 'cause she has no bread. Please, they don't make'm like Johnny. Keep in mind he paid the freight for your Uncle Eckley, buon' anema. And that was a major fuckin' nut.

TONY

Who? Who the fuck is Heckle?

JUNIOR
(fluffing Tony off)

Forget it. Keep thinkin' you know everything. Some people are so far behind in a race that they actually believe they're leading.

TONY

Ya, that's cute. Who's Heckle?

JUNIOR

Eckley, Eckley. Let's talk about something else.

TONY

Na, you opened this clam, my friend. Who is he?

JUNIOR

You don't know him. Water under the bridge. Just know that me an' your father looked out for him. He wanted for nothing.

TONY

Ayyy, fuck you and Heckley or whatever. I ain't got time for this.

JUNIOR

He was my younger brother. He was between me and your father in age. His name was Eckley – actually Ercoli – Hercules. Named after my grandfather.

TONY

Whoa, are you sayin' I had another uncle? Another uncle?

JUNIOR

Sharp as a fuckin' cue ball. Yes. I'm sayin' your father an' me had a brother that you didn't know about 'cause he was... it was different in those days. Mother and Father didn't even speak the language. They couldn't take care of a kid like that. But, God bless, your grandmother.

She went to every charity home in this fuckin' state till she found one that she felt would take good care of him.

> **TONY**
> Are you sayin' he was a retard?

> **JUNIOR**
> *(taking instant heat)*
> Why don't you go and fuck yourself. He was slow. He wasn't some mongoloid. He was strong as a fuckin' bull. And handsome. Like George Raft. If it was today they might've trained him to be a whatever or something. Get him a job. They didn't understand these things back then. If you had a fuckin' stutter they'd lock you away and say you were a reject. He wasn't that bad.
> *(more to himself)*
> Jesus, what were we thinkin'?

Silence. Tony is blown away.

> **TONY**
> Unbelievable. Don't take this the wrong way, but, I remember my mother and father arguing about something and my mother kept referring to my father's feeble-minded brother... I always thought she meant you.

Junior doesn't like this.

> **TONY (cont'd)**
> Talk about a kick in the balls. Eckley. How long ago did he die?

> **JUNIOR**
> Not long before your father.
> *(quickly)*
> The past is the past. This is the present. Let's talk about this game. What's my end?

Tony's still a little pensive.

> **TONY**
> I, I don't know. Ten percent.

> **JUNIOR**
> *(quickly)*
> Twenty.

Tony is still a bit numb from the Ercoli story.

> **TONY**
> Fifteen.
> *(beat)*
> And let your friends know the game is still happening.

Off Junior's signature smirk...

9: INT. SCATINO'S SPORTS – DAY

Richie is approached by Eric.

> **ERIC**
> Can I help you with something?

> **RICHIE**
> Yeah, I wanna boat with three propellers.

> **ERIC**
> What?

> **RICHIE**
> Kid, you see me ev'ry week. When you gonna stop askin'?

                    DAVID (O.S.)
          Ho, Rich.

Richie smirks as he walks away from Eric. He goes over to David who is at the register. As Richie approaches David opens the register, removes a small envelope.

                    DAVID (cont'd)
                    (re: Eric)
          There a problem?

                    RICHIE
          Nah. Just breakin' your kid's balls.

David hands Richie the envelope.

                    RICHIE (cont'd)
          Like the pimp said to his whores; "keep'm comin'."

                    DAVID
                    (on a chuckle)
          Hey, Rich, that envelope's 2 C's shy. I catch up on it next week.

Richie's face changes...

                    DAVID (cont'd)
          No problem, just got caught off guard a little this month. I took a second on the house and I forgot to calculate it in my budget. No biggie.

                    RICHIE
          No good, Davy.

                    DAVID
          A stutter step. Like I said "no biggie."

                    RICHIE
          The difference gets tacked on to the principal, you know that.

                    DAVID
          Yeah, sure. I understand.

                    RICHIE
          Don't take this personally, but, I don't want to see your face at any of my games until you're caught up.

                    DAVID
          C'mon Rich, that's not necessary.

                    RICHIE
          Kid, you think I just started this life ten minutes ago? A guy hands you a light envelope, it's just the beginning. Nothing personal.

                    DAVID
          I know, but, it's just this week...

                    RICHIE
          I know. Just a stutter step.
                    (beat)
          Remember, it's on the principal.

Richie turns and heads out. He grabs a baseball from a bucket of balls and tosses it over his head to ERIC who is waiting on a CUSTOMER...

                    RICHIE (cont'd)
          Ho...

Eric catches it. Without breaking stride –

                    RICHIE (cont'd)
          Sign him up.

10: INT. FISH STORE – DAY

Christopher, still limping from his broken toe, is with Matt and Sean buying fish for the game. A guy works the counter.

> **CHRISTOPHER**
> *(points)*
> What kind is that?

> **FISH MAN**
> Brazilian snapper.

> **CHRISTOPHER**
> Is it fishy?

> **FISH MAN**
> It's fish.

> **CHRISTOPHER**
> You know what I mean. It's for pizziola. Let me smell it.

The Fish Man pulls it out for Christopher. Christopher smells it.

> **FISH MAN**
> You want something or what?

> **CHRISTOPHER**
> Yeah, lemme get some of that, enough for fifteen people. And ten pounds of shrimp.

As the Fish Man is getting the fish out and trimming. Christopher pulls a pen out of his pocket and then nudges Matt. Christopher wedges the pen into the scale.

> **CHRISTOPHER**
> There's gonna be some serious money there. No nickel and dime shit. These motherfuckers can play for two days straight, sometimes. Once you start work, you don't go until the game breaks up and that fuckin' place looks like an operating room.

> **SEAN**
> We're, like, cleaning guys?

The Fish Man puts the Brazilian snapper onto the scale then looks at the weight. He squints as if to say "This can't be right." He TAPS on the scale.

> **CHRISTOPHER**
> Ho, what the fuck are you doin'?

> **FISH MAN**
> Something ain't right...

> **CHRISTOPHER**
> Fuckin-A. I caught you puttin' your finger on the scale.

The Fish Man is rattled.

> **FISH MAN**
> No I didn't.

> **CHRISTOPHER**
> Pull that shit with old ladies. Not with me, you fuckin' hump.

> **FISH MAN**
> I didn't put my finger on the scale!

> **CHRISTOPHER**
> I don't fuckin' believe this shit.

The Fish Man is about to remove the fish from the scale.

CHRISTOPHER
Where are you going? Wrap that up.

FISH MAN
But I gotta weigh it on the other –

CHRISTOPHER
What? You gotta what? Rob me?

The beleaguered Fish Man sighs and starts wrapping the fish. To Matt and Sean:

CHRISTOPHER (cont'd)
You'll serve some booze, empty ashtrays... oh, that reminds me, whatever you do, don't engage in conversation with Silvio. He can be a sick fuck when he gambles. One night he was losing like fifty large and at some point he sneezed, so Fritzi says "salut'."

SEAN
Fritzi Neste from Hoboken?

CHRISTOPHER
Yeah, you know him?

SEAN
No.

CHRISTOPHER
Then shut the fuck up and let me finish. Anyway, Fritzi says "Salut'," Sil' thinks he said something else and forget it, after that all night he blamed Fritzi for his losing streak, the fuckin' nut.

SEAN
What did he think he said?

CHRISTOPHER
You listenin' or what? He's a fuckin' nut. Who knows? Fritzi says "Salut'" Silvio hears "go fuck your mother" or something. He's a nut.

The Fish Man puts the wrapped fish on the counter.

FISH MAN
Here. But I didn't put my finger on no fuckin' –

CHRISTOPHER
Don't worry about it.
(slips him $5; to Matt)
Put that shit in the trunk so it doesn't stink up the car.

Christopher walks away. Matt wears a puss.

MATT
Is this guy for real or what? What're we, fuckin' piss boys?

He hands the bag to Sean.

MATT (cont'd)
C'mon, let's get the fuck out of here.

11: EXT. PAULIE'S CAR – NIGHT

PAULIE is driving when, suddenly, WE SEE a Police car pull up his ass, put the colored lights on, and give the SIREN a little toot. Paulie pulls over.

PAULIE
(to himself)
Prick.

WE SEE the COP get out of his car and walk to the driver's side window. Paulie rolls down his window.

145

PAULIE
Whatiya hear? Whatiya say?

COP
License and registration.

Paulie reaches under his seat, pulls out a 9mm, and cutely points it at the cop.

PAULIE
How 'bout I give you one of these instead?

The Cop doesn't even flinch.

COP
I'm wearing a vest.

PAULIE
Oh, yeah? If I shoot it's going in your squash.

COP
You're a sick fuck. You know that?

PAULIE
(smiling)
Danny Boy, how's your family?

COP
Not bad. My old man since they moved –

PAULIE
(cutting him off; an old ball breaker's joke)
Ayy! I got my own fuckin' problems.

Paulie cracks up.

COP
You fuckin' hard-on. How many times am I gonna fall for that?

The Cop scans the area. Paulie hands him a rolled wad of cash.

COP (cont'd)
Do me a favor. Tell your friends, player or no, they don't fuck with any tourists or motel guests, keep the noise down and no gunshots or we gotta take the call.

PAULIE
Yeah, yeah. Go play cops and robbers.

Paulie drives away...

11A: INT. FLYAWAY MOTEL – LOBBY – DAY

Things have certainly changed since Tony and company have inserted their presence. FURIO enters passing TWO street level HOOKERS and a businessman JOHN. There are a few vending machines one advertising soda and another, condoms. Furio hits the bell. A miserable HILLEL appears at the front desk.

FURIO
We want the room with the stove and the refrigerator.

HILLEL
The efficiencies are all booked to paying customers.

FURIO
(jerks thumb)
Muovono. And the two rooms on the sides. We may be here for some days.

HILLEL
You people have ruined this place.

FURIO
Atsa you father fault. He made the business deal. We want a lot of clean towelsa and bathrooms fresha smelling.

HILLEL
I should work for nothing?

We see yet a third HOOKER pass. Furio stops her.

FURIO
You ever suck his goshapic'?

HOOKER
I make that beanie spin when I work his thing.
(to Hillel)
Am I right?

Furio gives her the head nod to continue on her way.

FURIO
Don't bitcha to me.

12: INT. FLYAWAY MOTEL – EFFICIENCY ROOM – NIGHT

The Executive Game is in full swing. The Players: Paulie, Silvio, JOHNNY SACK, FRANK SINATRA, JR., and DOCTOR FREID, a penile implant doctor. The dealer is called SUNSHINE because he always looks like he has the weight of the world on his shoulders.

Tony is checking out the spread which consists of Pesce pizziola, deep fried battered fish, jumbo shrimp, a ham, Major League cold cuts, olives, caponata, chunks of provolone, peppers, lots of round Napolitan' bread, and of course, bottles of red and white wine. Matt and Sean work the room. Christopher floats around (DON'T FORGET THE LIMP) the card table like a pit boss.

TONY

samples some of the food.

TONY
Mike.

No one answers.

TONY (cont'd)
Ho, Mike.

Christopher realizes.

CHRISTOPHER
Matt, Tony wants you.

Matt double steps it to Tony.

MATT
Yeah, T?

TONY
Tony. Did you get the Macanudos?

MATT
You want one?

TONY
Yeah. And see if Dr. Freid wants one.

ON GAME

SUNSHINE
Four hundred to you, Sil.

SILVIO
How much is in the pot?

Sunshine scans.

SUNSHINE
About twenty-four hundred.

Silvio throws in his hand.

SILVIO
It's too early to chase an inside straight.

Matt is lighting Dr. Freid's Macanudo.

DR. FREID
(puffing)
Call.

Paulie fans the smoke.

MATT
Macanudos. You want one?

PAULIE
Go 'head, take a walk.

FRANK SINATRA JR.
Don't let him scare you, kid. He's not really a nasty fuck. He's an incredibly nasty fuck.

PAULIE
(good-natured)
Hey, chairboy of the board, read your fuckin' cards.

SUNSHINE
Two hundred to you, John.

JOHNNY SACK
(reading the table)
Shakespeare, straightening out, Paulie ain't got shit as usual, and the prick doctor, may be flushing.

ON TONY

He's giving instructions to Sean.

TONY
Put the T.V. trays out. One between two players. Then put some of this shit on them. Don't offer booze but if someone asks, get it. Go 'head.

There's a knock on the door. Christopher passes –

CHRISTOPHER
I got it.

Christopher pokes his head out.

13: INT. FLYAWAY MOTEL – HALLWAY – NIGHT

There is a man waiting. David Scatino.

CHRISTOPHER
Yeah?

DAVID
I heard Tony was here. Soprano. I'm a friend of his.

Christopher steps out into the hall, shuts the door behind him.

CHRISTOPHER
Do I know you?

> **DAVID**
> You know me. I own Ramsey's Sports and Outdoor.

Christopher stares at him for a beat then holds up his finger indicating 'wait a minute'. He goes back inside. David stands outside casually looks around. He is out of his element. Eyes him warily. A beat later Christopher comes out with Tony. Tony sees David.

> **TONY**
> Hey, hey! What're you doin' over here?

> **DAVID**
> I was just driving by and I thought I'd stop and say hello.

> **CHRISTOPHER**
> Is this guy whacked?

> **TONY**
> Nah. Known him for years. Legit guy.

Tony nods Christopher can go back inside. Christopher does. David is playing it cute. He hardly looks through the open door at the game.

> **DAVID**
> Some place.

> **TONY**
> Yeah, the Taj Mahal.

> **DAVID**
> Hey, have you heard the kids? Not bad.

> **TONY**
> Please, bad enough Carmela dragged me to that play. Now, if I never hear that song again it's too soon.

> **DAVID**
> The only area Eric's light in is the arts. This performance stuff'll put him over the goal line at most schools he's applying to.

> **TONY**
> Yeah? Just hope singin' on key isn't a requirement.

> **DAVID**
> *(play punches Tony)*
> You don't know, Tony. I thank God every night for that boy. Never gave us a minute of grief. Not like me at his age. Not like us.
> *(beat)*
> What's the game?

> **TONY**
> Seven card.

> **DAVID**
> *(sotto)*
> Is that Frank Sinatra, Jr.!

> **TONY**
> Yeah, he's friends with my uncle. He flies in.

> **DAVID**
> Wow. This really is an executive game.
> *(beat)*
> So... What do you think.

> **TONY**
> There's a resemblance.

149

DAVID
No, I mean the game. Can I take these guys, or what?

TONY
Trust me. It's not for you.

DAVID
C'mon, what's the odds of me being close to a game like this again? C'mon, Anthony, let me sit in. Just once.

TONY
Seriously, I don't do business with outside friends. You understand.

DAVID
Do I have to show your high school prom picture to these guys?

Chuckles...

DAVID (cont'd)
All kidding aside. I appreciate your position, but, Tony c'mon, I'm a big boy.

Tony stares at him for a beat, then...

TONY
What are you holding?

DAVID
Well, I didn't really expect to gamble tonight.

TONY
You gotta have at least five G's to sit.

DAVID
Can't you float me, y'know, short term.

TONY
David, don't say short if you don't mean short. All kidding aside. Do you understand what I'm sayin'?

DAVID
Of course. Hey, you don't have to explain business to me.

Tony looks him in the eye. Brings him in.

14: INT. FLYAWAY MOTEL – EFFICIENCY – NIGHT

TONY
Christopher...
(beckons)
Say hello to Davy Scatino.

DAVID
(they shake hands)
How you doing?

TONY
(eyes still on David)
Give him five boxes of ziti.
(to David)
Good luck.

Christopher turns to the table.

CHRISTOPHER
Ok, fellas, make room. New blood comin' in.

DISSOLVE TO:

15: INT. FLYAWAY MOTEL – EFFICIENCY – HOURS LATER

The players now look a bit disheveled. Paulie is asleep on the couch. A large pot is being played for. David has a pretty good stack of chips in front of him. Silvio seems to be losing big.

ON TABLE

David: Ace C, Queen H, Ten H.

Silvio: King H, King S, Ten D.

Dr. Freid: Deuce H, Deuce D, Eight H.

Frank Sinatra Jr.: Six D., Six H., Ace H.

And of course all have two cards in the hole.

> **FRANK SINATRA JR.**
> *(to David)*
> There's a lot of money in sporting goods, no?

Paulie stirs to half-wakefulness.

> **DAVID**
> Yeah, Frank. But, I tell you – Nike with their own stores, NBA has its own store, the fuckin' Yankee Store – it cuts in. Just temporary, though.
> *(taps head)*
> I got some ideas for next year.

> **PAULIE**
> Hey, Davy, ask the doc what his specialty is.

> **JOHNNY SACK**
> Hard-ons.

> **PAULIE**
> I wanted him to ask.

> **DAVID**
> Really?

> **DR. FREID**
> Penile implants.

> **PAULIE**
> Hey doc –

> **DR. FREID**
> Please, I've heard all the jokes.

While others chuckle, Sunshine quietly counts the pot and raises an eyebrow. It's a good one.

> **SUNSHINE**
> Pot's right. Sixth street. Here we go.

David: Four S.

> **SUNSHINE (cont'd)**
> No help.

> **FRANK SINATRA JR.**
> I'm out.

Silvio: Eight S.

> **SUNSHINE**
> Mysteries abound.

> **SILVIO**
> Shut the fuck up and deal.

Dr. Freid: Nine S.

Johnny: Three D.

> **JOHNNY SACK**
> This is unbelievable. Someone must've given me the horns.

> **SUNSHINE**
> Pair o'kings bets.

Silvio takes a bite of a chunk of cheese and drops the rest on the floor.

ON FLOOR

There are bits of bread and cheese all around Silvio's feet.

> **SILVIO**
> What's the bet?

> **SUNSHINE**
> Eight hundred.

ON TONY

> **TONY**
> *(sotto to Matt re: cheese)*
> Sweep that shit up.

Matt gets the broom and starts to innocently sweep around the table.

ON SILVIO

He reads the table.

> **SILVIO**
> *(to David)*
> What the fuck can you possibly have?

> **DAVID**
> Incredible luck.

> **SILVIO**
> You're not lying, you miserable cunt.

David is thrown. It's his first brush with ugliness tonight.

> **TONY**
> Be nice, be nice.

> **SUNSHINE**
> Bet or check.

> **SILVIO**
> *(angrily)*
> Don't rush me. You've been rushing me all fuckin' night.

> **JOHNNY SACK**
> He didn't study this hard in school.

> **SUNSHINE**
> John, please, you're not in the hand.

Dr. Freid tosses a ten dollar chip to Sunshine.

> **DR. FREID**
> Good. Dealer controls the game.

> **SILVIO**
> Do you fuckin' mind? Jesus, you don't shut the fuck up.

And blow that fuckin' smoke somewhere else.

Frank Sinatra Jr. nudges Johnny, then purposely blows a little cigar smoke in Silvio's direction. Just then Matt reaches the broom under Silvio's chair and he jumps up.

> **SILVIO**
> WHAT THE FUCK ARE YOU DOIN'!

All laugh, except David. Matt looks like a deer caught in headlights.

> **TONY**
> C'mon, Sil', take it easy.

> **SILVIO**
> I'm losin' my fuckin' balls here and this fuckin' moron is playing Hazel! Get the fuck outa here!

Christopher shakes his head as if to say 'I knew this was gonna happen.'

> **MATT**
> I'm sorry. I was just trying to get the cheese away from your feet.

> **SILVIO**
> *(snapping)*
> Why? Why now? Leave it there!

> **MATT**
> I just...

> **SILVIO**
> I don't fuckin' believe this idiot!
> *(to Tony)*
> Where do you get these fuckin'... sweeping cheese while I'm trying to...
> *(screams)*
> Leave the fuckin' cheese there! I love fuckin' cheese at my feet. I stick motherfuckin' provolone in my socks at night so they smell like your sister's crotch in the morning! Leave the fuckin', cocksuckin' cheese where it is!

Tony can't help but smile at this ridiculous display. Silvio grabs some more cheese and throws it on the floor, then sits. He tosses some chips in the pot.

> **SILVIO**
> Eight hundred.

Without missing a beat...

> **DR. FREID**
> Call.

> **SILVIO**
> Why don't you go fix a dick or whatever the fuck it is that you do?

Some chuckles.

> **PAULIE**
> Hey, Dr. Freid, you know about that Viagra shit?

> **DR. FREID**
> He won't quit this fucking guy –
> *(sighs)*
> Go ahead.

> **PAULIE**
> I heard they were sinking a crate of it down to the Titanic to try to raise it.

Hardly anyone laughs. And less because it's funny and more from the tension. David chuckles along but we get the feeling that he doesn't like the vibes in the room.

SUNSHINE
(to David)
Eight to you.

DAVID
Call.

SILVIO
Of course.

Chuckles. Sunshine counts the pot, takes five percent, and drops it into an empty coffee can. The can is half filled with chips. Christopher retrieves, pours the chips on the desk.

SUNSHINE
Down and dirty.

He deals one last card to each, face down.

SUNSHINE (cont'd)
Kings rule the kingdom. Last card automatic twelve hundred bump. Bet the raise makes it an even G. Kings?

SILVIO
Check.

SUNSHINE
Door wide open. Dr. Freid?

DR. FREID
Check.

SUNSHINE
David?

SILVIO
He checks.

DAVID
Bet. Twelve hundred.

Tony and Christopher stand nearby.

SILVIO
Call. You ain't got shit.

DR. FREID
(rhetorically)
Can I steal this fuckin' hand? I think I can. Raise twelve.

SILVIO
See? Why didn't you check? You got shit. Now it's gonna cost you an extra bet.

David just shrugs and throws in his chips. Pissed, Silvio follows in like.

SUNSHINE
Ok, fellas. Let's see them.

DR. FREID
Three of a kind.

SUNSHINE
Three deuces.

SILVIO
Huh, cry me a river. Three kings.

DAVID
Flush.

> **SILVIO**
> What? You motherfucker. You bought it last card. What the fuck were you doin' in that hand?

> **TONY**
> His money's good. If he wants to sail, it's his business.

Tony winks at David.

> **SILVIO**
> Fuck you too. I shoulda stayed with my goomah tonight.

Tony smiles. He loves to see Silvio mad.

> **SILVIO (cont'd)**
> (to Matt)
> Hey, cheese fuck. Get me some food.

16: EXT. SOPRANO HOUSE – EARLY MORNING

David's son Eric pulls up in an SUV, MUSIC. He BEEPS and Meadow comes out. She gets in and they drive off.

17: INT. ERIC'S SUV – EARLY MORNING

Meadow shuts the music.

> **MEADOW**
> I'm so pissed.

> **ERIC**
> Good morning.

> **MEADOW**
> Hunter just called and said that Rachel Weiss got an early acceptance to Weslyan.

> **ERIC**
> You didn't expect it?

> **MEADOW**
> No.

> **ERIC**
> Think about it. Did you ever see her mom?

> **MEADOW**
> Oh, please, I'm blacker than her mother.

> **ERIC**
> You should've mentioned it on your application.

Off Eric's smile...

18: INT. FLYAWAY MOTEL – EFFICIENCY – MORNING

Fortunes change. Silvio is way up (pile of chips) and in a better mood. A new guy is there and is holding his own. Frank Sinatra Jr. is losing. Johnny is in his "sleeveless tee" and is half asleep at the table while our boy David is really down as evidenced by the very few chips and the serious puss.

ALL look beat. Not the least of which is Tony who sits on the nearby couch "cat napping." Christopher walks over.

> **CHRISTOPHER**
> T?
> (nudges him)
> Ho, T.

> **TONY**
> Huh? Wha'? What time is it?

> **CHRISTOPHER**
> Almost 9.

> **TONY**
> How's it goin'?

> **CHRISTOPHER**
> Homestretch. Last five hands. Let's rough it up.

> **TONY**
> See if they wanna close the lights.

Christopher crosses over to Sunshine and whispers in his ear just as Sean brings Tony over a cup of coffee.

> **TONY (cont'd)**
> Thanks.
> *(to players)*
> Anyone want more coffee?

> **FRANK SINATRA JR.**
> Yeah. A little buca in it.

TABLE

> **SUNSHINE**
> Anyone for closing the lights?

> **DAVID**
> That a game?

Tired chuckles.

> **SILVIO**
> He's a pisser this kid. "Is it a game?"

> **SUNSHINE**
> Wanna close the lights means...

> **FRANK SINATRA JR.**
> Do you want to admit that you lost and pack it in?

> **DAVID**
> *(quickly)*
> Me, no.

TONY

> **TONY**
> *(to Christopher)*
> How much is he into us for?

> **CHRISTOPHER**
> About 25 boxes of ziti.

> **TONY**
> What?

> **CHRISTOPHER**
> He grabbed another five while you were sleeping.

Tony just sighs. A knock on the door.

> **TONY**
> Grab that, will ya?

Christopher disappears and returns a few beats later along with Richie.

> **RICHIE**
> Look at this fuckin' lineup.

ON DAVID

He looks like he may shit himself. Richie goes around the table.

          RICHIE (cont'd)
Johnny Sack. They must've had free tokens for the tunnel.
          (to others)
How'd you expect to make a dime with this stonewaller.

Richie only now notices David.

          RICHIE (cont'd)
How the fuck did you get in here?

          TONY
Same as you. Through the front door.

          DAVID
Hi Rich.

          RICHIE
Hi Rich?

          TONY
You want some lox? I got some nice fresh lox.

Richie is burning a hole in David.

          RICHIE
          (radioactive)
You gotta lot of balls, you know that?

          TONY
Whoa, what's goin' on here?

          DAVID
What did I do?

Richie goes over to David, who is blinking a mile a minute, and grabs him by the throat. The players all back away expecting punches to be thrown.

          RICHIE
I should stab you in the fuckin' eye.

          TONY
          (shouts warning)
Hey.

Christopher puts his hand on Richie about to move him.

          CHRISTOPHER
C'mon, Rich...

Richie turns like a mad animal.

          RICHIE
Get your fuckin' hand off me or I'll put one in your head.

          CHRISTOPHER
Don't fuckin' threaten me, Richie.

          RICHIE
Don't threaten you? I got a fuckin' hard-on for you anyway kid. Just gimme a reason.

Tony gets between them and talks with an angry whisper to Richie.

          TONY
Don't make me embarrass you. Outside now. I wanna talk.

ON MATT AND SEAN *who are taking it all in.*

> TONY (cont'd)
> *(to Matt)*
> Pour everyone a drink. I'll be right back.

Richie eyes Christopher.

> FRANK SINATRA JR.
> That's it. Cash me out.

> TONY
> Sit down, Frank. Doc, just a misunderstanding.

> FRANK SINATRA JR.
> No, I'm wiped. I'll square with you next game. My regards to your uncle.

> TONY
> C'mon, sit. At least let me get you some breakfast.

> DR. FREID
> Nah, really. I got seats for the Rueles-Harris fight tonight.

> FRANK SINATRA JR.
> *(to Matt)*
> Hey, kiddo...

He tosses Matt a chip.

> MATT
> Thank you, Mr. Sinatra. Junior. Sir.

He tosses another one.

> FRANK SINATRA JR.
> Give that to the other guy.
> *(to Christopher)*
> Cash me out.

19: EXT. FLYAWAY MOTEL – MORNING

Tony and Richie blink in the light. Salesmen and minor executives have checked out and are rolling sample cases toward rental cars.

> RICHIE
> *(livid)*
> I shut him the fuck off and he comes here and he sticks it up my ass.

> TONY
> What's all this got to do with you disrespectin' my fuckin' game.

> RICHIE
> Like you woulda done different.

> TONY
> You're fuckin' right.

> RICHIE
> Tony, I'm gettin' a little sick of this holier than thou act. And I'm not the only one.

> TONY
> Oh, really? Well, whenever anybody wants to make a move...

> RICHIE
> C'mon, Tony, don't be so fuckin' dramatic. I'm just sayin' sometimes you act like you're in a different business. Send that little prick out here so I can talk to him.

> TONY
> No.

          RICHIE
Do you realize that that motherless fuck is into me for over eight large? He's got money to play here? Let him pay me my fuckin' money. Send him out.

          TONY
Go home, Richie. This ain't gonna happen with one of my players.

After a stare down, Richie relents and walks away pissed.

20: INT. FLYAWAY MOTEL – EFFICIENCY – DAY

Tony re-enters.

          CHRISTOPHER
Everything alright?

Tony just nods.

          TONY
Where is he?

Christopher nods toward David who is throwing cold water on his face. Tony pours himself a shot of Brandy. Christopher says something to David, who comes out of his field trip and crosses to Tony.

          DAVID
Wow, he was pissed.

          TONY
I'll give you one day to sleep. Then, you're going to the bank and getting me my twenty five thousand.

          DAVID
Yeah, no problem. Jesus, how 'bout the luck on that Silvio...

          TONY
Shut the fuck up.

David is not sure how to take it and presses on.

          DAVID
I could use a schvitz. You want to go for a schvitz?

          TONY
If after one day I don't have every penny. Then every Saturday, someone will stop by your joint to pick up five percent interest. And you can never miss a payment otherwise it goes on top of the principal.

          DAVID
Listen Tony...

Tony doesn't respond.

          DAVID (cont'd)
I had a good run there for a while. I should of left then, huh?
    (Tony still ignores him, trying to get back to the other Tony)
So, you never told me how your kid made out with Bowdoin.

          TONY
Anything else?

          DAVID
No... no. Hey, Ton', did I do something to insult you?

          TONY
Two days. Y'understand?

          DAVID
Yeah, right.

David just sheepishly exits. Paulie enters with Cristal, glasses, cigars.

> **PAULIE**
> Skip?

> **TONY**
> How much?

> **PAULIE**
> Not finished counting but it's up there. At least forty boxes of ziti after expenses. Salut'.

They drink. Tony settles in.

> **TONY**
> Do you fuckin' believe it? We now run the executive fuckin' game.

> **PAULIE**
> Yep.

> **TONY**
> I remember me an' fuckin' Silvio peeking in through the scratch on the painted door when my ol' man and Junior had it. Junior was a prick even then. He'd chase us away. The executive game. How 'bout that.

Paulie, Tony, and Christopher are all smiles.

21: INT. SOPRANO HOUSE – MASTER BEDROOM – DAY

Curtains drawn, Tony is asleep. A THUDDING BASS is in the next room. Tony eventually awakens. He just lays there for a beat then BANGS on the wall just over his head. Nothing. And the music goes on... "Sun/Moon." Finally, he's had enough and gets out of bed.

22: INT. SOPRANO HOUSE – MEADOW'S ROOM – MOMENTS LATER

Meadow and Eric are working on their song. Eric plays Fender bass through a large amp.

> **TONY (O.S.)**
> Hey!

They stop and turn. Tony looks like shit.

> **MEADOW**
> Do you mind? God.

> **TONY**
> I'm trying to get some sleep. I was working all night. Hey, Eric. Sound good.

> **ERIC**
> Thanks.

> **MEADOW**
> Are you awake now?

> **TONY**
> Yes.

> **MEADOW**
> Good. Close the door.

> **TONY**
> *(snaps)*
> Hey!
> *(beat)*
> Where's your mother?

> **MEADOW**
> Store.

As Tony is about to close the door.

> **MEADOW (cont'd)**
> Oh, Aunt Barb called. Uncle Tom's Father died.

> **TONY**
> Whoa, whoa, whoa, what? Tom Sr.? When?

> **MEADOW**
> *(shrugs)*
> I don't know.

> **TONY**
> What the hell happened?

> **MEADOW**
> I don't know.

> **TONY**
> The guy's here almost ev'ry Christmas Eve. You don't ask? Someone says "Joe Blow died" and normal people say "how?"

Tony stares.

> **TONY (cont'd)**
> Jesus.

He shakes his head and closes the door. We stay with Tony. He stands outside the door, the music kicks in.

23: INT. MELFI'S OFFICE – DAY

Tony and Melfi.

> **TONY**
> Whoosh. A friggin' gust of wind comes and blows him off the roof. All for a satellite dish.

> **MELFI**
> It's very sad. How old?

> **TONY**
> 65. Guy lives his whole life, works hard, takes care of his family, and one day after he retires – one day – whoosh. Too freaky.

> **MELFI**
> Carlos Casteneda said live every moment as if it were your last dance in Earth.

> **TONY**
> Who the fuck listens to prizefighters? Ali, maybe. Had some wisdom.

> **MELFI**
> Well, at least Tom Sr. isn't a happy wanderer anymore.

> **TONY**
> The fuck's that supposed to mean?

> **MELFI**
> He got his. You don't have to pummel his ass. He joined the ranks of the unlucky.

> **TONY**
> Maybe you know what you're talking about but I don't.

He shoots her a look then gets lost in his thoughts.

> **TONY (cont'd)**
> You want to talk about unlucky – I only just found out I had a retarded uncle. My father's brother. Do you believe this shit?

161

> **MELFI**
> Was he seriously developmentally disabled?

> **TONY**
> Serious? No, it had the whole family in stitches back then.

She watches him.

> **MELFI**
> *(after a beat)*
> Now that you found out about a retarded family member do you feel better about coming here?

> **TONY**
> Say what?

> **MELFI**
> Is it permissible now? Is it enough of a sad tragedy that you can join the rest of the douchebags?

He just gives her a nasty smirk. But then his expression softens, to sadness.

24: INT. DRAGO'S FUNERAL HOME – TOM SR.'S ROOM – NIGHT

Tom Sr. lies in state. TOM JR. is at his post at his father's feet greeting mourners when they stand after genuflecting at the casket. The funeral parlor is pretty full with MOURNERS. Sitting at the front is Tony, Anthony Jr., and Meadow. Carmela is seated to the side of the room with the family, consoling BARBARA.

> **BARBARA**
> I was just talking to him a couple days ago.

Now Tony reacts to something. It gets Carmela's attention as well. As a matter of fact it's getting just about EVERYBODY'S attention... Parvati, pushing Livia in a wheelchair, and Richie have entered and are approaching the casket. As someone greets them, Livia lets out the old lady fake CRY.

> **TONY**
> Va F'ancula tu!

> **CARMELA**
> *(aside)*
> We knew we were bound to see them at some function. Just relax.

> **MEADOW**
> Wow, look at Aunt Parvati. She's stylin'.

Another little WAIL from Livia.

> **TONY**
> Fuckin' Bette Davis over there.

> **CARMELA**
> No scenes.

> **TONY**
> *(to kids)*
> C'mon, get up. We're leaving.

> **ANTHONY JR.**
> Thank you God.

She grabs Tony's arm and tugs him.

> **CARMELA**
> *(through her teeth)*
> I'll fuckin' kill you.

> **TONY**
> We said our respects. Let's go.

> **CARMELA**
> This may come as a shock to you, but, these people aren't here to see the Sopranos kill each other. Show some respect for Tom's father.

Just then Richie comes over.

> **RICHIE**
> *(kisses her)*
> Carm'.

> **CARMELA**
> Richie.

> **RICHIE**
> *(sotto to Tony)*
> Do I give the boost to your sister?

> **TONY**
> C'mon, I gotta give mine too.

ON TONY AND RICHIE

They go over to Tom and hand him envelopes. Each is given with a kiss. Tony is about to peel off in a different direction than Richie. Richie gestures for him to go with him.

25: INT. DRAGO'S FUNERAL HOME – EMPTY VIEWING ROOM – NIGHT

The room is dimly lit. A MAN is in a casket. His wake must've wrapped early. Tony and Richie enter.

> **RICHIE**
> How many rooms this place got?

> **TONY**
> It's a big joint.

> **RICHIE**
> Pretty good racket.

Tony lights a cigar.

> **RICHIE (cont'd)**
> I don't think you can smoke in here.

> **TONY**
> Who's gonna complain, him?
> *(to dead Man)*
> Mind?
> *(to Richie)*
> He doesn't mind.

> **RICHIE**
> Listen, Anthony, I'm sorry about blowin' up in your game.

> **TONY**
> You were outa line.

> **RICHIE**
> I know. I'm sayin' I apologize.

> **TONY**
> What am I supposed to do with you?

> **RICHIE**
> Wha'?

> **TONY**
> Back up and respect the title, you fuckin' jerkoff.

Richie stares at Tony, then...

RICHIE
You're right. You're right. It's your ball, you make the rules.

TONY
Hey, I didn't make them. They've always been there. Know this. Davy Scatino doesn't pay you a fuckin' penny till I get mine first.

RICHIE
Whoa, whoa...

TONY
Fuck you. That's your tax for raising your hands in my game. I get mine first, then you. That's how it's gonna be. I don't do something, how's it gonna look?

RICHIE
You're right, you're right.

TONY
You shouldn't have done that in my game.

RICHIE
I'm sayin' O.K. The fuck, can't you take "yes" for an answer?

26: INT. DRAGO'S FUNERAL HOME – TOM SR.'S ROOM – CONTINUED

Tony and Richie enter. As Tony passes by Livia all eyes turn, at least it feels that way to Tony. Carmela watching. Her face reads pain for Tony.

The Priest stands at the casket facing the mourners.

PRIEST
In the Name Of The Father...

TONY
(sign of the cross)
The Son and The Holy Ghost.

27: INT. TONY'S SUBURBAN – NIGHT

Kids in back, Carmela in front, Tony drives.

TONY
This guy... this fuckin' guy... a lot of balls bein' there.

CARMELA
Will you relax? You're getting worked up over nothing.

TONY
I mean, what is he part of this family now?

ANTHONY JR.
If he marries Aunt Parvati he will be.

CARMELA
(warning)
Anthony.

Silence, then...

MEADOW
Grandma looked good.

Carmela waits for a reaction. She gets it. After a beat, Tony hits the steering wheel.

TONY
He hardly knows Tom. And he definitely didn't know the old man. A lot of balls.

MEADOW
She stayed the whole time too.

CARMELA
We were there. We don't need a blow by blow.

TONY
I shoulda kicked him in the ass right there.

MEADOW
Sounds like displaced anger, if you ask me.

CARMELA
Well no one is asking you. Stay out of adult conversations.

Meadow wears a sarcastic little smile.

28: INT. RICHIE'S CAR – NIGHT

Richie drives, Parvati has shotgun, and Livia is half asleep in the back. After a moment Parvati leans in to Richie.

PARVATI
(half-whisper)
I'm just saying you shouldn't take any shit from him.

RICHIE
I heard you the first time.

Richie looks into the rear view mirror and SEES Livia is almost out.

RICHIE (cont'd)
Let's drop this subject.

PARVATI
(if you say so)
All right.

Long pause.

RICHIE
Tony put me back in action. Gave me fifty G's to put on the street. What's that? Huh? Nothing?

PARVATI
Please, I know how things work. Don't forget I was daddy's little girl.

RICHIE
The fuck are you talkin' about?

PARVATI
You're his responsibility. He didn't do you any favor. When my father was in Tony's position he gave Romeo Martin fifty thousand dollars when he got out of jail.
(beat)
And I'm talking almost thirty years ago. Thirty years ago. Today that's like a half a million. Fifty thousand. Mailmen make more than that.

Richie just shakes his head like an old husband.

29: INT. RAMSEY'S SPORTS AND OUTDOOR – OFFICE – DAY

David is behind his desk doing paper work when a KNOCK comes to his door.

DAVID
(without looking up)
Come in.

WE HEAR the door open then close. After a beat David looks up. The look on his face tells us this isn't someone he wants to see... Tony.

TONY
What's this fuckin' doctor's appointment you had all the sudden when my friend came to see you? You must think I'm still a kid on the school bus.

> **DAVID**
> Please, Tony, I'm doing my best here. I fucked up. Ok. I'm gonna make it work somehow. I swear.

> **TONY**
> Whatiya got for me?

> **DAVID**
> I'm tapped.

> **TONY**
> Maybe you gave it all to Richie Aprile.
> *(beat)*
> Stand up.

> **DAVID**
> Why?

> **TONY**
> 'Cause I just said so. Stand up or I'll rip your fuckin' head off your shoulders.

David timidly stands. Tony just stares at him until he can't take it.

> **DAVID**
> *(starts his whine)*
> I'm sorry Tony, really. I wouldn't do anything to insult you. Our kids go to school together...

Tony hits him with an OPEN HAND SLAP. He YELPS like a woman. The slap knocks him to the floor. He pulls himself to his feet.

> **DAVID (CONT'D)**
> *(crying)*
> Tony, I'm sorry. I'm sorry. I'm just having some bad luck.

> **TONY**
> It just got worse.

He SLAPS him again.

> **DAVID**
> *(whimpering)*
> Really, I'm gonna come back. My luck's gonna change.

Another SLAP sends him flying to the floor. Tony stands over him. David WHIMPERS which only brings out more rage in Tony. Tony reaches down, grabs David by the hair, and yanks his head back.

> **TONY**
> I want something tomorrow. Y'understand? Tomorrow.

30: INT. RAMSEY'S SPORTS AND OUTDOOR – MOMENTS LATER

Tony emerges from the office and is heading for the door. He looks up and there on display is an inflatable boat with small outboard. He goes over to it and hefts it off the wall and casually exits the store with it resting on his head as the dumbfounded sales staff looks on.

31: INT. NUOVO VESUVIO – DAY

Standing there is David. Artie emerges.

> **ARTIE**
> Ho, David.

They shake hands.

> **ARTIE (cont'd)**
> Where's the wife?

> **DAVID**
> She's home... Can I talk to you?

> **ARTIE**
> Yeah, sure. Is everything alright? C'mere, sit down.

They do.

> **ARTIE (cont'd)**
> Talk to me.

> **DAVID**
> I got myself in a little bind. Jesus, I feel ashamed.

> **ARTIE**
> What happened? What's going on?

David is about to weep.

> **DAVID**
> I'm in a jam, Artie. A bad one. This could cost me big. My marriage, my business...

> **ARTIE**
> Alright, relax, I'm sure there's something we can do. What kind of jam?
> *(beat, realization)*
> Aw, Jesus, you didn't knock up that Tae Bo broad you had working?

> **DAVID**
> God no, Artie.

> **ARTIE**
> Talk to me. I'm your friend.

David again looks like the tears may flow.

> **DAVID**
> I need money. Money, Artie.

Artie pulls back slightly.

> **DAVID (cont'd)**
> Not much. I swear on my kid I'll get it back to you before you even miss it.

Artie sighs.

> **ARTIE**
> How much we talking?

> **DAVID**
> Just enough to buy me some breathing room till I can put the rest together... twenty thousand.

> **ARTIE**
> *(bull)*
> Davy, Davy, my God. Bad timing. Do you believe it? I gotta put a new roof on this place. God forgive me for saying this, but, what about Chapter 11?

> **DAVID**
> I don't think Tony Soprano will buy that.

> **ARTIE**
> Tony?
> *(beat)*
> Jesus Christ. Davy.

32: EXT. SCATINO HOUSE – DAY

David pulls into the driveway alongside of Eric's SUV. He gets out of his car. He's miserable. As he passes Eric's SUV something catches his eye. He walks over to the SUV and notices a little mud on the tires. He marches into the house. We hear some yelling then the front door of the house flies open. David comes out followed by an upset Eric.

> **ERIC**
> This is bullshit!

Mrs. Scatino stands in the doorway. It has all the earmarks of an embarrassing family fight.

> **MRS. SCATINO**
> Eric... Eric, get in the house.

> **DAVID**
> I warned you. No off-roading! I gave you enough chances.

> **MRS. SCATINO**
> Dave, this is not the place...

> **ERIC**
> Dad, I didn't do anything!

David turns to Eric.

> **DAVID**
> I'm sorry, Eric. Accountability is everything.

> **ERIC**
> Off-roading?! I drove it onto the field at school! To bring some girls up to cheerleading practice!

> **DAVID**
> There's mud all over those doors. I warned you and I warned you, Eric.

David climbs in the SUV and starts it.

> **ERIC**
> I didn't do anything!

David peels out...

> **ERIC (cont'd)**
> (yells)
> I didn't do anything!

> **MRS. SCATINO**
> Eric, get in this house.

> **ERIC**
> I fucking hate all of you!

Eric storms off.

> **MRS. SCATINO**
> You apologize right now. Eric...

Eric just continues his march into oblivion...

33: INT. SOPRANO HOUSE – GARAGE – NIGHT

The light goes on and there is Eric's SUV. Tony enters with Meadow, Carmela next. Meadow has her eyes closed, Tony guides her by her shoulders.

> **MEADOW**
> I know it's a car.

> **TONY**
> No, it's not, smart ass. Ok, open'em.

Meadow focuses and for a fleeting moment she looks like she may get excited.

> **MEADOW**
> I knew it was a car.

> **TONY**
> It's a Sport Utility Vehicle. Get in.

Meadow hops in behind the wheel. Tony gets in the passenger seat. Meadow examines the interior.

> **TONY**
> You like it?

> **MEADOW**
> *(realizing)*
> This is Eric's jeep.

> **CARMELA**
> Oh, my God, is this Eric Scatino's jeep?

> **TONY**
> *(smiling)*
> It's yours now.

> **MEADOW**
> *(curiously)*
> He sold it to you?

> **TONY**
> Something like that.

> **MEADOW**
> What do you mean, 'something like that'?

She turns on her heel and goes back in the house.

> **CARMELA**
> Jesus, Tony!

34: INT. SOPRANO HOUSE – KITCHEN – CONTINUING

Tony and Carmela come up the stairs after her.

> **TONY**
> If you don't want it, fine. Don't take it. But, I'll eat it before I give it back. What am I, a sucker?

> **MEADOW**
> What does Eric have to do with his asshole father? He didn't do anything to you.

> **TONY**
> I didn't strong arm him. He owes me and he did the right thing and offered it up as partial payment.

> **MEADOW**
> Yeah, right.

> **TONY**
> Jesus Christ.
> *(to Carmela)*
> That's you talking.

> **CARMELA**
> I hope you know his wife is very close to the brother-in-law of a provost at Georgetown.

> **TONY**
> The who?

> **MEADOW**
> Oh, great.

> **TONY**
> Go 'head. You want to act holier than thou, well, guess what? I'm not giving it back. I'm gonna sell it to Pussy. Then I'm gonna take the money he gives me and buy food and clothes and CD players and shoes and

shit like I've been doing since you were born. Everything this family has came from the work I do.

> **CARMELA**
> Ok, Tony, that's enough.

> **TONY**
> *(running it down)*
> Hey, a grown man made a wager. He lost. He made more. He lost. End of story. So take that high moral ground and go sleep in the fuckin' bus station if you want.

35: INT. SCHOOL AUDITORIUM – NIGHT

The auditorium is filling with FAMILY and FRIENDS of the performers. Tony sits there holding a bouquet of flowers for Meadow. Carmela is scanning the room, Anthony Jr. next to her.

> **CARMELA**
> *(beat)*
> Oh, Jesus.

> **TONY**
> *(he knows)*
> Where?

> **CARMELA**
> A few rows back.

TONY'S POV

Livia sits in her wheelchair in the aisle alongside Parvati.

> **RICHIE (O.S.)**
> Tony.

They turn and there is Richie also holding a bouquet only bigger than Tony's.

> **RICHIE (cont'd)**
> I almost didn't make it. Where's Janice?

> **TONY**
> *(re: flowers)*
> Didn't I see those at the wake the other night?

> **RICHIE**
> Funny.

> **CARMELA**
> They're in the next aisle.

Tony and Richie notice David and his wife seated a few rows behind Parvati. David makes eye contact. It is a very uncomfortable moment, then...

> **RICHIE**
> *(to Tony)*
> I'll see you after the show.

Richie walks away.

> **CARMELA**
> Just keep thinking 'Meadow'.

36: INT. BACKSTAGE – SAME

Eric, dressed in Marine Corps. fatigues, is storming away from Meadow, who is dressed as Miss Saigon. Eric bumps into other "PERFORMERS" as he is making his way toward an exit.

> **MEADOW**
> Eric! Eric, c'mon. Let's talk.

Meadow grabs him by the arm and turns him. He's been crying.

MEADOW (cont'd)
You're just going to leave me here.

ERIC
I thought you were my friend.

MEADOW
I am. I can't stop my dad from selling it.

ERIC
Your dad's an fucking asshole. You know that? A real lowlife, fucking asshole.

Family is family.

MEADOW
Oh, and I suppose yours is completely innocent in all this? For your information, he gave it to my dad. It's not like my dad stole it.

ERIC
You know what Meadow?
(he removes his Marine shirt)
Fuck you. Fuck your gangster father and fuck this!

He throws his shirt into backstage refreshments causing eyes to turn. On that he's out the door into the night leaving Meadow standing there. Mrs. Gaetano comes running over.

37: INT. AUDITORIUM – CONTINUING

ON TONY and CARMELA. FEEDBACK from a backstage microphone pierces everyone's ears.

MALE VOICE (O.S., SOOTHING TONE)
Welcome everyone to Verbum Dei High School's Cabaret Night. As we are recording tonight's performance we'd like to remind everyone, please, no talking, no pictures or videotaping, and please remember to turn off those pagers and cell phones. If you're worried about coughing and feel a nice lozenge might help, may we suggest that now would be the time to unwrap it –
(mild audience laughter)
– as opposed to during the performance.
(beat)
A program note – "Sun/Moon" to be performed by Eric Scatino and Meadow Soprano has been canceled. Regretfully, Mr. Scatino will not be performing tonight. Instead Miss Soprano will be singing "My Heart Will Go On", the theme song from "Titanic."

Carmela lights up.

CARMELA
Oh, that's a lucky break. I wonder what happened.

As the house lights start to fade.

VOICE (O.S.)
Enjoy the show.

Tony looks over at David and his wife. They are making their way out of their seats and down the aisle, ostensibly, to go backstage. Before the lights are completely black he focuses on Livia, Richie, and Parvati.

House lights out – stage lights up. WE HEAR APPLAUSE. Gudren begins her German leid.

THE END

FADE OUT

"The Knight in White Satin Armor"

S212

Written by
Robin Green & Mitchell Burgess

Directed by
Allen Coulter

Soprano Productions, Inc.

Production Draft	11/22/99
1st Revision (Full Blue)	11/24/99
2nd Revision (Pink Pages)	11/29/99
3rd Revision (Full Yellow)	12/1/99
4th Revision (Green Pages)	12/2/99
5th Revision (Goldenrod Pages)	12/3/99
6th Revision (Buff Page)	12/6/99
7th Revision (Salmon Pages)	12/7/99
8th Revision (Cherry Page)	12/13/99
FINAL SHOOTING SCRIPT	

CHARACTER LIST

TONY SOPRANO
CARMELA SOPRANO
DR. JENNIFER MELFI
CHRISTOPHER MOLTISANTI
MEADOW SOPRANO
LIVIA SOPRANO
UNCLE "JUNIOR" SOPRANO
PUSSY BONPENSIERO
SILVIO DANTE
ADRIANA
JANICE "PARVATI" SOPRANO
RICHIE APRILE

Irina
Skip Lipari
Harold "Mel" Melvoin
Victor Musto
Furio
Lilliana
Bobby "Bacala" Baccilieri
Frank Cubitoso
Gabriella Dante
Dick Barone
Rosalie Aprile
Ramone
Svetlana
Albert Barese
Jackie Aprile, Jr.
Richard "Rick" Aprile, Jr.

SETS

INTERIORS

Janice and Richie's New House – Great Room	D
Janice and Richie's New House – Foyer	D
Janice and Richie's New House – Living Room	D
Irina's Apartment	D
Irina's Bedroom	D/N
Melvoin's Office	D
Junior's House – Den	N
Junior's House – Kitchen	D
Soprano House – Kitchen	D/N
Soprano House – Basement	D
Soprano House – Foyer	D
Soprano House – Bedroom	N
Soprano House – Living Room	D/N
Soprano House – Family Room	N
Hospital – Hallway	N
Hospital – Room	N
Hospital – Emergency Bay	N
Bridal Salon	D
Federal Building – Office	D
Albert Barese's Social Club	D
Paint Store	D
Melfi's Office	D
Stock Brokerage – Christopher's Office	D
Dentist's Office	D
Livia's House – Living Room	D/N
Livia's House – Kitchen	D/N
Dr. Schreck's Office	D
Bada Bing – Back Room	N
Pork Store – Middle Room	N

EXTERIORS

Janice and Richie's New House	D
Roadside	D
Soprano House – To Establish	D
Stock Brokerage Parking Lot	D/N
Diner Parking Lot	N
Street Somewhere	D
Pork Store – To Establish	N
Livia's House	D
Bus Station	D
Park	D

1: INT. JANICE AND RICHIE'S NEW HOUSE – GREAT ROOM – DAY

A big, vacant, suburban monstrosity. No furniture to speak of yet, a few boxes, a broom. To music from a boom box, a man and woman in ballroom dancers' workout clothes waltz gracefully. This is Richie's son, RICHARD "RICK" APRILE JR., 28, and his DANCE PARTNER. As the couple dips and twirls –

2: INT. JANICE AND RICHIE'S NEW HOUSE – FOYER – SAME

TONY and JANICE carry a loveseat through the front door.

>   **JANICE**
> I used to take some great naps in this settee.

>   **TONY**
> You okay over there?

>   **JANICE**
> Hey, shades of Starving Students. Santa Monica. Summer of '78.

>   **TONY**
> You were a mover? How many jobs you had in your life?

>   **JANICE**
> Enough to know I don't want another one.

In b.g., Rick waves to Janice while dancing.

>   **RICK**
> Jan, these floors have excellent glide!

>   **JANICE**
> Lookin' good, Rick. Beautiful, Juliet.
>   *(then, to Tony)*
> Phoo. Gimme a sec.

They stop to rest.

>   **TONY**
> Richie's son is still "Flying Down to Rio"? Dad must be proud as punch.

>   **JANICE**
> He is. Those two made top ten in the Embassy Ball Championships last year.

>   **JACKIE JR. (O.S.)**
> Tony! Hey, man!

Tony turns to see –

3: INT. JANICE AND RICHIE'S NEW HOUSE – LIVING ROOM

Jackie Aprile's son, JACKIE JR., 23, a recent college dropout, approaches with open arms, THREE BUDDIES lounging on lawn chairs in b.g., smoking and drinking Fosters and watching Monster Trucking on a 16.9 Ratio T.V.

>   **TONY**
> Jackie, how's your rash?

They embrace, throw some light lefts and rights.

>   **JACKIE JR.**
> Wanna beer, T?

>   **TONY**
>   *(smiling)*
> Nah, go join your wastrel friends.

Tony watches Jackie Jr. head back into the living room.

TONY (cont'd)
Jackie Aprile was a man who loved knowledge. He was dying of the cancer. He was praying that kid would go to medical school. Break his heart if he knew he'd dropped out of college.

JANICE
Didn't hurt the Beatles, Bill Gates. His Uncle Richie's watching out for him.

TONY
Easier to deal with than his own son.

JANICE
Tony, don't do that. Richie gets along with everybody but you. Did you know he's taking AJ to the dirt bike championships at Giant Stadium?

TONY
Anthony can't go. He got a C in Algebra.

JANICE
Does Carmela know about this? Because I just think it's punitive and how many fuckin' hours did you help him with his mathematics?

TONY
You really wanna know? I don't want him around my kids.

JANICE
Who? Richie?

TONY
You heard me.

JANICE
What the fuck are you talking about?

TONY
Ask Gia Gaeta.

JANICE
Richie told me all about that. The transmission slipped out of gear. Richie was lucky he wasn't crushed by the car too. And for your information, Beansie Gaeta owed him major dollars for ten years and Richie wasn't even asking for the interest.

TONY
Why not?

JANICE
And if we're so awful, why are you throwing us an engagement party?

TONY
You're my sister, I try to do what's right. Anyway, it's my wife's thing.

JANICE
'What's right'? How welcoming. 'What's right' include planking that little Russian girl of yours on the side?

TONY
Be in denial. Be a codependent to a shit bag? Who cares?

JANICE
You can't stand for me to be happy, can you, you motherfucker!

TONY
Take this settee and cram it up your ass.

Tony leaves.

4: INT. IRINA'S BEDROOM – DAY

Tony is fucking IRINA. He finishes and rolls off her onto his back. She slides out of bed and goes to the bathroom. He relights a half smoked cigar. Irina comes out of the bathroom, sips her vodka, slips on a pair of pony boots.

> **IRINA**
> I love my new pony boots, Tony.

> **TONY**
> Yeah, nice. Wear 'em when you go on some of these interviews.

She cuddles up and throws a leg over him.

> **IRINA**
> Feel, Tony, how soft. Mm.

> **TONY**
> Did you call Sy Littman yet?

> **IRINA**
> No. I'm doing it.

> **TONY**
> There's good money in modeling. You don't wanna spend the rest of your life behind a perfume counter at a department store, right Rina?

> **IRINA**
> What you care what I do?

> **TONY**
> Don't start with that moody shit.

Irina decides on a different tack. She picks up a slender volume and starts reading.

> **TONY (cont'd)**
> What's that?

> **IRINA**
> "Chicken Soup for the Soul."

> **TONY**
> You should read "Tomato Sauce for Your Ass." It's the Italian version.

> **IRINA**
> Hah hah. Somebody give me this I met at work.
> *(when Tony doesn't react)*
> He drive for Runway Limos, he broughts Karl Lagerfeld to the store for the trunk show. Why? You jealous?

> **TONY**
> You fucking him?

> **IRINA**
> I can't have a conversation with you! You're horrible!

> **TONY**
> *(means it)*
> It's a fucking question. Maybe it's something you should think about.

> **IRINA**
> What?

> **TONY**
> Finding somebody that can give you everything you want.

> **IRINA**
> I told you, he drives a fucking limo.

TONY
I don't mean those kinds of things, I mean getting married, having children.

IRINA
No, I don't want to find someone. I have you.

TONY
What, to go to dinner and screw your fucking brains out? What's wrong with you?

Tony hauls himself out of bed and starts to dress.

IRINA
Tony, no, don't go.

TONY
You don't know what the fuck you want.

IRINA
(crying)
Don't yell at me! Please! You know this is a bad time! My new boss is so mean to me!

TONY
It's always a bad time with you. With the cousins and the landlords and the black eyes and the legal shit. You people, you don't know how to behave in this country. Fucking serfs crawling out of the fucking dark ages.

IRINA
Tony, no! Please, NO!

She's hysterical now, grabbing at him. He sits down.

TONY
Come on, Rin'. You know it hasn't been any good for a long time. For either of us. I'm worn out here.

IRINA
I'll die without you.

TONY
You'll be fine. In two weeks you'll forget all about me.

IRINA
No. I'm telling you, if you go I'll kill myself.

TONY
Don't fucking threaten me, Irina. This is over. I can't do it anymore. I don't wanna do it anymore. You call that guy about the modelling like I told you. I'll take care of you until you get on your feet. But I'm not gonna do this any more. Understand?

IRINA
I hate you.

Tony goes. Hurting, Irina throws a figurine after him.

5: EXT. PARK – DAY

Tony and DICK BARONE meet with ALBERT BARESE (40), Richie, and Jackie Jr. who sits behind him.

TONY
So that's it. Albert splits Nutley with D'Alessio Brothers, Barone keeps everything north of Patterson.
(to Dick)
What else we gotta talk about?

DICK BARONE

Fairfield township's taking bids next week.

RICHIE

What's to fuckin' talk about there? Fairfield's mine.

TONY

Was yours. I don't give bids to the handicapped.
(off Richie's confusion)
You're obviously fuckin' deaf, Rich. Ten times I told you, then I find out
you're still sellin' blow on your garbage routes?

RICHIE

For this I'm losin' a fuckin' bid? You fuckin' kiddin' me?

TONY

Next time you'll find yourself in the back of one of your trucks. That
sound like I'm fuckin' kiddin'?

A very tense moment. Richie struggles to stay composed.

JACKIE JR.

Those are my father's garbage routes.

RICHIE

Ssh. Kid.

ALBERT

Actually, all due respect, but Larry wants the Fairfield contract – the
hardship of his family and whatnot while he's in jail awaiting trial.

TONY

See? That's why we have the fixed bid <u>club</u>. Everybody's got a story
why they should go to the head of the line.

RICHIE

I was in line for ten fuckin' years.

JACKIE JR.

My uncle is asking for what my dad would of given him when <u>he</u> was
boss if Richie got out of prison. And it has nothing to do with they were
brothers. You respected my father, you should respect Richie.

TONY

Those who want respect give respect.

RICHIE

He just told you to shut the fuck up, kid.
(beat)
And he told me to go fuck myself.

6: INT. MELVOIN'S OFFICE – DAY

JUNIOR, reading papers, is with his lawyer, HAROLD "MEL" MELVOIN.

JUNIOR

Your bill, Mel. Jesus. I wish this fuckin' trial would happen already. I'm
hemorrhaging sponduliks here!

MELVOIN

The Minimization Process could be very good for us. Hire experts to
study the wiretap tapes. Former Bureau guys. Very thorough. If they
find abuses we take those findings to the judge and possibly get <u>all</u> the
wiretap evidence thrown out.

JUNIOR
(delighted)
That's fuckin' great. I know the Feds stay on the phone longer than the
twenty seconds they're allowed to see if the call is relevant. I hear a

click. I could be talkin' about root beer and sometimes they'll stay on forty, fifty seconds before they hang up. Pricks.

> **MELVOIN**
> But it'll cost – the study.

> **JUNIOR**
> How much?

> **MELVOIN**
> Two hundred-plus hours of tapes to analyze. And I wanna bring on specialized counsel to handle the wiretap litigation – ballpark figure?

> **JUNIOR**
> Yes, yes, Wrigley fucking Field, for Christ sake.

> **MELVOIN**
> Four hundred thousand.

Junior goes pale.

7: INT. JUNIOR'S HOUSE – DEN – NIGHT

Bacala, Junior, and Richie. Junior fulminates.

> **JUNIOR**
> Did my nephew say where I'm allowed to move the coke?

> **RICHIE**
> He doesn't give a shit about anybody but himself. This country's in boom times. There's more fuckin' garbage than there ever has been and he won't let me eat.

> **JUNIOR**
> You wanna cry money problems? I'm facing twenty years. I could die in the fuckin' place.

> **BACALA**
> You're gonna beat it, Skipper.

> **JUNIOR**
> You don't fuckin' know that.
> *(beat)*
> That coke is my lifeline right now.

> **RICHIE**
> Break it down, Jun'. What choice does he leave us?

> **JUNIOR**
> You need allies to do what you're thinking about.

> **RICHIE**
> Albert Barese did not like what he was hearing. And by extension Larry Barese. Biggest fuckin' crew in the family.

> **JUNIOR**
> Doesn't surprise me. Larry's had as much time as me to think about why he's under indictment and some other people ain't.

> **RICHIE**
> What do you want me to do?

> **JUNIOR**
> Go talk to Ally Boy. Feel him out. But he's a slippery fuck. Don't commit.

> **RICHIE**
> I'll go see him.

They embrace deeply. Richie goes.

> **JUNIOR**
> He's got tremendous moxie for his size.

> **BACALA**
> Tell me about it, he's a fighter.

8: EXT. ROADSIDE – DAY

LIPARI is in his car. PUSSY pulls up, gets out, comes over and gets in. He hands Lipari a gift box of Johnny Walker.

> **LIPARI**
> What's this?

> **PUSSY**
> *(excited)*
> Open it.

> **LIPARI**
> I can see it's JW Gold. But we can't accept gifts, Sal. I'll pass it along to the guys at the Fireman's home.

> **PUSSY**
> See? That right there. You guys have a policy and it's fucking stuck to. You don't get distracted. Look what happened with those Egyptians, those motherless World Trade Center fucks. Serial numbers on an axle and you put everyone of them behind bars.

> **LIPARI**
> The fuck is all this?

> **PUSSY**
> I owe you, Skip. The rest of my life I'll never forget. You looked the other way on that Bevilaqua beef, my ass would of been fried.

> **LIPARI**
> What?! The Bureau would never turn its head on a murder charge.

> **PUSSY**
> All right. What else can you say at this point, right? What do you know about Scottsdale?

> **LIPARI**
> Arizona?

> **PUSSY**
> I was thinking I would pick there to live. When this assignment is over.

> **LIPARI**
> Assignment?

> **PUSSY**
> You know, when I'm in witness protection. They got more than 300 days of sunshine, golf, Giant's Spring training.
> *(beat)*
> Naturally, I'm talking about <u>after</u> I do my two years in Atlanta. I been thinking I'll take some courses in the can. Psychology, criminology. Get my degree when I get out. Maybe travel around and give lectures at police departments on O.C.

> **LIPARI**
> *(thin smile)*
> Yeah, well, that's an idea...

Pussy hands Lipari a blank airline ticket.

> **PUSSY**
> An airline ticket. From the Scatino bust-out. Tony made the guy order blocks of these things through the sporting goods store.

181

LIPARI
I'll put it on file.

PUSSY
(sensing his disappointment)
You could use it as probable cause for a warrant, couldn't you?
Evidence of extortion, intent to defraud? Those are RICO predicates,
right?

LIPARI
First you'd have to tie the ticket to Tony. And he's too smart to use any
of them himself. He probably moved them by now.

PUSSY
(dejected)
Oh.

LIPARI
However. This engagement party for the sister. We're gonna wanna wire
you up. I know you're sensitive.

PUSSY
Fuck that. What was I, his fuckin' errand boy?

LIPARI
(bored)
The Saturn. Yeah.

PUSSY
Running all over looking for his kid's science teacher's car? What the
fuck is that? Any faith I had went out the window that very day.

9–10: OMITTED

11: INT. SOPRANO HOUSE – BASEMENT- DAY

*Carmela sets the laundry basket on the dryer, opens the washing machine to start
putting in a dark load when she notices something in the tub. She reaches in and pulls
it out – a shirt of Tony's – and is about to toss it aside when something stops her. A
familiar smell. She brings the shirt up and sniffs it. Her face floods with sadness,
anger and disappointment. Over which – PRELAP – PARTY CHATTER, A RINGING
DOORBELL.*

12: INT. SOPRANO HOUSE – FOYER – DAY

*A party is underway. LILLIANA walks through carrying a big fancy cake with wedding
bells and the words: "Love Forever, Janice & Richie." MEADOW greets SILVIO and
GABRIELLA who holds a present.*

MEADOW
Hi, Uncle Silvio, Auntie Gab'.
(off present)
Fortunoff's?

GABRIELLA
Three of her Haviland place settings.

SILVIO
What's it gonna be, Mead – B.U. or Columbia?

MEADOW
I may take a year off.

13: INT. SOPRANO HOUSE – LIVING ROOM – SAME

ADRIANA is looking at Janice's engagement ring.

ADRIANA
Gorgeous. So, are you out of your mind with all the arrangements?

JANICE
My planner did Rick Cerone's wedding.
(Adriana gasps)
All I do is hand out money. I have his card for you.

CHRISTOPHER
Your father's disappeared and I'm not paying for something like that.

Putting on her best face, Carmela comes up with a tray of hors d'oeuvres.

ADRIANA
Carmela, I love the new wallpaper.

JANICE
You think I should do my den? Do you have that guy's number?

Carmela moves on, passing –

AT THE BAR

Pussy and Tony fixing drinks. Tony's got his eyes on Richie, who is with Jackie Jr., and Meadow, laughing about something.

PUSSY
T, you still got any of those airline tickets you got from the Scatino bust out?

TONY
(watching Richie)
Fuckin' creep. What happened to that man in the can?
(calling)
Meadow, go help your mother.

PUSSY
You're in a little bit of denial here, T. Richie was always a disturbed kid.
(Janice comes up.)
So Janice, I really don't have a shot anymore?

Janice laughs. Pussy moves off.

JANICE
(pouring wine)
Having a good fucking time?

TONY
What do you want me to say, Janice? I'm sorry. I'm glad for you.

JANICE
You shoulda seen Ma when we left the house. She really wanted to be here.

TONY
Could we go back to where I was glad for you?

JANICE
You don't even give her a chance. She is a completely different person since the doctor has her on Prozac.

TONY
(thrown)
Has her on what?

RICHIE
Janice!

Janice moves off.

AT THE FOOD TABLE

Carmela is setting out a chafing dish as Lilliana removes an empty one. Tony comes up.

> **TONY**
> You believe this shit? They got the old lady on Prozac. She's 'changed'. My ass. She's just too senile to remember who she hates.
> *(when there's no response –)*
> What's the matter with you today?

> **CARMELA**
> What do you care?

Tony just looks at her. We HEAR a TINK, TINK of fork against glass.

FIND RICHIE AND JANICE

His arm around her as the group quiets.

> **RICHIE**
> Everybody? I wanna thank my future in-laws for a great party and thank you all for coming and celebrating with us this historic-making union of the Apriles and the Sopranos.

Tony is pensive on the sidelines. Rosalie and Jackie Jr. beam at Richie. As does Rick. And Carmela, caught up in the romance of it all.

> **RICHIE (cont'd)**
> They say it's never too late and they say that good things come to those who wait and they are right on both counts.

"Here, here," "yo," etc.

> **ROSALIE**
> Got anything to add, Little Ricky?

> **RICK**
> *(raises glass)*
> Glad for you, Dad. Stepmom.

Richie glowers.

> **JANICE**
> Thanks, Rick. I just wanna share my happiness with everybody. I've been looking for my soulmate all my life. Madonn' have I looked. I don't know what made me think I was gonna find anybody halfway decent at an ashram in Pradesh. But look where I found it, right here at home. You knock my socks off, baby.

The happy couple kiss deeply. Carmela can't take it any more. She slips away to –

14: INT. SOPRANO HOUSE – KITCHEN – SAME

With sounds clapping and well-wishing wafting in from the next room, Carmela cries.

15: INT. SOPRANO HOUSE – BEDROOM – MIDDLE OF THE NIGHT

Tony is sleeping, when the PHONE RINGS. He opens an eye, answers.

> **TONY (on phone)**
> Yah?

16: INT. SOPRANO HOUSE – FAMILY ROOM – SAME

Carmela's in her bathrobe, watching a black and white Ronald Colman romance on AMC. Tony comes down, throwing his clothes on. He seems rattled.

> **TONY**
> I gotta go out.

Carmela merely turns up the volume. He goes out.

17: INT. HOSPITAL – HALLWAY – NIGHT

Tony hurries down the hall, but not so fast that the limping SVETLANA, Russian, 30's, can't keep up with him.

> **SVETLANA**
> Thank God I'm home. I'm in the shower, I almost didn't hear the phone.
> She's drunk, she's crying, she's took twenty sleeping pills.

> **TONY**
> The fuck did she think she was doing?

> **SVETLANA**
> Is not her fault.

> **TONY**
> Please.

> **SVETLANA**
> She has hard life.

> **TONY**
> Look at you, you got one leg, you don't behave like that.

> **SVETLANA**
> Her parents, both of them were alcoholics in Petrozavodsk, horrible
> industrial city. The father died, fifty-five years old. Lung cancer,
> cirrhosis of the liver. It was probably good thing, he wasn't working
> anyway. The factory was close down. The mother didn't have any teeth.
> Also dead. She had to go to Kazakhstan to live with uncle, crude,
> miserable man.

Svetlana opens the door to a room. They go into –

18: INT. HOSPITAL – ROOM – NIGHT

Irina lays in bed, pale and wan. Tony and Svetlana enter.

> **TONY**
> Jesus Christ, Irina.

> **IRINA**
> I don't care no more what happen.

> **TONY**
> Don't say that shit. You got your whole life in front of you.

> **IRINA**
> I'm sorry, Tony.

> **SVETLANA**
> The ambulance, emergency room, how she gonna pay? You think they
> give her medical insurance at that department store she works in?

> **TONY**
> I'll take care of it.

> **IRINA**
> What kind of life is there for me without you, Tony? To go back to
> the Bada Bing? Be a dancer? Be prostitute after that? I don't want to.
> I don't want to.

She breaks down in tears. Tony is moved and sits on the bed and holds her.

> **TONY**
> It's all right. Come on, ssh. It's gonna be all right. Don't worry.
> Everything's gonna be all right.

Trapped by his genuine sympathy, he comforts her.

19: INT. BRIDAL SALON – DAY

Janice in a wedding dress. Reveal her mirror-image, full length. Carmela prods and fluffs the dress.

JANICE

Look at that cleavage. Thank you, Jesus. I'm only doing this for the presents. No, I'm doing it for Richie. He says he'd rather go to Vegas but you gotta have the ritual, right?

CARMELA

This is such a happy time. The flowers and all the excitement. Remember how radiant I looked, walking down that aisle? I remember how I felt. And the honeymoon, the hope chest...

JANICE

You're working overtime here, Carmela.
(realizes)
You're depressed, aren't you?

CARMELA

(won't admit it)
Depressed? I leave that to others. I'm just being realistic. Because in a year tops you'll have to accept a goomar.

JANICE

Oh, yeah?
(beat)
I'd like to see the goomar that's gonna let him hold a gun to her head when they fuck.

CARMELA

What?

JANICE

What?

CARMELA

Do you let him hold a gun to your head during sex?

JANICE

If that's what gets him off. Is that so different from garter belts or nurse's uniforms?

CARMELA

It's a gun, Janice. I thought you were a feminist.

JANICE

Usually he takes the clip out.

CARMELA

Well, Jesus, I hope so.

JANICE

It's a ritual. It's fetishistic, that's all.

20: INT. FEDERAL BUILDING – OFFICE – DAY

Federal-Agent-in-Charge FRANK CUBITOSO is at his desk, writing on a yellow pad. There's a deli platter with "Happy Birthday" balloons on a side table. Skip Lipari pokes his head in. He holds up a file folder.

LIPARI

My three-o-two's from last week.

CUBITOSO

Sure, c'mon in.
(of yellow pad)
I've been invited to speak at a State Prosecutors retreat, in Atlantic City no less.

LIPARI

Nice duty if you can get it.

> *(notices balloons)*
> Happy birthday, Chief.

Cubitoso moves to the deli platter, takes a slice.

> **CUBITOSO**
> From Tony Soprano. Never misses an occasion, Christmas, Columbus Day. Grab a sandwich before I send it over to St. Ambroseus Shelter.

> **LIPARI**
> My CW on that just gave me a bottle of Johnny Walker.

Lipari takes a slice of copa.

> **CUBITOSO**
> CW Sixteen.

> **LIPARI**
> Bonpensiero, yeah. Fuckin' guy thinks I'm his friend now.

> **CUBITOSO**
> *(nibbling at tray)*
> I know poor people are gonna get it, but I can't resist this lard bread.

> **LIPARI**
> He's turned some corner. One minute he's crying because he loves Tony Soprano so much, and in the next breath he's a Junior G-Man.

> **CUBITOSO**
> *(nibbling)*
> Well, it's prosciutto bread now. But in the old days it was real bits of friggin' lard. Delicious.

> **LIPARI**
> Talking about RICO predicates and probable cause. Suddenly we're the fuckin' good guys. Worse case of Stockholm Syndrome since Patty Hearst.

> **CUBITOSO**
> That was sad. Psychologically identifying with a shit bag like Donald DeFreize, robbing banks.

> **LIPARI**
> Tell you, though, I'm worried about Sal with these fantasies of law enforcement.

> **CUBITOSO**
> 'Sal'?

> **LIPARI**
> What?

> **CUBITOSO**
> This thing can work two ways, Skip. You can find yourself getting too close.

They are helping themselves to further nibs of cold cuts as an assistant carries the platter from the room –

21: INT. ALBERT BARESE'S SOCIAL CLUB – DAY

Was Larry Barese's social club. Vanity shot of Larry looking down from the wall on Albert Barese and Richie.

> **ALBERT**
> Getting married, settling down. Different Richie Aprile.

> **RICHIE**
> One door opens, another door closes. Fuckin' expensive proposition though. I didn't need that shit that happened the other day.

ALBERT
You don't need that shit that happened the other day.

RICHIE
(nods to Larry's photo)
You talk to the king of dermabrasion about what went down?

ALBERT
I'm talking, he's looking at his reflection in the Plexiglas.

RICHIE
Imagine, getting a fuckin' face lift and a week later you're in jail.

ALBERT
He gets a face lift and a week later he's in jail.

RICHIE
Anyway, I had a feeling that you didn't like what you were hearing.

ALBERT
Larry expected to get fucked outta that bid.

RICHIE
Now there's a sad commentary.

ALBERT
Richie, what's Larry gonna do? The fucking guy is a guest of the government.

RICHIE
While some people stuff themselves.

ALBERT
Some people are out there stuffing themselves.

RICHIE
(patiently)
Right.

ALBERT
Only Larry's got a trial coming up. He's not in a position to go into the unknown not knowing.

RICHIE
What about you, Albert? Weigh in anytime.

ALBERT
I'm with him. He could beat this.

RICHIE
But all things being equal...?

ALBERT
No. No way. I don't know what to tell you.

22: INT. PAINT STORE – DAY

A can of paint vibrates in the electric paint mixer. Scanning the aisles, Carmela "runs into" VIC MUSTO.

CARMELA
Vic!

VIC
(taken aback)
Carmela!

CARMELA
Imagine running into you here! How are you?

VIC
I'm fine. Fine. How are you?

CARMELA
Good. Shopping for a roller...
(steels herself)
Look, Vic, truthfully? I'm not just running into you. I saw the name of this store on your supplies and I've been waiting for you. I wanted to talk to you.

VIC
I'm sorry, Carmela, I should have called you that day.

CARMELA
No, no, believe me, you have nothing to be sorry about.

VIC
I should have told you I wasn't coming for lunch.

CARMELA
It's all right. I got the message when you didn't show up. That's why I wanted to see you. To thank you.

VIC
For what?

CARMELA
Maybe someday I'll be free... but if you had come that day, I might have done something that I would be sorry for forever. So I wanted to thank you for thinking for the both of us. For being strong for the both of us.

VIC
Carmela –

CARMELA
No, I mean it. Okay? I just needed to say that. Thank you.

VIC
(lame)
You're welcome.

CARMELA
Goodbye, Vic. Take care of yourself.

Carmela puts her hand on his arm, kisses Vic's cheek. Beat. No response from Vic. She turns and goes. RAMONE comes up, sees his boss shaken there, watching her go. He breathes relief.

VIC
Thank Christ.

23: INT. MELFI'S OFFICE – DAY

The beginning of a session. Tony and MELFI.

TONY
I need you to give me the number of a good shrink.

MELFI
Oh?

TONY
Look, this has nothing to do with any O.C. shit, okay?
(beat)
It's for the girl that I was seeing.

MELFI
Was?

TONY

I broke it off with her and she tried to kill herself. And this was no small cuttings. This was twenty halcyon and a quart of vodka. Fuckin' ambulance, they pumped her stomach. It cost me three grand.

MELFI

She should have been seen by a psychiatrist at the hospital.

TONY

He was Romanian and they got some beef goes back centuries. She wouldn't talk to him.

MELFI

Do you feel responsible for her suicide attempt?

TONY

This is gonna be about me now?

MELFI

You're my patient.

TONY

I was banging her for two years!

MELFI

Was that a hardship on her?

TONY

Cute. You know how many women I been through? I don't know why I fuckin' don't say 'fuck it' with this one.

MELFI

Why do you think?

TONY

Listen, she's a sweet kid underneath it all and I think she's seriously depressed.

MELFI

You feel for her.

Silence.

MELFI (cont'd)

I'm interested in why you're ending it.

TONY

What do you mean, why? That what I'm supposed to do, aren't I? Isn't that what you're always saying in here?

MELFI

I don't think I've ever passed judgement per se on a patient's sex life.

TONY

Even if the girl's twenty years younger than me and I'm married? What's wrong with you?

MELFI

Why now?

TONY
(levels)

Why? Because it's not fun anymore, okay? So you gonna recommend somebody or not?

24: INT. JUNIOR'S HOUSE – KITCHEN – DAY

Junior sits at the table not eating the rest of a sandwich, waiting. Bacala comes in, followed by Richie, followed by Jackie Jr.

BACALA
He's eating lunch.

JUNIOR
(to Richie)
So?

RICHIE
Larry's out.

JUNIOR
Shit. Fuck. I knew it. I fuckin' knew it.
(waves food away)
Bobby, take this. I can't eat.

Bacala clears Junior's dish and cleans up at the sink.

RICHIE
Albert and Larry are not the problem. The fuckin' problem is Tony. He's taken out of the picture and believe me, everybody else will come along. Where else are they gonna go?

JUNIOR
I'm sick.

RICHIE
And fuckin' Larry Barese too. I got friends in Federal holding that'd like nothing better than to do that weak fuck.

JACKIE JR.
He was a great friend to my father but he doesn't care who he follows now. I'd do him myself.

JUNIOR
Who's that speaking here? Is someone speaking?
(then)
Listen, kid, lemme think about this alright? But we can't be too fucked up by this set-back. We gotta screw our courage to the post.

They embrace emotionally, then look into each other's eyes.

JUNIOR (cont'd)
You're a good boy, Richie.

RICHIE
It's gonna be good.

JUNIOR
(emotional)
Go on home. We'll talk.

They hug again. Richie goes. The air is heavy with the weight of the occasion. The outer door closes.

BACALA
Fuckin' guy's fearless for his size.

JUNIOR
That's nice. Then what? I can't even wear his shoes.

BACALA
The fuck you talking about?

Junior paces slowly, thinking. He makes a cool assessment. He's not angry.

JUNIOR
Fuckin' loser. He couldn't sell it.

BACALA
Richie?

JUNIOR
Pay attention, you just may learn something here.
(thinking, worrying)
Who'm I best off with? We best off with?
(beat)
Old man Profaci, he knew how to split his enemies.
(thinking; re Richie)
He couldn't fuckin' sell it. He's not respected.
(beat)
But Tony with his impulsiveness and selfishness. He's locked in that fuckin' head of his.
(decides)
I'm better off with Tony.
(decides again)
Definitely. I wanna see Anthony at the doctor's office tomorrow.

Bacala stares at Junior, stunned and disgusted.

JUNIOR (cont'd)
What are you looking at?

BACALA
(seriously)
I'm in awe of you.

25: INT. STOCK BROKERAGE – CHRISTOPHER'S OFFICE – DAY

Christopher is watching financial news on a T.V. Pussy comes to the door, touches a place on his chest where a recording device would be, and sticks his head in.

PUSSY
Hard at work.

CHRISTOPHER
Fuck you, it's financial news. The fuck are you doing here?

PUSSY
I got a line on a car for Adriana.

CHRISTOPHER
You want anything? They got sodas, coffee. I got a bottle in the drawer.

PUSSY
I'm good. How's it going here?

CHRISTOPHER
This racket, we dumped Webistics and whacked up the payoff? Fuckin' license to steal.

PUSSY
Anything you can get me into?

CHRISTOPHER
A pharmaceutical. They have a fuckin' root from the Amazon, cures glaucoma. It's all bullshit.
(searching)
I got a brochure. Hey tonight, Puss? I got something hard-edge for you.

PUSSY
What?

CHRISTOPHER
Pokemon cards. Me and Tommy Mac are taking down a truckload.

PUSSY
Yeah? Where?

> **CHRISTOPHER**
> Tommy knows. You in?

> **PUSSY**
> What? Me?

> **CHRISTOPHER**
> Yeah, c'mon, old times.
> **PUSSY**
> (thinking fast)
> You don't want a fat fuck like me around.

Pussy starts to leave.

> **CHRISTOPHER**
> I can't find the fuckin' brochure. Anyway what difference does it make? Go in for five, ten grand. At the time we dump the piece of shit you'll be in six figure territory.

Pussy nods, starts to leave again.

> **CHRISTOPHER (cont'd)**
> Puss?

> **PUSSY**
> Yeah?

> **CHRISTOPHER**
> The fuckin' car?

> **PUSSY**
> What car? Oh, yeah, right, for Adriana. It's an M3 convertible. Clean. I'll keep you posted.

26: EXT. STOCK BROKERAGE – PARKING LOT – DAY

Pussy gets in his car. Dials his cell phone.

27: INT. DENTIST'S OFFICE – DAY – INTERCUT AS NECESSARY

Lipari is in the chair. A HYGIENIST cleans his teeth. His cell phone rings. With instruments in mouth –

> **LIPARI**
> Thcuze me.

When she removes the instruments, he answers phone.

> **LIPARI (cont'd)**
> Lipari.

> **PUSSY**
> This is Fat Man.

> **LIPARI**
> Who?

> **PUSSY**
> You know.

> **LIPARI**
> Sal?

> **PUSSY**
> I just heard about they're gonna jack a load of cigarettes. Moltisanti and another individual.

> **LIPARI**
> Good. Where?

PUSSY
I don't know yet. I should ascertain, right?

LIPARI
(to hygienist)
Could you excuse me, dear?

The Hygienist goes out.

LIPARI (cont'd)
You're a cooperating witness. You wear a wire. That's what you do. So ask around, see what you can find out. But I in no way want you going along on any hijack, you hear me? We let you earn, but no violent crimes, right?

PUSSY
Okay.

28: INT. IRINA'S BEDROOM – NIGHT

Irina is dressed and hysterical when Tony comes in. She starts beating him with her fists.

IRINA
Get out of here! I hate you, you fucking bastard!

Svetlana limps in.

SVETLANA
(in Russian)
I told him this was not a good time.

TONY
Fuckin' mood swings. I liked her better when she committed suicide. At least she was quiet.

SVETLANA
(in Russian)
Ssh. Ssh. Is all right.
(to Tony)
Was very bad day for her.

TONY
When isn't?

IRINA
(holding back tears)
I went to modeling agency like you told me. I waited four hours to see Mr. Littman.

TONY
So...?

SVETLANA
(don't ask)
Wasn't good.

TONY
She didn't get a job? So what? She can model somewheres else.

IRINA
It was catalogs there. To be a model for catalogs for salad spinners.

TONY
You gotta start somewhere.

IRINA
I went into to see him, he told me I am too old!

TONY
Jesus. I'm sorry...

> SVETLANA
I go make the tea.

Svetlana limps away. Irina wails. Tony sits with her.

> IRINA
I told you. I told you. Is all over for me.

> TONY
No it isn't. It's gonna be fine.

> IRINA
Look at Svetlana, her prosthetic leg fall off in Gap store and her Bill pick her up and carry her. Where is my knight in white satin armor?

> TONY
I got the number of somebody I want you to talk to.

> IRINA
I don't wanna go on no more fucking interviews.

> TONY
This isn't that. This is a shrink.

> IRINA
A shrink?

> TONY
A psychiatrist.

> IRINA
I know what is.

Svetlana comes back with a glass of tea, sugar cubes.

> TONY
He comes highly recommended and I think you'll feel better if you talk to him.

> IRINA
I'm not going to no shrink.

> TONY
Yeah, you are, because that's what I want you to do.

> IRINA
You're not the boss of me.

> TONY
Okay, you know what? Go fuck yourself then. I'm being a nice guy here. I went to a lot of trouble to get this guy's number.

> IRINA
Why? So you can send me to hospital? Lock me up?

> SVETLANA
Psychiatrist is scary for Russian. Means being sent to Gulag. Political rehabilitation.

> TONY
This is too fucked up.

> IRINA
Kiss off then.

He heads out.

29: INT. LIVIA'S HOUSE – LIVING ROOM – NIGHT

Richie is drinking and watching boxing on HBO. His mind is full of thought. Janice is scanning a brochure.

LIVIA'S VOICE
Janice? How do you open this Advil?
(then)
Oh. Never mind.

Rick comes through from the kitchen, carrying hedge clippers, garden hose, hoe, and rubber shoes.

RICK
Dad, I'm gonna get started on your gutters tomorrow.

RICHIE
(eyes on T.V.)
Great, kid.

Rick goes out. Janice proffers the brochure to Richie.

JANICE
Richie, take a look at this. I picked it up at the Kuchensysteme yesterday. Very Bauhaus. And not bad. You can get the basics for twenty thousand.

RICHIE
Janice, maybe you better slow down on some of this spending time being.

JANICE
Why?

RICHIE
Because I said so.

JANICE
Something wrong? What happened?

RICHIE
It'll be taken care of. But things could be fucked up for a while.

JANICE
Richie, if something's happening to you, it's happening to me.

RICHIE
A decision went against me which impacts me a great deal financially.

JANICE
Fuck, I knew it.

RICHIE
The shit with your brother, it's been building since I got out.

JANICE
But we're still going ahead with everything at the house, right?

RICHIE
We'll see.

JANICE
Richie, they're tiling the pool on Friday. And the atrium window, I'll lose my deposit.

RICHIE
I told you, I'm taking care of it.

JANICE
He can't handle that our house is going to be nicer than his.

RICHIE
I don't know what to do with this guy. Give him a coat that you treasure and he gives it to his fuckin' Polack maid.

Janice's lip starts to tremble. She tries not to cry.

RICHIE (cont'd)
What's the matter with you?

JANICE
Nothing.

RICHIE
What?

JANICE
Nothing. It's just sad that's all.

RICHIE
What?

JANICE
AJ didn't have the flu. He didn't go with you because Tony wouldn't let him. He doesn't want you around his kids.

Richie picks his beer bottle up and throws it across the room. Livia's voice comes from a table-top intercom box.

LIVIA'S VOICE
What happened? What was that?

30: EXT. DINER PARKING LOT – NIGHT

Pussy waits in an old beater. Take-out pizza box and soda cans say he's been in the car a while. Watching the door of the diner, he speaks into a tape recorder.

PUSSY
Searchlight Diner. Five fifteen a.m. Subject vehicle has still not left location. Sun coming up.

Pussy sees Christopher and Tommy Mac come out, ducks back into shadow.

PUSSY (cont'd)
Five sixteen. Subjects departing Searchlight Diner.

Christopher and Tommy Mac get in Christopher's car. They drive out. After a beat, Pussy follows.

31: EXT. STREET SOMEWHERE – DAY

Pussy follows the Mercedes at a discrete distance. Christopher drives fast. Pussy has to hump to keep up with him. The Mercedes easily takes a corner at high speed. When Pussy follows, he doesn't make the turn, skids sideways, and hits a worker on a bicycle. The man and his lunch box land on Pussy's windshield. Pussy's car plows into a parked car. Stunned, knee very hurt, Pussy extricates himself from the wreck. He starts to stagger away but finally, in pain and defeat, lowers himself onto the curb as a few bystanders approach.

32: OMITTED

33: INT. SOPRANO HOUSE – KITCHEN – MORNING

Lilliana dry mops. Dressed for the gym, Carmela and Gabriella finish coffee and bagels as the PHONE RINGS.

CARMELA
Get that, Lilliana?

LILLIANA (phone)
Hello, Soprano residence?

34: INTERCUT AS NECESSARY – IRINA

Drunk, on the phone. Tony enters the Soprano kitchen.

> **IRINA**
> Is Tony there?

> **LILLIANA**
> May I ask who is calling?

> **IRINA**
> Just put him on.

> **LILLIANA**
> Who is calling please?

> **IRINA**
> What are you, that Polish maid? I wanna talk to Tony.

> **LILLIANA**
> *(in Russian)*
> *Who is this? The Russian whore? You're not the first one you know.*

> **IRINA**
> *(in Russian)*
> *Put him on the fucking phone, you bearded Polack hag!*

Tony grabs the phone from Lilliana.

> **LILLIANA**
> Is for you.

> **TONY**
> Hello?

> **IRINA**
> Tony, I miss you. I love you.

> **TONY**
> You got the wrong fucking number. Don't call here again.

> **GABRIELLA**
> I'll wait out there.

She heads to the foyer. Tony slams the phone down. Carmela glares at him.

> **CARMELA**
> Who's that, your little Russian girlfriend?

> **TONY**
> Carmela, it's over between us. It has been for a long time.

> **CARMELA**
> *(furious; wounded)*
> Oh, bullshit. How come your clothes still stink of perfume?

> **TONY**
> Okay, I saw her, but not the way you think. She tried to commit suicide, Carmela.

> **CARMELA**
> Oh, fuck you.

> **TONY**
> After I broke it off with her, she tried to kill herself because she didn't wanna go on without me, the poor kid.

> **CARMELA**
> *(long beat; breathing heavy)*
> You're putting me in a position where I'm feeling sorry for a whore who fucks you. And what's even stranger, for a second I believed you.

Carmela goes. Tony goes in a different direction.

35: INT. SOPRANO HOUSE – FOYER – DAY

Gabriella waits for Carmela at the front door.

> **CARMELA**
> Goddamn him, goddamn him.

> **GABRIELLA**
> They're all the same, Carm.

> **CARMELA**
> No they're not. The man who did my wallpaper, there was a male person you could respect and... and...

> **GABRIELLA**
> Victor Musto? Carmela, he didn't show up that day because of who your husband is. Face it. Use your head. He pissed his pants.

> **CARMELA**
> *(leaves, drops bag)*
> I don't want to go to the gym.

She runs upstairs. On Gabriella –

36: INT. DR. SCHRECK'S OFFICE – DAY

Junior waits. Tony comes in.

> **TONY**
> This better be good. I'm in the middle of World War III over there.

> **JUNIOR**
> When you're lying in the street in a pool of your own blood, don't say your uncle didn't try to tell you.

> **TONY**
> The fuck are you talking about?

> **JUNIOR**
> Richie Aprile is moving against you.

> **TONY**
> I didn't know if he had the balls.

> **JUNIOR**
> He has a legitimate beef with you. You're fuckin' high-handed with everybody.

> **TONY**
> Stick to what you fuckin' know and leave your opinions wherever the fuck.

> **JUNIOR**
> He approached Albert Barese. Albert said no.

> **TONY**
> Albert told you this?

> **JUNIOR**
> No, I got it from Richie himself. At my house yesterday. He's gonna take you out, and Larry Barese or anybody else who doesn't go along.

> **TONY**
> Wait a minute, why's he telling <u>you</u> all this?

> **JUNIOR**
> He thinks I'm with him.

TONY
Oh really?
(studies him)
What gave him that idea?

JUNIOR
It's what I wanted him to believe. I've been playing him. I saw this coming early on. That's why I made a big deal of that coke. I raised a non-issue and he fell for it.

TONY
Oh. I see. You're a double agent. Fuckin' Matt Helm.

JUNIOR
Fuck you.

TONY
How do I know you're not playing me?

JUNIOR
You don't. Believe what you want, my little nephew. But if I didn't come to you, your fuckin' wife would be a widow and your children wouldn't have no father. So go fuck yourself.

TONY
Stop. I'm grateful to you. I am.

Junior just looks at him.

TONY (cont'd)
I gave you five percent on the action that was left to you. I'll kick it up to seven and a half. But no drugs on the routes. It's shortsighted.

A beat. Then Tony and Junior hug. Emotional. Junior teary-eyed. Then they break.

TONY (cont'd)
The asshole's marrying my sister.

JUNIOR
You gotta wonder where she is in all this.
(sour)
My little niece.

37: INT. BADA BING – BACK ROOM – NIGHT

Tony's pouring a drink, Silvio comes in.

SILVIO
What's up, T?

TONY
My future brother-in-law's causing a serious problem.

SILVIO
How serious?

TONY
He's not satisfied with the current leadership. He wants to have me popped.

SILVIO
Motherfucker.

TONY
So now I gotta decide what to do about him.

Silvio thinks, walks, smokes. Then –

SILVIO
I genuinely don't think there's anything to gain by keeping him around.

                    TONY
Get it done.

38: INT. LIVIA'S HOUSE – KITCHEN – NIGHT

Janice is straining penne. Gravy simmers. Sausages fry. Richie is opening a bottle of wine.

                    JANICE
The planner checked the Almanac and there's a 65 percent historical chance of rain on the twelfth. He wants a tent as backup. What do you think?

                    RICHIE
I can't decide that shit, Janice, c'mon.

                    JANICE
Okay, but when you start bitching when you see the bill, don't.

                    RICHIE
My fuckin' kid today, he hit me up for ten grand to go to England for one of these fuckin' dance contests.

                    JANICE
Little Ricky's still coming to the wedding isn't he?

                    RICHIE
It's Rick. <u>Rick.</u> <u>Richard.</u> How many times do I have to tell you? He was Little Ricky when he was fuckin' twelve.
     (beat)
Keep the heat down on my sausages.

                    JANICE
     (turns heat down)
Awright. Jesus.
     (then)
But he's still coming, right?

                    RICHIE
He's not gonna miss a chance to tango and foxtrot in front of everybody.

                    JANICE
Ballroom dancing is a legitimate art form.

Janice brings bread and Parmesan to the table.

                    RICHIE
He carries my name. <u>Richard.</u> Fuckin' disgraziata. My nephew Jackie, why couldn't I of had a son like that?

                    JANICE
You came home with a fuckin' attitude. I been in this house fuckin' cooking your dinner and taking care of that fuckin' black hole upstairs all day!

                    RICHIE
Keep your fuckin' voice down. You know she hears everything.

                    JANICE
Not tonight. I gave her two Nembutols because I thought we'd wanna have sex. Not likely.

                    RICHIE
Just put my fuckin' dinner on the table, okay, and shut your mouth.

                    JANICE
You shut up.

> **RICHIE**
> You shut up.

> **JANICE**
> Just because he's a ballroom dancer you think your son is gay? And even if he was, what difference would it make? You feel threatened?

> **RICHIE**
> Fucking sow. What'd I just tell you?

Richie punches her in the mouth. She's rocked. Her hand goes to her mouth. She stands there, stunned as Richie goes to the stove and prepares a plate of food. Janice looks at her hand, sees blood.

> **RICHIE**
> What are you looking at? You gonna fuckin' cry now?

Richie comes and puts his plate of pasta and sausages down on the table and sits. While he eats, Janice calmly goes into –

39: INT. LIVIA'S HOUSE – LIVING ROOM – SAME

Janice comes in and reaches behind the VCR and pulls out a gun. She turns and goes back into –

40: INT. LIVIA'S HOUSE – KITCHEN – SAME

Janice comes in and stands over Richie while he eats. He looks up and sees her and the gun.

> **RICHIE (cont'd)**
> Get the fuck out of here, I'm not in the mood for any of these fuckin' dramat –

Janice fires. Hits him in the chest. He goes over backward. Struggles to his knees, blood oozing from his mouth. He goes to grab for her ankle and she fires once more getting him square in the face. She stands there. The silence roars.

It takes her a moment before she looks at the gun in her hand. Then she listens. Not a sound. She goes to –

41: INT. LIVIA'S HOUSE – LIVING ROOM – SAME

Janice stands at the foot of the stairs and listens. Nothing. She goes and looks and listens out the door. Nothing. Then she calls outside, loud –

> **JANICE**
> Jeremy! Put those cherry bombs away!

She turns back and looks to the kitchen, at Richie. Omigod.

42: INT. SOPRANO HOUSE – KITCHEN – NIGHT

Carmela is doing dinner dishes. Tony comes home, the weight of the world, goes straight to the fridge.

> **TONY**
> Any left of whatever that was?

> **CARMELA**
> Bottom shelf.

Tony takes out a dish of stuffed shells. A fork.

> **TONY**
> Where is everybody?

> **CARMELA**
> AJ's upstairs. She's out.

The PHONE RINGS. He's eating, looks to her.

> **CARMELA (cont'd)**
> You get it. Maybe she's slit the other wrist.

He answers the phone.

> **TONY**
> Hello?

43: INTERCUT AS NECESSARY – JANICE

Hysterical. Hyperventilating. Trying to contain it.

> **JANICE**
> Tony? You've gotta help me. You gotta come over here. Please.

> **TONY**
> What's the matter? Is it Ma?

> **JANICE**
> No. Tony...

> **TONY**
> Tell me what happened.

> **JANICE**
> *(sobbing now)*
> I can't say.

> **TONY**
> What do you mean you can't say?

> **JANICE**
> I can't say right now, Tony. Think!

> **TONY**
> Jesus. Okay take it easy, I'll be right there.

He hangs up. Sees Carmela watching.

> **TONY (cont'd)**
> It was Janice.

> **CARMELA**
> *(pissy)*
> Right. What happened?

> **TONY**
> I dunno. But I gotta go.

Tony heads out, looks back and sees Carmela watching, turns and continues on. She throws the dishtowel down.

43A: EXT. LIVIA'S HOUSE – NIGHT

Tony parks. Checks clip on 9mm automatic. Sticks it in his waistband. Warily approaches house.

44: INT. LIVIA'S HOUSE – NIGHT

All the curtains are now pulled shut. As we left him, Richie lies in a pool of blood. Janice is kneeling near Richie, smoking, crying and keening, occasionally reaching out and touching him tenderly. Her lip is now swollen.

> **JANICE**
> He hit me. It was an accident.

> **TONY**
> Where's Ma?

> **JANICE**
> Upstairs. Out. She took two Nembutols.

TONY
Ma?

JANICE
I didn't mean to do it, Tony.

TONY
Where's the gun?

JANICE
Under the sink.

Tony takes out a handkerchief and retrieves the gun.

TONY
If anybody called anything in or there's any shit about this, you don't have to talk to anybody.

Tony takes out his cell phone, dials.

JANICE
What are you doing?

TONY
Take a shower, then gimme the clothes and the shoes you got on.
    (into phone)
It's me.

45: INT. HOSPITAL – EMERGENCY BAY – NIGHT

Pussy sits on an exam table. His leg's in a plastic cast over cut-away pants. He's buttoning his shirt as Lipari comes in, bleary-eyed.

LIPARI
What the fuck, Sal?

PUSSY
(hangdog)
They got away.

LIPARI
What did I tell you? Huh? What did I tell you?

PUSSY
I didn't go with them. I was following them to the boost and then I was gonna call you.

LIPARI
And if they spotted you, Moltisanti and his friend, what was your plan for that?

PUSSY
(lights up)
That was the beauty part. I wasn't even in my own car. I switched with my son.

LIPARI
You hit a fuckin' 7-11 clerk.

PUSSY
How is he?

LIPARI
In a coma.

PUSSY
Fuck.

LIPARI
They were gonna pinch you for leaving the scene, but I got you out of it.

PUSSY
I owe you again.

LIPARI
Sal, listen to me. No – look at me. Look up.
(beat)
You're not an FBI employee, Sal. Okay? That's not gonna happen.

PUSSY
But... I got a lot to offer. And I fuckin' hate l.c.n. I know I misspent most of my life. I know that. I know fuckin'-A well we live in a society of laws and –

LIPARI
Sal, you're gonna help us make a case against Tony Soprano. And then do your time for selling heroin and then you're gonna make a new life for yourself somewhere.
(beat)
It's a good thing, Sal. It's a lucky thing.

PUSSY
How fucking long until they find out about me?

LIPARI
C'mon, let's not think that way. I can show you statistics.

Pussy nods. But the life has gone out of him.

46: INT. LIVIA'S HOUSE – NIGHT

Janice sits and smokes. Her hair is in a towel, she wears a terry robe and is barefoot. Tony's gotten started with the clean-up. There's bloody paper towels, garbage bag, bucket of bloody suds. Richie's been moved a little to help the clean-up. Mop in hand, he lets in FURIO and Christopher, who carry a tarp. Christopher sees Richie.

CHRISTOPHER
Whoa.

TONY
Awright, I know. We don't have time for that. Get him out of here, get rid of him and get his car to the salvage place.

FURIO
(saddened)
Cadillac. Managia la marina.

JANICE
It was an accident.

TONY
Janice.

They spread the tarp, load Richie onto it. The PHONE RINGS. Janice too freaked, Tony answers.

TONY (on phone)
Hello?

Whoever it is hangs up.

47: INT. SOPRANO HOUSE – KITCHEN – SAME

Carmela is hanging up the phone.

48: INT. LIVIA'S HOUSE – SAME

Christopher and Furio lift up the wrapped body and head to the door. Tony puts Janice's shoes in the hefty bag and takes it and the gun and follows the men out.

JANICE
Where are you going? Don't leave me. Don't leave me.

TONY
I'll be right back.

Tony goes out with the men and body. Janice sits alone. Begins to weep.

49: EXT. PORK STORE – NIGHT – TO ESTABLISH

Dim night-lights within. Nothing unusual – except for the BUZZ of a BAND SAW cutting through something.

50: INT. PORK STORE – MIDDLE ROOM – NIGHT

Wearing blood-splattered rubber aprons and bloody gloves and working in focussed silence, Furio and Christopher move something we do not see through a vertical saw.

CHRISTOPHER
We gotta move faster here. You know what time these humps show up for work? Fuckin' meat delivery at six a.m.

FURIO
We almost done.

Furio takes a black garbage bag from a dispenser, snaps it open and holds it below view. We hear the PLOP, THUD of parts they throw in.

CHRISTOPHER
It's gonna be a while before I eat anything from Satriale's.

FURIO
Get-a the hose. Start-a wash the room.

51: INT. LIVIA'S HOUSE – LIVING ROOM – DAWN

The place is spic and span. Janice is on the couch, bawling.

LIVIA'S VOICE
Janice? Are you down there? What are you doing up so early?

JANICE
Go back to bed, Ma.

But Livia's chair starts down the stairs.

LIVIA'S VOICE
I don't know what happened to me. I had the strangest dreams all night. People were coming and going and I couldn't get up from the bed.

Tony comes in from outside as Livia lands. She walks with a four-legged cane. Janice tries to warn him.

JANICE
Tony –

LIVIA
Anthony? What are you doing here?

TONY
(cold)
Nothing. C'mon, Janice, let's go.

LIVIA
What's wrong with her?

TONY
Richie didn't come home last night and she's worried about him.

LIVIA
Sure, I bet he jilted her. It's the story of her life.

TONY
What kind of a fuckin' chance did she have with you for a mother? Always nagging her about her weight. She'd come home from a date, you'd call her a tramp.

JANICE
(flees, crying)
I'm going out to the car.

Janice goes.

LIVIA
I never said anything of the kind.

TONY
I heard you. I heard all that shit.

LIVIA
You make things up. You tell me. Tell me one thing I ever did to any of you.

He just looks at her, incredulous.

TONY
You don't fuckin' know, do you? You don't fuckin' have a clue.

LIVIA
(crying now)
I wasn't always perfect. But I did the best I could. You didn't like it – any of you – that I tried to tell you what to do. But little babies are animals. They're no different from dogs. Unless someone teaches them right from wrong. I was your mother. Who else was going to do it? And if you ask me, I did pretty darn good. That big palace you live in up there.
(weeping)
I gave my life to my children on a silver platter.

TONY
This is too crazy for me.

Tony just shakes his head and heads for the door. She gets up and follows.

LIVIA
So now you won't even give me a kiss I suppose.

TONY
What?!

LIVIA
You're cruel, that's what you are.

52: EXT. LIVIA'S HOUSE – SAME

As Tony comes out – so eager to flee that he trips – falls – tumbles down the stairs. In the doorway, Livia can't help laughing, covers her mouth. Tony stares in disbelief, picks himself up – and his fallen 9mm – and heads toward Janice and the Suburban.

53: INT. IRINA'S BEDROOM – DAY

Irina languishes in bed with tea and magazines. Svetlana limps to the doorway.

SVETLANA
(in Russian)
Irina, a man is here to see you.

IRINA
(in Russian)
Who?

SVETLANA
(in Russian)
The one who has the club. Mister Dante.

> **IRINA**
> *(in Russian)*
> *He can come in.*

Silvio comes in. Svetlana lingers at the doorway.

> **SILVIO**
> How you doing, hon?

> **IRINA**
> Who send you, Tony?

> **SILVIO**
> He asked me to bring you this.

Silvio holds out a bulging envelope to her.

> **IRINA**
> What it is, money? I don't want it.

> **SILVIO**
> Yes you do. There's seventy-five thousand dollars in here.

> **IRINA**
> *(crying)*
> Seventy-five?

> **SILVIO**
> I'm gonna give you a little piece of advice, Irina. In my business, I see girls
> come and go, so I know. Time is the great avenger. You got a short window.
> It's not good to get too hung up on any one thing. Men, jobs, whatever.
> *(beat)*
> On the other hand, something new always comes along. I've seen it
> happen a million times. It's called 'Passages'. There's a book.

> **SVETLANA**
> He's right, Irinushka. He is very smart man.

*Irina pouts. Silvio puts the envelope down on the bed and leaves. Svetlana limps after
to open the door for him. At the door –*

> **SILVIO**
> Look, far as I'm concerned, she really can't kick.

He turns and leaves.

54: EXT. BUS STATION – DAY

A Greyhound idles curbside. Destination: Seattle. Janice says goodbye to Tony.

> **JANICE**
> I'm not gonna forget this, Tony. I owe you. God, do I owe you.

> **TONY**
> Chilly, huh?

> **JANICE**
> What's wrong with our family, Tony?

> **TONY**
> I go to a shrink says we have the type of personality that has to keep
> moving forward so we don't have to think about shit we done, like a
> shark. I mean, that's not all she says...
> *(beat)*
> Our mother is... a narcissistic personality. Why she came out that way,
> who the fuck knows. And then Dad... Jesus.

> **JANICE**
> You go to a shrink? I used to suggest that you'd fuckin' blow your stack
> at me.

> **TONY**
> Maybe you should think about going back into therapy.

> **JANICE**
> *(can't help asking)*
> What did you do with him?

> **TONY**
> We buried him. On a little hill, overlooking a river. There's pine cones all around.

> **JANICE**
> You did?

> **TONY**
> C'mon Janice. The fuck? What do you care, what do you think we did with him? You really want to know?

> **JANICE**
> *(starts to blubber)*
> I loved him so much.

> **TONY**
> You'll miss your bus.

He stands.

> **JANICE**
> Tony, you don't know how much I don't wanna ask.

Tony takes out his wad of bills. Peels some off.

> **JANICE (cont'd)**
> Could you front me another four? I'm gonna need first and last for an apartment. It's gonna be at least a couple weeks to find a job.

He keeps a few bills and gives her the wad.

> **JANICE (cont'd)**
> I'll pay you back, Tony. I promise.

They kiss goodbye. She gets in the bus. The bus pulls out.

55: INT. SOPRANO HOUSE – LIVING ROOM – DAY

Carmela's reading "Memoirs of a Geisha." Brochures and pamphlets on the coffee table next to her. She hears someone come in.

> **CARMELA**
> *(calling)*
> Meadow, you have a UPS. It's up in your room.

But it's Tony who finds her.

> **TONY**
> What are you doing in here?

> **CARMELA**
> Oh, it's you. You've been gone all night, half the morning. What happened over there?

> **TONY**
> Janice decided to go back to Seattle.

> **CARMELA**
> You're kidding. What about Richie? He must be devastated.

> **TONY**
> Richie's gone.

CARMELA
What do you mean, gone?

TONY
Gone.

CARMELA
Where?

TONY
Carmela, after twenty years of marriage don't make me make you an accessory after the fact.

CARMELA
Accessory after the...?
(beat)
Holy shit.

TONY
Stop asking.

CARMELA
Oh, my God. Oh, my God.

TONY
I took care of it.

What can she say? He did. Only he could – and would. She shakes the cobwebs out of her head.

CARMELA
That... that was not a marriage made in heaven.

She stares off, grows quiet. Tony notices the travel brochures.

TONY
What's this?

CARMELA
(beat)
After Meadow's graduation, me and Rosalie Aprile are going to Rome. For three weeks.

TONY
Excuse me?

CARMELA
We're gonna stay at the Hassler. Shop. Try and see the Holy Father, maybe go on a tour of Tuscany.

TONY
What are people gonna say if you take off for three weeks?

CARMELA
You'll have to chauffeur AJ around to his dentist and whatnot. And you've gotta find a tennis clinic for Meadow to join. Because if I have to do it, Tony, I just might commit suicide.

She smirks. Then the smirk fades. Not smiling, she leaves the room. Tony sits there.

THE END

"Proshai, Livushka"

S307

Written by
David Chase

Directed by
Tim Van Patten

Soprano Productions, Inc.

Production Draft 7/24/00
1st Revision (Full Blue) 7/28/00
2nd Revision (Full Pink) 7/31/00
3rd Revision (Yellow Pages) 8/2/00
4th Revision (Green Pages) 9/13/00
5th Revision (Goldenrod Pages) 9/18/00
6th Revision (Buff Pages) 9/29/00
7th Revision (Salmon Pages) 10/27/00
8th Revision (Cherry Pages) 11/3/00
9th Revision (Tan Pages) 11/4/00
FINAL SHOOTING SCRIPT

CHARACTER LIST

TONY SOPRANO
CARMELA SOPRANO
DR. JENNIFER MELFI
CHRISTOPHER MOLTISANTI
ANTHONY SOPRANO, JR.
MEADOW SOPRANO
UNCLE "JUNIOR" SOPRANO
SILVIO DANTE
PAULIE WALNUTS
ADRIANA LA CERVA
ARTIE BUCCO
FURIO GIUNTA
BOBBY "BACALA" BACCILIERI
JANICE SOPRANO
RALPH CIFARETTO

Pussy Bonpensiero
Noah Tannenbaum
State Assemblyman Ronald Zellman
(previously Councilman Greenspan)
Svetlana Kirilenko
Barbara Giglione
Mary DeAngelis
Hugh DeAngelis
Gigi Cestone

Vito Spatafore
Gabriella Dante
Jackie Aprile, Jr.
Rosalie Aprile
Reverend James Jr.
Johnny Sack
Father Felix
Charmaine Bucco
Patsy Parisi
Herman "Hesh" Rabkin
Fanny
Tom Giglione
Raymond Curto
Albert Barese
Cozzerelli (previously Palumbo)
Man
2to5/7to9 (previously 2to4/7to9)
Young Man
Tech
Other Tech
Eugene Pontecorvo
The Giglione kids – should be at
the funeral – no lines
Lilliana
Bobby Zanone
Joe Zachary

SETS

INTERIORS

Soprano House – Kitchen	D
Soprano House – Family Room	D/N
Soprano House – Breakfast Area	D
Soprano House – Anthony Jr.'s Room	N
Soprano House – Master Bedroom	N
Soprano House – Basement	D
Soprano House – Front Door	D
Soprano House – Hallway	D
Soprano House – Living Room	D/N
Livia's House	D/N
Livia's House – Kitchen	N
Livia's House – Cellar	D
Barbara's House – Kitchen	N
Janice's Apartment	N
FBI Surveillance Van	D
Cozzerelli Funeral Home	D/N
Cozzerelli Funeral Home – Viewing Room	N
Cozzerelli Funeral Home – Lobby	N
Melfi's Office – Waiting Room	D
Melfi's Office	D
Dante House – Bedroom	N
Christopher's Apt.	N
Hospital Room – Existing Footage	

EXTERIORS

Garbage Company Yard	N
Soprano House – Driveway	D
Livia's House	D/N
Soprano House – Pool	D/N
Soprano House	N
Soprano House – Vegetable Garden	N
Seattle (stock)	N
Cozzerelli Funeral Home	D
Office Depot	D
Cemetery	D
Suburban Home	N

1: EXT. GARBAGE COMPANY YARD – NIGHT

The sides of sleeping garbage trucks say: SANI-CRUISER. Two mechanics are at work on different trucks. An EXPLOSION goes off in the bin of a third truck; a massive ball of flame. A mechanic is thrown to the ground. He scrabbles away on his knees, shielding his face.

2: INT. SOPRANO HOUSE – KITCHEN – DAY

PAN ACROSS to kitchen floor. Past a crumpled Star Ledger someone has dropped – headline: "2ND FIREBOMBING ALLEGED IN SANITATION DISPUTE – RETALIATION EXPECTED" – to a bedroom slipper – overturned. More floor. To a shard of glass. To –

The soles of two feet, one bare, the other wearing a slipper. Then two legs sprawled. More shattered glass. A terricloth bathrobe belt – a pool of red liquid – bathrobe splayed, boxer shorts, then the undershirt, TONY'S undershirt. Tony's torso. Lying face down. Not moving. Not good.

3: EXT. SOPRANO HOUSE – DRIVEWAY – DAY

Carmela pulls into the garage. The door lowers.

4: INT. SOPRANO HOUSE – KITCHEN – DAY

Carmela enters lugging groceries. Sees her husband.

> **CARMELA**
> Tony! Oh, my God...

Runs and drops to her knees, lifts his head.

> **CARMELA (cont'd)**
> Tony!

TONY'S POV – CARMELA

The image swimming.

> **CARMELA (cont'd)**
> What happened? Tony...?
> *(he mutters)*
> What? I can't understand you?

> **TONY**
> *(mutters)*
> Uncle Ben...

> **CARMELA**
> What? Are you all right?

> **TONY**
> I... brsmn...

5: FREEZE FRAME.

Then starting slowly, everything RUNS IN REVERSE – Carmela backs out the door...Tony miraculously hops up from the floor – the shards of glass coalesce into a drinking tumbler which flies up into his hand – as does the newspaper – he puts cheese and capicolla back in fridge – all in REVERSE – moonwalks backward away from fridge and out of the room – EVERYTHING GOING FASTER NOW – into the entry – Meadow backs into the front door – then a YOUNG MAN – the pair talk with Tony – Meadow moonwalks backwards upstairs leaving Tony and the young man talking – then Meadow returns again – but it's going so fast now it's almost a blur – Tony moonwalks backwards up the stairs and FREEZE. Then –

FORWARD

Normal speed – Tony comes down the stairs. A typical day in the Soprano house, carrying his morning Star-Ledger. He sees –

6: FAMILY ROOM

MEADOW, curled on couch, Skechers off. Pair of Vans beside them. T.V. on – Meadow is rewinding James Cagney in "The Public Enemy". He smooches her.

> **TONY**
> Hey. What are you doing here?

> **MEADOW**
> We had to drive all the way out because some shmuck stole the VCR out of the common room.

> **TONY**
> *(of movie)*
> This is a good one. Been years.

> **MEADOW**
> *(rises; ejects tape)*
> For a class. Just finished. We're outta here.

> **TONY**
> Forty grand a year to watch old movies? Who's we?

> **MEADOW**
> *(slightly tense)*
> A friend from class, okay?

> **NOAH**
> *(entering)*
> Whewf, your mom likes lavender.

NOAH, 20, lanky, light-skinned African American Columbia sophomore – wire glasses, generic T-shirt.

> **MEADOW**
> I'll be ready to bolt in a sec.

A flash of a look passes from Tony to Meadow – a tight displeased smile.

> **NOAH**
> *(to Tony; easy, confident)*
> Mr. Soprano? Hey, I'm Noah Tannenbaum.

> **TONY**
> Hey. How ya doin'?

> **NOAH**
> I'd shake your hand, but –
> *(holds his up)*
> Damp, just washed 'em. Appreciate you letting us screen here. Those Bose direct reflectors make all the difference. You a film buff?

Tony nods. Staring at Noah. He shows the box for "Public Enemy."

> **NOAH (cont'd)**
> People say Hawks invented the genre with "Scarface" but Cagney was modernity. Muni was not. So I give the nod to William Wellman.

> **MEADOW**
> Noah, I'm gonna grab that 'Barenaked Ladies' CD then let's hit the road.

Meadow exits. Tony watches Noah puts his shoes on.

> **NOAH**
> The last year this course is being offered. "Images of Hypercapitalist Self-Advancement in the Era of The Studio System."

7: INT. SOPRANO HOUSE – FRONT DOOR – DAY

They start walking toward the front door. Tony drapes a hand on his shoulder.

> **TONY**
> So you guys, you and Meadow, you're... you know.

> **NOAH**
> *(laughs)*
> Little early to say.

> **TONY**
> What's your background, Noel?

> **NOAH**
> Noah. I'm from Los Angeles. West L.A.

> **TONY**
> No, what I meant was –

> **NOAH**
> My family's in the business.
> *(apologetic)*
> Show business, not <u>the</u> business.

> **TONY**
> Those old Tarzan movies?

> **NOAH**
> *(confused)*
> My dad's an entertainment lawyer.

> **TONY**
> *(smiling)*
> No, no I mean, like we're Italian...?

> **NOAH**
> My dad is Jewish, my mom's family is African-American.

> **TONY**
> *(patient chuckle)*
> 'Tannenbaum', sure. But on your application to Columbia – you didn't check Jewish, did you?

> **NOAH**
> No. They can't ask about religious affiliation.

> **TONY**
> No, right, of course not. What'd you check?

> **NOAH**
> *(shrugs)*
> What'd I check? African-American.

> **TONY**
> Well, sure, you wanted to get in. That's what I meant. See, we <u>do</u> understand each other – you're a ditsoon.

Tony is still smiling. Noah isn't.

> **NOAH**
> Excuse me?

> **TONY**
> A charcoal briquette. A mulignan.
> *(off silence; 'helpfully')*
> A nigger.

Noah jerks his shoulder out from under Tony's hand, turns and faces him.

> **NOAH**
> What's your problem?

> **TONY**
> *(still smiling)*
> You know what my problem is. Your little friend up there, she didn't do you any favors bringing you into this house. I don't know what the fuck she was thinking – we'll get to that later. But anyway, I got business associates who are black but they don't want my son with their daughters and I don't want their sons with mine.

> **NOAH**
> *(flabbergasted)*
> Fuck you.

> **TONY**
> *(smile hardens)*
> See, that's what I'm trying to avoid – that kind of thing. So when my little girl walks down those stairs, you're going to say how nice it was to meet me, go drop her off at school, say goodbye, and then whenever you see her on the campus find a place to hide. Maybe a wood pile.

Now Noah has seen the scary Tony. Meadow comes down.

> **MEADOW**
> Come on if you want to see the Garden State.
> *(busses Tony)*
> We're dropping by Hunter's. I want her to meet Noah, then we'll be back to pick up my laundry.

They move to the front door. Big smile –

> **TONY**
> All right, Noah, keep cracking those books.

Noah's outside already, his face all rage and confusion.

> **MEADOW**
> Later, Dad.

Tony, closes door, walks with growing anger, toward –

8: INT. SOPRANO HOUSE – KITCHEN – DAY

opens the refrigerator, looks in. Breathing angrily. Sees capicolla, cheese. Slams them on counter. His breathing grows labored. He takes a drinking tumbler from a cabinet... opens another cabinet for new jar of mayo – sees box of Uncle Ben's rice – everything starts to get blurry, spin. The mayo jar falls from his hand. The drinking glass falls, shatters. He goes down – we HEAR glass crunch.

CUT TO BLACK:

9: INT. SOPRANO HOUSE – BREAKFAST AREA – DAY

Tony is seated at the table, robe hanging open, head between his knees. He holds a towel to his cut arm. Carmela holds a cold cloth to his forehead.

> **TONY**
> I don't have time for these attacks.

> **CARMELA**
> It's been so good for months. If you didn't instigate things...

> **TONY**
> Bleeding's stopped...
> *(realizes)*
> I instigate?

> **CARMELA**
> He's just a new friend, Tony.

TONY
You didn't see the way they looked at each other.

CARMELA
You listen to me, Tony – and listen carefully because I am very serious. You want her to be with him, just keep it up. Keep playing the race card, you'll drive her right into his arms.

TONY
Not if I cut off those fuckin' arms.

CARMELA
Stop it! You let me deal with this, if anybody's going to deal with it. You make things worse with your bullshit I am going to be really pissed. I mean it. I'm talking about a major problem between you and me.
(looks at cut)
I'm gonna call Cusamano. You might need stitches.

TONY
Some parenting we do. Always fuckin' soft pedaling –

CARMELA
She's got free will.

TONY
When my sisters were young, if either one of them brought home a fuckin' butterhead, I can tell you right now what my old man –

Carmela just leaves the room.

10: OMITTED

11: INT. LIVIA'S HOUSE – DAY

Tony enters. LIVIA sits in a living room chair over the remains of lunch.

TONY
Hey, Ma.

LIVIA (O.S.)
Look who calls.

TONY
Actually, I'm here standing in front of you.

Livia disgustedly waves Kleenex. SVETLANA KIRILENKO comes from the kitchen, clears dishes.

TONY
Hey.
(to Livia)
So how's it going?

LIVIA
What do you care? Out of sight out of mind.

TONY
(empties bag)
I got you some Books On Tape. You say you can't concentrate to read.

LIVIA
I wish the Lord would take me now.

TONY
Yeah, well in the meantime – you got 'The Horse Whisperer', 'Omerta'... And look we gotta talk.

LIVIA
What's wrong? Tell me.

> **TONY**
> *(impatient)*
> We just gotta talk, that's all. You have to freak out because I brought you something nice?
> *(sees writing tablet)*
> What's this?

Livia disgustedly waves the Kleenex.

> **SVETLANA**
> She is going to finish baby journals from long time ago. My suggestion.

Livia sneers. Tony sees a book.

> **TONY**
> I remember these...

He lifts front cover. Little lambs, flowers, and in a pretty font, *"A Grandmother Remembers..."*.

> **TONY (cont'd)**
> The fuck!? Carmela gave you one of these for each of our kids when they were born!
> *(fans blank pages)*
> Look at that. You were supposed to fill these out. Twenty years. Fat fuckin' nothin'.

> **LIVIA**
> Now look here. I don't like that kind of talk. Now just stop it. It upsets me.

> **TONY**
> Carmela's mom, she returned these books to the kids <u>filled</u> with memories. You couldn't write down stuff from your life for your grandchildren?

> **LIVIA**
> *(weepy)*
> That's none of anybody's business.

> **TONY**
> You're so busy feeling sorry for yourself –

> **SVETLANA**
> She will do it. Is good for her, she realize that. Keep her mind active.

> **TONY**
> Yeah, why do anything if there's not something in it for <u>her</u>?

Livia sighs. Svetlana pats Tony's shoulder, trying to broker peace. She goes into the kitchen.

> **TONY**
> *(still annoyed)*
> Awright, listen up – I want you to concentrate. Remember the airline tickets?

> **LIVIA (O.S.)**
> The tickets were stolen.

> **TONY**
> Did <u>you</u> say that? Or the Feds? What'd you tell them when they had you in the lock-up?

> **LIVIA**
> What? Who-me? What, what did I do?

> **TONY**
> 'Cause it's important – they're trying to build a RICO case against me.

Livia looks off.

> **TONY (cont'd)**
> What are you going to say if they put you on a witness stand? They only let you go to get your cooperation.

Livia disgustedly waves the Kleenex.

> **TONY (cont'd)**
> *(annoyed)*
> No don't wave your hanky. What are you gonna say from <u>now on</u>? I never stated to you those tickets were stolen. Capisce?

Livia ignores.

> **TONY (cont'd)**
> Barbara will testify I didn't say it but you have to back her up.

> **LIVIA**
> *(tearful)*
> I suppose I should have kept my mouth shut. Like a mute.

> **TONY**
> *(louder)*
> No matter what kind of deal they try and cut with you. Right?

Livia shrugs. Tony blows up.

> **TONY (cont'd)**
> Fuckin' year I didn't speak to you! I should have kept it that way! Fuck it! Do what you want!

He leaves disgustedly. Livia scowls.

12: EXT. LIVIA'S HOUSE – DAY

Tony heads down the walk. Svetlana opens door.

> **SVETLANA**
> Tony.

He turns. She descends stairs.

> **TONY**
> Don't ask me how, but I think you actually get through that four inches of oak in her fuckin' head.

> **SVETLANA**
> *(shrugs it off)*
> Childhood in Russia, leg amputated at hip – she knows she better not fuck with me.

> **TONY**
> *(laughs)*
> Yeah. Bet she loves your stories.

> **SVETLANA**
> More pain, more better. Listen, if you want me to go to judge and say you didn't tell mamochka tickets was stolen, you just tell me. I say I was here, I back up your sister Barbara.

> **TONY**
> You weren't here.

> **SVETLANA**
> When my elder-care agency fail, you hire me to take care of mama. You let me set up office here. I owe you.

> **TONY**
> Let's hope it don't come to that. But thanks.

SVETLANA
I make her finish book. Don't worry.

Tony turns and goes. Svetlana limps upstairs.

13: CLOSE ON TV SCREEN – 'THE PUBLIC ENEMY'

The movie is just beginning – under stentorian music the weasel studio disclaimer crawl: "PERHAPS THE TOUGHEST OF THE GANGSTER FILMS, 'PUBLIC ENEMY' AND 'LITTLE CAESAR' HAD A GREAT EFFECT ON PUBIC OPINION. THEY BROUGHT HOME VIOLENTLY THE EVILS ASSOCIATED WITH PROHIBITION AND SUGGESTED THE NECESSITY OF A NATION-WIDE HOUSE CLEANING."

TONY

smirking. He's in the family room, kicked back in his lazy boy with a scotch, in the dark.

SCREEN

crawl continues – "TOM POWERS IN 'PUBLIC ENEMY' AND RICO IN 'LITTLE CAESAR' ARE NOT TWO MEN, NOR ARE THEY MERELY CHARACTERS – THEY ARE A PROBLEM THAT SOONER OR LATER WE, THE PUBLIC, MUST SOLVE."

TONY

chuckles, sips. The main titles fade up scored by a martial version of "I'm Forever Blowing Bubbles". Cagney appears in trolleyman's uniform next to 'James Cagney as Tom Powers'. He grins his Cagney grin, punches the air and winks. Tony is in heaven.

ANGLE

to include front door. Meadow enters, heading toward the basement, she realizes Tony is in the family room. She comes over. He doesn't look up.

MEADOW
Did you say something to Noah?

TONY
If you're smart you'll keep going down those stairs.

MEADOW
You <u>did</u>. What did you say? He was all quiet at Hunter's, so she thinks he's a snob. And now he's just sitting out in the car.

TONY
(yells)
You didn't hear me? Maybe if I said it in Swahili.

CARMELA (O.S.)
Meadow? Come up here, please.

MEADOW
What?!

CARMELA (O.S.)
I need your help with this clasp.

Meadow glares at Tony. But folds her tent. Leaves.

SCREEN

Cagney and his sidekick Matt slap a bartender around.

TONY

agitated. Looks at his watch, gets up.

14: EXT. SOPRANO HOUSE – VEGETABLE GARDEN – NIGHT

Back by the pool cabana in a cleared patch of woods. An oscillating sprinkler bathes sweet corn, arugula, tomatoes. Tony, with cigar, enjoys the peace a few seconds, then ducks under the gentle rain to move the sprinkler.

15: INT. SOPRANO HOUSE – FAMILY ROOM – NIGHT

He enters through a rear slider. Turning, he sees Carmela, Meadow, and Anthony Jr. in the family room, looking at him. A beat –

> **TONY**
> What?

The kids glance at Carmela.

> **TONY (cont'd)**
> What?

> **CARMELA**
> *(quietly)*
> Your mother died.

A long strange beat. Then, almost flat –

> **TONY**
> You're kidding.

They stare at him.

> **TONY (cont'd)**
> I mean – Jesus Christ. What happened?! How?

> **CARMELA**
> Svetlana just called, she said after dinner your mother went upstairs to get ready for bed – you know, for TV time – when Svetlana came up, your mother was under the covers, in her nightgown. Svetlana thought she was asleep but...

It goes quiet.

> **TONY**
> Wait. Lemme get this straight. So in the end, after everything, she calmly changes into her nightie, plumps her pillow and just shuffles off to Buffalo?

> **CARMELA**
> *(holds his hand)*
> Svetlana's waiting for us over there.

> **TONY**
> *(sinks into chair)*
> She's dead. My God.

His lips purse. His brain is a blur. Carmela strokes his hair. Tony's eyes meet Meadow's. She's the only one with tears.

> **MEADOW**
> I'm sorry, dad.
> *(beat)*
> That your mom died.

> **ANTHONY JR.**
> Me too.

> **TONY**
> *(emphatic)*
> Hey. She loved you very much.
> *(pointing to AJ)*
> Your grandmother loved both you two. Very much.

> **ANTHONY JR.**
> We know.

Tony shakes his head – shocked disbelieving. Dead.

16: EXT. LIVIA'S HOUSE – NIGHT

Tony and Carmela pull up. Getting out they see the Paramedic wagon back out of the driveway and head – very slowly, no lights or siren – down the street. Some neighbor KIDS and a dog are the only spectators.

17: INT. LIVIA'S HOUSE – NIGHT

Tony and Carmela enter. Svetlana comes out of the kitchen with a cup of tea, sees them.

> **SVETLANA**
> They just remove.

> **CARMELA**
> We saw.

> **SVETLANA**
> She was in no pain, Tony.

> **CARMELA**
> What about the cause of death? Did they say?

> **SVETLANA**
> *(shrugs)*
> Old age. Massive stroke.

> **TONY**
> Yeah.

> **SVETLANA**
> So...
> *(sighs)*
> ...she will not be finishing journal. I break promise to you, Tony. Does not happen often with me – that these old ones get away with something.

> **CARMELA**
> Journal?

> **TONY**
> Nothing.
> *(then)*
> Those 'Granny Remembers' books you gave her when the kids were born. She never touched them.

On Carmela –

18: INT. SOPRANO HOUSE – ANTHONY JR.'S ROOM – NIGHT

Anthony Jr. is hunched over a text book, miserable, twiddling a pencil. "Slipknot" blares from his system. Suddenly, he flings the pencil hard. It leaves a mark. Meadow is passing with laundry bag.

> **MEADOW**
> What's your beef?

> **ANTHONY JR.**
> A-hole Robert Frost! How do I know what this means? Like I even care.

> **MEADOW**
> *(reads; laughs)*
> 'Stopping By Woods on A Snowy Evening'. Oh my God, I am so glad I'm not in high school anymore.

> **ANTHONY JR.**
> You read this?

> **MEADOW**
> Sure.

ANTHONY JR.
Well, what does it <u>mean</u>? I have to turn in a 'close read' by tomorrow.

MEADOW
What does it 'mean'?

ANTHONY JR.
I don't get it. 'The woods are lovely, dark and deep/But I have promises to keep/And miles to go before I sleep.' <u>I</u> want to go to sleep. We got speed trials at practice tomorrow.

MEADOW
Okay, look – where is he?

ANTHONY JR.
The guy?

MEADOW
Yeah.

ANTHONY JR.
He's in the fields or something. He's on his horse.

MEADOW
He's not <u>on</u> the horse. The horse has bells.

ANTHONY JR.
So?

MEADOW
What kind of horse has bells?

ANTHONY JR.
I don't know! Just give me the fucking answer so I can write this!

MEADOW
A horse pulling a sleigh.

ANTHONY JR.
(struggles)
So it's a Thanksgiving poem? Like –
'Over the river and through the woods to grandmother's house we go'?

MEADOW
(contempt)
No, it's not a 'Thanksgiving' poem. Frost isn't Norman Rockwell.
(beat)
He's in a field. What's covering the field?

ANTHONY JR.
(reads)
Snow?

MEADOW
Yeah! And what does snow symbolize?

ANTHONY JR.
Christmas?

MEADOW
Oh, shit. Hello? Cold? Endless white? Endless nothing?

ANTHONY JR.
I don't know!

MEADOW
Death!

ANTHONY JR.
I thought <u>black</u> was death!

> **MEADOW**
> He's not going to stay in the field. He has 'miles to go before he sleeps'.

> **ANTHONY JR.**
> He must be a long way from his house.

> **MEADOW**
> The sleep of death. The Big sleep. He's talking about his own death. Which has yet to come but <u>will</u> come.

Anthony Jr. is creeped out. Looks at poem.

> **ANTHONY JR.**
> Fucked <u>up</u>.

> **MEADOW**
> *(horn blows outside)*
> I gotta go.

> **ANTHONY JR.**
> I thought <u>black</u> was death.

> **MEADOW**
> *(out the door)*
> White too.

And he's alone. Still confused. Starts writing. Hears the FRONT DOOR CLOSE. A CAR DRIVE-OFF. He reads the poem. Hunches over it. But then he HEARS something. Or thinks he does. AGAIN. He gets up. Goes to his doorway.

18A: INT. SOPRANO HOUSE – HALLWAY – NIGHT

He peers into the dark empty hall. Listens. Beat.

> **ANTHONY JR.**
> Grandma?

19: INT. BARBARA'S HOUSE – KITCHEN – NIGHT

20: INTERCUT

with Tony in Livia's kitchen. BARBARA is crying. Tony is sadly philosophical.

> **TONY**
> Yeah. Whaddaya gonna do.

> **BARBARA**
> I'll call Janice.

> **TONY**
> Awright. I'll meet you at Cozzerelli's tomorrow. Noon. I already called them.

> **BARBARA**
> Ma didn't want any kind of service, Tony. No remembrance. At all.

> **TONY**
> Okay, so we'll just pick out a simple... urn or whatever.

> **BARBARA**
> *(crying)*
> See you there.

Tony hangs up. Svetlana enters with Russian vodka and glass. She pours him one. Carmela enters, shot glass in hand. Beat. Svetlana jerks her shot glass.

> **SVETLANA**
> Proshai, Livushka.

Down the hatch, all three.

TONY
Which means.

SVETLANA
Good-bye, little Livia.

21: INT. SOPRANO HOUSE – FAMILY ROOM – NIGHT

SILVIO, PAULIE, CHRISTOPHER, and Anthony Jr. watch pro skateboarding. Anthony Jr. eats a sundae, chortles at the action. When Tony and Carmela enter, Christopher, Paulie, and Silvio stand with long faces.

SILVIO
(embraces Tony)
Ton', I'm sorry. We all know how much you loved her.

TONY
(uneasy)
Thanks.

PAULIE
(hugging)
I can imagine how you feel.

TONY
Yeah, well... whaddaya gonna do?

CHRISTOPHER
(hugs him)
I'm sorry, T.

TONY
(stymied; repeats)
Whaddaya gonna do?

Awkward silence. To fill it...

TONY (cont'd)
At least she didn't suffer.

Awkward silence. Phone RINGS. Tony goes off to get it. KNOCKING at door. TRACK with Carmela as she opens door on her mother and father, MARY and HUGH DeANGELIS. They embrace.

MARY
My God. What next, huh?

HUGH
How's Tony taking it?

TONY (O.S.)
The fuck!? Goddamn fuckin' bitch.

22: INTERCUT – BARBARA/TONY ON PHONE

23: INTERCUT – BARBARA'S DIALOGUE

BARBARA
(sobbing)
She was so awful. What do I tell my kids when their own aunt –

TONY
Take it easy. I'll handle it.

24: EXT. SEATTLE – NIGHT – STOCK

25: INT. JANICE'S APARTMENT – NIGHT

JANICE lays home fried eggs before a pimply 19 year old. They both wear Kenny Rogers' Roasters uniforms.

YOUNG MAN
Then he goes, 'You gotta work Columbus Day weekend.'

JANICE
I'll threaten Warren with an OSHA over that burn you got from the deep fat fryer. I'll write to Kenny Fucking Rogers himself if I have to.
(smooches him)
Eat your eggs, baby.

Phone RINGS.

JANICE (cont'd)
Ace Garage.

TONY (O.S.)
Not coming to your own mother's fuckin' funeral?

JANICE
(calmly)
May I speak?

TONY (O.S.)
You got your sister sobbing!

JANICE
May I speak?

TONY (O.S.)
Go the fuck ahead!

JANICE
(wary glances toward Drew)
You may recall, Anthony, that I have very good and valid reasons not to present myself in the state of New Jersey.

TONY (O.S.)
Aw, Jesus. That case is colder than your tit.

26: INTERCUT – TONY.

TONY (cont'd)
Do you good to show up here at this point. Nothing to hide.

JANICE
(working up tears)
I don't do well at funerals, Tony.

TONY
Who does? You just don't want to get your ass out of whatever chair it's in.

JANICE
Let each grieve in his own manner.

TONY
You don't have manners.

JANICE
I'm going to hang the fuck up, you –

TONY
She didn't want a funeral, Janice. But how 'bout you come sit with your family at this stressful time. I know she mopped the fucking floor with you but she was your mother.

JANICE
You can afford to just hop on a plane. But for ordinary working folks –

TONY

Oh, listen to this. Fucking Woody Guthrie over here. The airlines have special rates for a family death.

JANICE

Half of full-fare coach, which at this late date still comes to one thousand one hundred dollars.

TONY

All researched and everything, huh? All right, Janice, I'll pay it.

JANICE

Can I bring my fiancé?

TONY

What?! Fiancé?! Fuck that. One seat. Coach. And if you don't show, lemme tell you right now, give up any ideas of breezin' in when it's time to carve up the estate. I'll put Mink on it right now, tonight. I'll cut you the fuck out.

JANICE

What are you telling people about that other thing?

TONY

That he vanished into the witness protection program. The truth, right Janice?

JANICE
(likes this)

Ummm.

TONY

Cozzerelli's Mortuary. Noon tomorrow. Does Harpo know his grandmother died? 'Cause him I'll pay for – bring him down from Montreal.

JANICE
(tears)

Hal's on the pavers, Tony. He's a street person.

TONY

Aw, geez... I'm sorry.

JANICE

See, you're not the only one with problems.

TONY

What's this Ace Garage shit?

JANICE

Long story.

TONY

Be there tomorrow.

27: INT. SOPRANO HOUSE – MASTER BEDROOM – NIGHT

Tony sits on bed undressing. Carmela comes out of bathroom. Sees him staring off. Comes, takes his hand.

CARMELA

How you doing?

TONY

I can't get there, Carm. I don't feel anything. When your grandmother died, you were ripped to shreds.

CARMELA

Well... who's to say you're not the lucky one? You want to feel all that pain?

TONY
You're supposed to!

CARMELA
There's no rule book.

TONY
People come up to me, 'I'm sorry, I'm sorry'. I feel like a fraud.

CARMELA
Tony, your mother wanted <u>you</u> dead.

TONY
Those people don't know that. If I don't act sad enough, they look at me like, 'Jesus Christ, what the fuck's with you?'

CARMELA
Oh, please, of course they know. Ninety percent of them. All they had to do was meet her once.

TONY
(lies down)
Maybe that's why I'm so down on Janice. Because who am I to talk?

28: INT. SOPRANO HOUSE – MASTER BEDROOM – NIGHT

Carmela sleeps. Tony can't. Gets up, takes his pillow.

29: INT. SOPRANO HOUSE – FAMILY ROOM – NIGHT

Tony is in the lazy boy watching –

'THE PUBLIC ENEMY'

Brother Mikes's homecoming party. The Powers family celebrates the war-hero brother's return with bootleg beer that gangster brother Tommy (Cagney) brought.

MIKE
Ya murderers. There's not just beer in that keg. There's beer and blood! The blood o' men!!

He hurls the keg. Sweet Ma Powers stops Tommy/Cagney from hitting him.

MA POWERS
Oh, please Tommy, he ain't himself.

TOMMY
Come on, Matt. Let's get outta here before I go screwy too.

MA POWERS
Aw, please, Tommy.

Cagney walks out on his family. Cut to: – Hotel suite. Tommy, in silk pajamas, goes to a breakfast table.

GIRLFRIEND
Gee, Tom, I wish –

TOMMY
(sneers)
There you go with that wishin' stuff again. 'I wish you was a wishin' well' – so I could tie a bucket to ya and sink ya'!

GIRLFRIEND
Maybe you found someone you like better.

Cagney slams her in the puss with the famous grapefruit. Tony smiles with recognition. He's growing sleepy.

30: EXT. SOPRANO HOUSE – NIGHT

The blue glow of the TV goes off. Then the last light.

31: VEGETABLE GARDEN

The forgotten sprinkler continues its soft rain. The ground is a pond.

32: INT. FBI SURVEILLANCE VAN – DAY

The TECH reads a book. A REPLACEMENT TECH enters with coffee. Changing of the guard.

> **TECH**
> His mother died last night.
>
> **OTHER TECH**
> No shit?

Over speakers they hear... WHISTLING.

33: INT. SOPRANO HOUSE – BASEMENT – DAY

Tony is whistling like a lark while taking several large cereal boxes from shelves. He hears VOICES upstairs, catches himself.

34: INT. SOPRANO HOUSE – BREAKFAST AREA – DAY

Tony comes up from the cellar. The house is filling with mourners including the Soprano crew and ALBERT BARESE. GIGI, RALPH CIFARETTO, and VITO SPATAFORE have just entered. The long faces and hugging start.

> **GIGI**
> Ton', I was so sorry to hear.
>
> **TONY**
> Yeah.
> *(beat)*
> Whaddaya gonna do?

A big silence. Ralph has <u>genuine</u> <u>tears</u>.

> **RALPH**
> I know how you feel. We lost Mom last year. You remember.
>
> **TONY**
> Yeah.

Another big silence.

> **VITO**
> At least she didn't suffer.
>
> **TONY**
> Right. Hey.
>
> **PATSY**
> God needed her with <u>Him</u>. And –
>
> **TONY**
> *(wants to change subject)*
> I need to talk to you, Ralphie. You too, Albert. Vito, have a schfuyadell.

35: INT. SOPRANO HOUSE – FRONT DOOR – CONTINUOUS

Anthony Jr. and Carmela arrive at the same time. Carmela opens door, Janice rushes into her arms, sobbing.

> **JANICE**
> Carmela... she's gone...
>
> **TONY**
> *(watching this)*
> Jesus fuckin' Christ.
> *(to Ralph & Albert)*
> C'mon.

36: EXT. SOPRANO HOUSE – POOL – DAY

Tony, Albert, and Ralph walk.

> **TONY**
> *(to Ralph)*
> Who gave the order to torch one of Albert's trucks?

> **ALBERT**
> One of the trucks.

> **TONY**
> Be quiet, Albert.

> **RALPH**
> Talk to <u>him</u>. He lit up two of my dumpsters.

37: INT. FBI SURVEILLANCE VAN – DAY

Nothing coming over the speakers but CLOTHES DRYER NOISE. The Tech is reading a book, working a hand exerciser.

38: EXT. SOPRANO HOUSE – POOL – DAY

> **TONY**
> The fuck's the matter with you? Both of you. We're all over the papers, every fuckin' week with this shit.

Gigi comes, joins them.

> **RALPH**
> My crew's in line for the Raritan Township contract, and this guy over there is whispering to Albert –

> **TONY**
> *(cocks ear)*
> Wait. Your what? What did you say?

> **RALPH**
> Take it easy. You're the boss, you get to put in who you want over the crew. But –

> **TONY**
> You're a captain, Ralphie, when I say you're a captain.

> **RALPH**
> I'll turn up my hearing aid so I don't miss it.

> **TONY**
> Gonna get cute with me now? With my mother lying dead?

> **RALPH**
> Raritan Township – the recycling manager down there, Joe Zachary? He knows who's in line for the contract but he's playing footsie with Albert, the next minute he's threatening to go to the EPA, bust us all –

> **TONY**
> He said <u>that</u>?

Ralph nods. Albert too. Tony mulls this.

> **TONY**
> Fix it.

They nod. He jabs a finger in Ralph's chest.

> **TONY**
> <u>No</u> – <u>more</u> – <u>fires</u>.

ALBERT
(to Ralph)
Fires – none of those.

Tony shoots Albert a look, walks off. On Ralph –

39: INT. FBI SURVEILLANCE VAN – DAY

The Tech hears FEET ON STAIRS. Someone DIALS A CELL PHONE. Tech switches on recorder.

39A: INT. SOPRANO HOUSE – BASEMENT – DAY

Anthony Jr. comes down the last of the stairs dialing a cordless phone. He is in the vicinity of The Lamp. (Perhaps prominent in <u>b.g.</u> of shot.) He speaks low so they can't hear him upstairs.

ANTHONY JR.
Dude, I'm gonna ditch Spanish. I'll meet you by the trophy case...

39B: INT. FBI SURVEILLANCE VAN – DAY

This is all coming out over the speakers.

39C: INT. SOPRANO HOUSE – BASEMENT – DAY

ANTHONY JR.
How could we possibly get busted?
(listens)
Don't worry about it.
(listens)
The boys room behind the stage? They never check in there –

40: INT. COZZERELLI FUNERAL HOME – DAY

Undertaker COZZERELLI waits unctuously as his SON opens front door, admitting Tony, Janice, Barbara.

COZZERELLI
Mr. Soprano, Janice, Barb... please accept my condolences.

ALL
Thank you, etc.

COZZERELLI
(to Tony)
I'll use all my powers. All my skills.

TONY
(begging off)
Don't go crazy. I mean... you know.

COZZERELLI
(quietly)
So then we're not envisioning any visitation hours for Mom.

TONY
See, she didn't want any service of any kind...

JANICE
(crying)
I find that hard to accept.

TONY
Is she still at the hospital morgue?

COZZERELLI
We brought Mom here this morning. She's downstairs.

Screaming silence.

BARBARA
Wait, there's going to be priest or something though, right?

TONY
Well, yeah, a priest I guess but...
(to Cozzerelli)
When would that be?

COZZERELLI
You're not having a funeral mass? And I'm not trying to sell here...

BARBARA
Well, she was Catholic but not religious.

TONY
I figured I'd have some kind of shindig at the house. Y'know – after. So the grandchildren get to... I dunno.

This makes Janice weep harder. Barbara comforts.

BARBARA
Harpo.

JANICE
Shindig after what? I know what Ma's wishes were but not to have a wake and a funeral. It seems...

BARBARA
Cold.

JANICE
It looks like we're unloving children. Not to mention cheapskates.

TONY
Who gives a shit how it <u>looks</u>? The woman expressed her wishes.

JANICE
(cries)
I wish to honor my mother.

TONY
There's a lot I could say right now that I'm not going to say.
(to troubled Barb)
What – <u>you</u> think we should do something now?

BARBARA
(conflicted)
Ma said all kinds of things – so much of it was for effect.

JANICE
When she was younger she used to picture her funeral.

TONY
(quickly)
Awright, fine – let's do it, let's stop talking about it. Cozzerelli, you arrange it, wake, funeral, send me the bill.

COZZERELLI
We can discuss the payment schedule another time.

JANICE
(sniffling)
We're doing the right thing here.

COZZERELLI
(quietly)
Did you wish to pick out a casket?

41: EXT. COZZERELLI FUNERAL HOME – DAY

Tony, Janice and Barbara come out.

> **JANICE**
> I want you to know, Tony, that it all won't fall on you. I'll do a painting for the overleaf of the program at the service. Motifs from the Mexican Day of the Dead.

> **TONY**
> She was in the country legally, Janice.

> **JANICE**
> Thank God we still have our humor, huh?

He's not laughing.

> **JANICE**
> One thing I'd like to suggest very strongly. At the house, we create an interval where everybody gathers and each one can voice a remembrance or feeling about Mom.

> **TONY**
> No. I don't want any of that California bullshit. People can drink, eat some Gorgonzola. If they want to yak about Ma with each other, that's their business.

42: INT. MELFI'S OFFICE – WAITING ROOM – DAY

Tony waits. MELFI opens her door.

> **MELFI**
> Anthony?

He gets up.

43: INT. MELFI'S OFFICE – DAY

Before she can take her seat, before he is fully seated –

> **TONY**
> Well – my mother died.

She sits. Just looks at him, giving him clean slate. He has an odd smirk. After long silence –

> **TONY (cont'd)**
> No, 'I'm sorry', 'my condolences', nothing?

She nods once in acknowledgement. Beyond that, nothing. Silence. He crosses his legs. Uncrosses them.

> **TONY (cont'd)**
> No, actually it's good. Everybody else, all bullshit. By fuckin' rote. Good for you. It's a relief you not saying nothing, you want to know the truth.

She nods. He nods. Then laughs. Shrugs. Shakes his head. Crosses his legs.

> **TONY (cont'd)**
> All right, here's the thing. I'm glad she's dead. No, not just glad... I wished she'd die. Wished. I had this court case coming up. She might have testified against me. When they told me she was dead fuckin' relief flooded my veins.

Silence. Nothing. He fidgets.

> **MELFI**
> How do you feel about the fact that your own mother would have testified against you?

                     TONY
                     (taken by surprise)
Oh, you're good.

                     MELFI
You sound angry at me.

                     TONY
Well, is that right? Being glad she's dead? Is that a good son?

                     MELFI
                     (amazed)
A 'good son'.

                     TONY
Yeah, a good son. Bad sons...

Trails off.

                     MELFI
Bad sons what?

                     TONY
They should fuckin' die. That's a miserab' disgusting thing to be, a bad son. Be anything, be a fuckin' scumbag hits women on the head with bricks, but a bad son...
                     (beat)
That son of yours. Up at Bard. He better be a good son, right?

She nods conditionally, not really answering.

                     TONY (cont'd)
No, you know what? You're right. Why the fuck should I have been a good son? To that demented old bat? That fuckin' selfish cunt.
                     (beat)
She ruined my father's life, y'know? Oh, yeah. Wouldn't let him move to Reno where he had a wonderful opportunity waiting for him.

                     MELFI
I remember. But he wasn't her son. What did she do to <u>you</u>?

                     TONY
That's a matter of public record in here. We both know.

                     MELFI
You don't like to say it, do you?

                     TONY
Who even knows if she really knew what she was doing.

                     MELFI
You're letting her off.

                     TONY
My uncle denies it, y'know. That she took part.

                     MELFI
Your uncle loves you.

                     TONY
                     (yells)
I never said he didn't.

It's pretty confusing for Melfi. But she presses on.

                     MELFI
Grown children often secretly wish for an aged parent to die. And it's not necessary for the parent to be a 'witness for the prosecution'. It's a

taboo thought, but common. Particularly if the parent has lost all capacity for joy at being alive.

> TONY
> That's her, all right. I think that happened at her sweet sixteen.

> MELFI
> I just want to make sure you know that.

> TONY
> Anyway, the wake's at Cozzerelli's. The hours are two to five and seven to nine.
> *(beat)*
> You can use the name Lento. Distant cousins.

> MELFI
> I wouldn't be going.

> TONY
> *(amazed and angry)*
> You don't even pay your respects? I'm in here fuckin' twice a week.

> MELFI
> It's not appropriate.

> TONY
> Right. You're a friend for hire.

It affected her but she maintains poker face. More silence.

> TONY (cont'd)
> Awright, so I'm probably done here, right? She's dead.

But Melfi doesn't answer him. On Tony –

44: INT. LIVIA'S HOUSE – CELLAR – DAY

Janice is tapping on the wall with a knife handle, listening through a drinking glass for hollow spaces in the wall. She hears FRONT DOOR and FOOTSTEPS. Ditches the gear and sits on a folding chair, sorting through keepsakes. Tony comes down the stairs.

> TONY
> Hey.

> JANICE
> Ma would want a closed casket, don't you agree?

> TONY
> Definitely.

> JANICE
> They usually put a picture on the casket. What do you think?

An 8x10 of Livia in her bridal headpiece.

> TONY
> Hunh. Look at that.

> JANICE
> She's smiling.

> TONY
> She looks normal.

> JANICE
> Maybe it was us kids that turned her into a friggin' sourpuss.

> TONY
> *(grabs her in headlock)*
> Maybe it was one of us.

> **JANICE**
> *(laughing)*
> Let go you fuckin' asshole.

He does. She sucker punches him in the stomach.

> **TONY**
> Get the –
> *(serious)*
> You could be right. My shrink told me not all women are cut out to be mothers.

> **JANICE**
> Is that a slam at me?

> **TONY**
> <u>No</u>. Look, if my father was in friggin' Cirque du Soleil, maybe I'da turned out like Har – Hal.

> **JANICE**
> *(sorting through stuff)*
> Y'know this is fuckin' weird...

> **TONY**
> What?

> **JANICE**
> None of my kid artwork or schoolwork or anything is here anymore. Barb's either.
> *(produces old report cards)*
> Just yours.

> **TONY**
> Get the fuck outta here.

> **JANICE**
> *(reads old term paper)*
> 'Anthony Soprano. 7th Grade. Mr. Martino.' Hey, I had him. "Why 'Fear Strikes Out' by Jim Piersall Is a Good Book."

He starts to go through the boxes.

> **JANICE**
> Take a look. She only saved yours.

> **TONY**
> No, look – here's Barb's communion certificate. Her baby shoe.

> **JANICE**
> Yeah. That's <u>it</u>. Nothing here of mine. When everybody agreed I had extraordinary visualization skills. Those pencil drawings I made of Grandpa...

Tony is silent. He even touches Janice gently on the shoulder. He is staring at a varsity letter "W/O" with stitched football. He can't take his eyes off it.

45: EXT. OFFICE DEPOT – DAY

Huge highway store. RAYMOND CURTO waits behind the wheel of his Cadillac. A MAN gets in.

> **MAN**
> How you doin'? What's happening?

> **RAYMOND**
> Tony Soprano's mother's wake is tonight.

> **MAN**
> Oh, yeah?

> **RAYMOND**
> Want me to wear a wire?

> **MAN**
> Why not. Got a few minutes? I brought some new batteries for you.

Raymond nods. They get out and walk to the man's car.

46: INT. DANTE HOUSE – BEDROOM – NIGHT

A furious Silvio flings a troublesome cufflink against the mirror.

> **SILVIO**
> Fuckin' motherfuckin' pain in the fuckin' ass!

> **GABRIELLA**
> *(getting dolled up)*
> Could we not? Huh? With the tantrums?

> **SILVIO**
> For this shit I miss the Jet's first home game?!

47: INT. COZZERELLI FUNERAL HOME – NIGHT

Silvio walks right up to Tony, hugs him, big long puss.

> **SILVIO**
> Ton'. The sadness accrues.

> **TONY**
> At least she didn't suffer.

> **SILVIO**
> Very important. Crucial.

Carmela and Gabriella hug.

48: INT. CHRISTOPHER'S APT. – NIGHT

Christopher takes a hit from a large bong, passes off to Furio who hits.

> **ADRIANA (O.S.)**
> Are they saying when your making ceremony might happen now with this delay?

> **CHRISTOPHER**
> *(does some coke)*
> Stop asking fucking questions. Even if I knew I couldn't tell you.

> **ADRIANA**
> *(comes out; in black)*
> Hit me, hit me...

Furio is now snorting the coke. Christopher hands Adriana the bong. She sucks it dry. Furio snargles up the cocaine.

> **ADRIANA (cont'd)**
> *(breath held)*
> Every little bit helps. Anything. To get through these events.

49: INT. COZZERELLI FUNERAL HOME – VIEWING ROOM – NIGHT

Livia's casket is quite regally surrounded with flowers. Her picture graces the polished mahogany top. The room is very hushed. People sit silently. Meadow and Anthony Jr. Barbara's kids. Janice tidies. Tony looks at –

FLORAL DISPLAY ENCLOSURE CARD

"Our deepest sympathies. Federal Bureau of Investigation, Organized Crime Division. Newark Field Office."

TONY

smirks. Reads another.

CARD

"Sweets for the sweet. Lest we never forget". Signed "Yogi".

TONY

puzzled. Turns to show Carmela but she is laughing softly with Ralph Cifaretto. Something about this sits wrong. JACKIE APRILE, JR. comes up.

          JACKIE JR.
          (terse)
     Ton'. Sorry.

He only shakes hands, cold. Leaves abruptly. ROSALIE hugs Tony. She's <u>partly</u> apologizing for her son.

          ROSALIE
     Tony. I'm sorry.

          TONY
     Thanks for coming.

Tony notices many have turned toward the entrance. JUNIOR is arriving with BACALA. Surprised, Tony crosses. Junior seems shaken, pale.

          JUNIOR
          (embraces Tony)
     What a fuckin' blow.

          TONY
          (sotto)
     Put away the frosting gun, okay? Not you too.

          JUNIOR
          (shaken)
     I'm serious. What you don't know could fill a fuckin' book.

          TONY
     You breaking the terms of your house arrest?

          JUNIOR
     Got a dispensation from the Marshals. She's my sister-in-law for Chrissake.

Junior is drawn to the casket. Tony and Bacala do the hugging thing. By way of consolation –

          BACALA
     My dad's very ill too.

          TONY
          (autopilot)
     Thank you. Thanks for coming.

Tony goes onto the next mourner, STATE ASSEMBLYMAN ZELLMAN.

          ZELLMAN
     Mr. Soprano, allow me to express my condolences and those of the 13th ward.

          TONY
     Thank you, Assemblyman.

          ZELLMAN
     I met your mom once or twice. That was a proud Newarker.

> ### REV. JAMES JR.
> *(shaking hands)*
> Tony, my sympathies. We talked about this day, did we not.

MEADOW

watching Tony warmly shaking a black man's hand with both of his own.

> ### TONY
> Yep. We did. You know State Assemblyman Zellman from the 13th ward?

> ### ZELLMAN
> Do I know this guy? Ha, ha. You bet!

> ### REV. JAMES JR.
> Yes, we go way back. How are you, Assemblyman?

WITH JUNIOR AT THE CASKET

He stares at Livia's picture, speaks sotto voce.

> ### JUNIOR
> Ma che cosa?

Livia seems to look back at him. Tony comes up.

> ### TONY
> Uncle Jun', you all right?

> ### JUNIOR
> They're dropping like fuckin' flies.

> ### TONY
> All that charcoal-broiled meat you people ate.

> ### JUNIOR
> *(heartsick)*
> Nobody told us till the '80s.

> ### TONY
> I'm kidding, ya old fuck. S'matter with you?
> *(beat)*
> Bacala says you want to see me?

> ### JUNIOR
> I gotta talk to that wife of yours first.

> ### TONY
> Uncle Jun' –

> ### JUNIOR
> I don't give a fuck. This is a funeral. Enough of her *soigne** attitude –

* *pr. – swanyea*

> ### JOHNNY SACK
> Tony...

> ### TONY
> Hey, John...

> ### JOHNNY SACK
> *(they hug, kiss)*
> I'm so sorry.

> ### TONY
> You didn't have to fight that tunnel.

> ### JOHNNY SACK
> I wanted to. By all reports, she was one great lady.

Junior has moved to Carmela who is whispering with Rosalie and her parents. She feels Junior's presence.

> **CARMELA**
> What do you want?

> **JUNIOR**
> *(not so feisty)*
> I'm hoping that we can use this sad occasion to put bitterness and sore-headed feelings aside.

> **CARMELA**
> *(terse)*
> I'll behave how Tony wants. I don't want to add to his stress.

> **JUNIOR**
> *(to Hugh)*
> Hugo, this is some girl you got here.

> **JUNIOR (cont'd)**
> *(to Meadow and AJ)*
> There they are.

> **KIDS**
> Hey, Uncle Jun'...

> **JUNIOR**
> How's that surfboard I gave you?

> **ANTHONY JR.**
> *(Junior pinches his cheek past point of pain)*
> Oww!

> **JUNIOR**
> You two miss your uncle?

> **BACALA**
> *(comes up)*
> Junior, Tony's waitin'.

50: INT. COZZERELLI FUNERAL HOME – LOBBY – NIGHT

Junior comes out. Tony is smoking a cigar, idly going through the "la posta" envelopes.

> **JUNIOR**
> Ralphie Cifaretto got word to me.

> **TONY**
> Yeah, so?

They move into a side room.

> **JUNIOR**
> Yeah, <u>so</u> – he's lookin' for a bump. Kid's been a top fuckin' earner since that rat bastard went in the program. You can't deny it. Ralphie's whipped Richie's crew into shape over there.

> **TONY**
> And three months ago, by you, that 'rat bastard' was the second fuckin' coming. Why do you do this to me?

> **JUNIOR**
> Because I am the boss of this family. You forget.

> **TONY**
> I forget fuckin' nothing. Don't make me say things we'll both regret.

> **JUNIOR**
> Go ahead. I'm fuckin' fed up.

> **TONY**
> I'm on the street. That's the arrangement. Clip your coupons, be a happy man.

> **JUNIOR**
> Things are good, I'll give you that. But this economy's so robust, you get credit for shit you had nothing to do with. Fuckin' chinks and housewives are betting football.

> **TONY**
> You better be finished.

Junior says nothing else. Tony turns on his heel, walks back toward the viewing room. We see Raymond Curto expressing his condolences to Barbara.

51: INT. SOPRANO HOUSE – FAMILY ROOM – NIGHT

Tony, wake tie loosened, watches "Public Enemy". On screen, GALE (Jean Harlow) holds Tommy/Cagney to her.

> **GALE**
> Oh, Tom the men I know – and I've known... lots of them – oh, they're so polished, so sweet. Most women like that type I guess. They're afraid of the other kind. I suppose I was too. But you – you're different – you don't give, you take. Oh, Tommy, I could love ya to death!

They kiss. Tony sails pleasantly. He's back in another time. Film continues; his head drops in sleep – jerking him awake. He shuts off the set, yawns. Goes upstairs.

52: EXT. CEMETERY – DAY

Quite a turnout for Livia's funeral.

> **FATHER FELIX**
> ...The Lord bless her and keep her, the Lord make his face to shine upon her and be gracious to her, the Lord lift up his countenance upon her and give her peace. Amen.

Sign of the cross. Crowd stirs to life. Tony stands staring at the casket as it lowers. Carmela pats his shoulder. Tony notices Meadow staring at the casket. Their eyes meet. He takes a step toward her but Meadow coldly walks off.

> **TONY**
> Did you talk to her?

> **CARMELA**
> She's sure you said something to him but he won't discuss it, he clams up.

Small smile. It's how Tony wanted it to go. He notices –

> **TONY**
> Look at this. Fuckin' Jackie Onassis.

Janice has gone dramatic, rooted center stage at the lowering casket, her hand touching the cold metal, bidding it a silent farewell.

> **PAULIE**
> *(comes up)*
> T. Beautiful send off.

> **TONY**
> *(spots Junior)*
> Uncle Jun...

A line is moving slowly, throwing dirt on the casket but Junior is headed out. Junior stops. Bad mood, impatient to leave.

BEYOND THE FENCE

FBI agents taking pictures.

GRAVESITE

> **TONY**
> Did my mother ever meet Yogi Berra or something or know him...?

> **JUNIOR**
> Meet?
> *(trying to place, recalls)*
> She dated the Yog.

> **TONY**
> My mother...?

> **JUNIOR**
> Frankly, it was between Yogi and your dad for a little while. It was a brief whirlwind thing. And your dad –
> *(chuckles)*
> – Berra never knew it, but he came this close to getting acid thrown in his face.

> **TONY**
> Janice, you hearing this?

Janice, talking with Svetlana, waves Tony off. He corrals Barbara.

> **TONY**
> Come here. Tell her.

> **JUNIOR**
> What's the big deal? At one time your mother considered marrying Yogi Berra. I know he proposed anyway. She was a huge Yankee fan. For awhile. And then... she turned on it like she did with things.

> **TONY**
> *(yells)*
> AJ. Your grandma was engaged to Yogi Berra!

> **ANTHONY JR.**
> Who's that?

> **JUNIOR**
> *(annoyed)*
> I didn't say engaged. But she was an attractive woman, your mother.
> *(to Barb)*
> Looked like you, but more Juno-esque.

He goes.

JANICE AND SVETLANA

after Janice tosses dirt into grave.

> **JANICE**
> I want to thank you for all you did for her.

> **SVETLANA**
> She was much work. Interesting. But in end, she defeated me.

> **JANICE**
> Anyway, we won't be needing your services anymore obviously and I'll be moving into the house. So if you could get your things out of there by the weekend, I think that'd be good.

> **SVETLANA**
> I only stay there during week. When my fiancé has his children with him. Tony says I can continue situation till me and Bill find house.

> **JANICE**
> But... see Tony should have consulted me. I'm going to be living at 55 Benedek. While we deal with the estate.

> **SVETLANA**
> Mm.

> **JANICE**
> Speaking of which. My mom had this – kind of extensive record collection. Caruso, Robert Merrill, shitload of Broadway shows. Old '78's. Some of them were in mint condition. You know where they are? They used to be stacked over by the Grundig.

> **SVETLANA**
> She give to me, those records.

> **JANICE**
> What?

> **SVETLANA**
> She know I like American show tune so she give to me. I didn't ask. But you know how she was, she insist I take.

> **JANICE**
> *(tightass smile)*
> But those are my mother's records and I feel very close to them –
> *(lying)*
> Many of them were gifts from me to her.

> **SVETLANA**
> I don't want to make trouble. But Miss Janice, I feel I have to respect her wishes.

> **JANICE**
> Oh, come on. This is just about you bogarting all those discs for your ass. They're worth a fortune to the right collector.

> **SVETLANA**
> *(stiffens)*
> I will not answer such here.

> **JANICE**
> *(tight smile)*
> I want that entire discography back in the house by this weekend.

She walks off.

53: INT. HOSPITAL ROOM – DAY – EXISTING FOOTAGE

> **LIVIA**
> How's your mother? You call her every day.

> **ARTIE**
> Well... Mom, passed away.

> **LIVIA**
> *(tsks)*
> Really? When?

> **ARTIE**
> Oh, it's about six months now.

> **LIVIA**
> Well, you give her my regards. Is she still on that crazy diet?

> **ARTIE**
> I brought you something. From my restaurant.

He extends the plate. Livia looks at the pasta, suddenly tears up.

> **ARTIE**
> Mrs. S, what's the matter?

She shakes her head, waving the Kleenex, crying.

> **LIVIA**
> It's just that... after what my son did, how can I look you in the face?

> **ARTIE**
> *(laughs)*
> Tony? What'd he do now?

> **LIVIA**
> You don't blame him for setting the fire? Well... you're a bigger man than some. I guess we should be grateful no one was incinerated to death.

54: ARTIE – PRESENT DAY

staring into space in the Soprano kitchen. Vesuvio waiters bring food up from the garage. Artie wears an apron over shirt, tie, slacks. CHARMAINE(in a dress) works with the waiters.

> **CHARMAINE**
> What are you doing, Artie? People are starting to arrive.

Artie snaps out of the memory, starts to work.

55: INT. SOPRANO HOUSE – LIVING ROOM – DAY

A subdued non-party, the house crowded. Tony, with Carmela, watches Meadow do the sad-smile thing, pressing the flesh like Hillary Clinton.

> **2TO5/7TO9**
> I'm so sorry about your grandma.

> **MEADOW**
> *(plastic smile)*
> At least she didn't suffer.
> *(turns to another)*
> Ohhh, Louise. Hi. Thank you for coming.

> **TONY**
> Look at her. She's already become a fuckin' robot like the rest of us.
> *(beat)*
> All her innocence is gone.

POV – ANTHONY JR.

Next to Meadow. Bored, picking his nose.

> **CARMELA**
> There's always something in life to balance everything out.

Meadow's eye happens to catch Tony's. They look at each other then she turns away coldly. Tony feels it.

> **CARMELA (cont'd)**
> Who's that Meadow was talking to? She was at the wake both nights.

> **PAULIE**
> *(looks over)*
> That's 2to5/7to9.

> **TONY**
> The fuck you talking about?

> **PAULIE**
> Mickey Massucco's wife. He's doing twenty in Lewisburg so she goes to every fuckin' wake. Rain, sleet, snow. They call her 2to5/7to9.

POV

the woman is stuffing her face on Vesuvio delicacies.

CARMELA, TONY, PAULIE

get a laugh.

56: INT. SOPRANO HOUSE – HALLWAY – CONTINUOUS

Hesh, Vito, Gigi, Silvio, Christopher, Ralphie, Patsy.

> **HESH**
> (sotto)
> Reminds me. Jewish guy's funeral in the synagogue. Comes to the part in the service where the rabbi is supposed to extol the good points of the deceased. Rabbi says, 'Alas, I did not know this man. I'm new here. You all knew him. Why don't you say something good about him'. Dead silence. Goes on for one whole minute, two minutes. Silence! Finally, out of the silence, there's this voice from the back, 'His brother was worse.'

Uproarious laughter. Tony passes and they throttle their laughter, look at him with long pitying faces. They stand silently, 'mourning', even after he's gone.

57: INT. SOPRANO HOUSE – FAMILY ROOM – NIGHT

Some people including Rosalie, 2to5/7to9, are chatting, laughing. Anthony Jr. and Meadow pass; the women stifle.

58: EXT. SOPRANO HOUSE – NIGHT

Some people are leaving, respects paid.

59: INT. SOPRANO HOUSE – NIGHT

Things are picking up in gaity and energy, as always happens at these affairs.

CARMELA

really putting away the drinks. LILLIANA passes by.

TONY

knocking back the scotch, chuckling with Paulie and Furio.

> **FURIO**
> This "Survivor" show. Somebody should finda the winner, stick a pistol in the face and say 'You not gonna survive this unless you give me 25 percent of that fuckin' million dollars.'

> **PAULIE**
> That's not bad. We could find out where they live.

> **FURIO**
> (points imaginary gun)
> See how good you survive this, you pezzo di merda.

Under the above, Tony opens an armoire for a special grappa and in the mirror on the inside of the door, WE SEE, as it swings by, for a flash, PUSSY reflected. Just standing there. Only a flash. Tony has not seen it. Only US. When Tony closes the door again, there is no Pussy in the mirror. When he turns to the guys to pour, there is no Pussy. But a heavy thought passes over him, before he resumes laughing.

A FORK on GLASS is heard. TINK, TINK.

> **JANICE (O.S.)**
> Everybody? Could I have your attention?

She's in the entrance to the living room.

> **JANICE (cont'd)**
> At this time we'd like to ask you all to gather in the great room – bring

247

your drinks, bring each other – and form a circle, sit anywhere, floor, whatever, get comfortable – so we can be together and each of us share a remembrance or a feeling about the woman who has brought us all here today.

> **TONY**
> *(furious, sotto)*
> Goddammit –

> **JANICE**
> Everyone? Please? Paulie Gualtieri, join us please?

Murmuring. People shuffle. Tony goes up to Janice.

> **TONY**
> *(sotto)*
> What the fuck did I say?

> **JANICE**
> *(dewey-eyed)*
> If you rather, I'll invite everybody back to her place.

> **TONY**
> This is not a good idea, Janice.

> **CARMELA**
> *(comes up)*
> Janice, what are you doing?

> **JANICE**
> *(to the condemned entering living room)*
> That's right! Very good! We can take a break from eating for five minutes, it won't kill us.

FROM UPPER BALCONY

The living room fills.

60: INT. SOPRANO HOUSE – LIVING ROOM – NIGHT

People file in. 'If I Loved You' ('Carousel') is playing. Janice has CD in hand. Tony remains in the entry, watching, in shadow. When the room settles:

> **JANICE**
> Most of you will remember this was her favorite song. I thought maybe it'd help get us rolling.

Livia's bridal picture is atop the CD player. Janice waits for volunteers. There are none. Finally –

> **JANICE (cont'd)**
> Herman? Rabkin? You two went back. Almost to the pyramids.

All heads swing to Hesh. He is <u>fucked</u>.

> **HESH**
> I… guess what struck me most was… she never minced words.
> *(silence demands more)*
> Between brain and mouth, there was no interlocutor.

Some people nod. Silence. Silence. Janice scans.

> **JANICE**
> Anthony Jr.?

> **ANTHONY JR.**
> *(freaked; near tears)*
> I don't know what to say!

JANICE
Come on, your –

CARMELA
Lay off him, Janice. Move on.

Janice scans. Silence. Silence. Finally –

FANNY (O.S.)
She was my best friend.

Everybody turns. It's the woman Livia ran over. She's in a wheelchair.

FANNY (cont'd)
If anybody died or was in the hospital, I could be sure I'd get a call from Lee letting me know.
(flat)
After my accident I didn't see her as much.

JANICE
(after silence)
Thank you, Fanny.

More silence. Carmela knocks back a shot.

JANICE (cont'd)
Okay... what's good for the goose. Most of you probably remember that I have an extraordinary visual sense. When I was a child my mother didn't let me rest on those laurels. She didn't flatter me.
(fighting crying)
She knew that wildflowers blossom best among rocks, with little water. She was tough. But she was right. She's the reason I make videos today.

Silence. Some coughs.

JANICE (cont'd)
Tony? Maybe you'd like to tell them how Ma saved your childhood schoolwork and varsity letters and none of mine or Barbara's?

Hearing this for the first time, Barbara is crushed. Carmela sucks air over the fiery whiskey on her tongue.

TONY
You just did. Wrap it up, Janice.

Janice extends her hand for more speakers. Nothing. Christopher and Adriana are on a couch. Ripped. Pinned, red eyes. They crane around. Then –

CHRISTOPHER
(suddenly)
They say there's no two people on earth exactly the same. No two faces. No two sets of fingerprints. But do they know that <u>for sure</u>? 'Cause they would have to get everybody together in one huge space and check it out and obviously that's not possible. Even with computers. Not only that, they'd have to get all the people who were <u>ever</u> alive, not just the ones now. So they got <u>no</u> proof. <u>Nothin'</u>.
(beat)
Mrs. Soprano may have passed. But who's to say there isn't another Mrs. Soprano just like her – or <u>will</u> be? Maybe not with the same fears and paranoia but the same. What I'm saying is...
(finds it)
...death be not proud.

ADRIANA
Tell it.

Silence. Janice dabs her eyes.

> **JANICE**
> Thank you, Chris.

Tony leaves in disgust.

61: EXT. SOPRANO HOUSE – POOL – NIGHT

Tony stands at pool's edge, hands in pockets. Rear door opens. Artie comes out, dragging trash can toward the side of the house. Sees Tony.

> **TONY**
> *(calls)*
> Hey.

> **ARTIE**
> *(calls out)*
> Well, Ton' – she's dead.

> **TONY**
> What?

Artie comes across the patio. Brings his nose inches from Tony's face. He's been boozing.

> **ARTIE**
> And I guess our little secret dies with her.

Tony goes to say something. But doesn't. He and Artie just stare into each other's eyes, Artie weaving slightly. Then he goes off. Kicks the trash can over. Crap, garbage, grease go all over the patio.

> **TONY**
> Pick that up!

> **ARTIE**
> What am I doing out here when they're telling stories of her? I got a beaut!

He goes back into the house. Tony hurries after –

> **TONY**
> Artie!

62: INT. SOPRANO HOUSE – LIVING ROOM – NIGHT

Everyone still trapped. Finally –

> **2TO5/7TO9**
> I hear she didn't suffer. For that we can be grateful.

> **JANICE**
> Thank you.

The fucking silence again. Charmaine, seated across the room, sees Artie. Artie is about to break the silence when –

> **CARMELA**
> This is such a crock of shit.

All eyes turn to her.

> **CARMELA (cont'd)**
> We're all a bunch of friggin' phonies.

> **MARY**
> Carmela!

> **CARMELA**
> I'm sitting here thinking I should protect my children from the truth about their grandmother on the one hand. And on the other saying to myself, what kind of example am I setting – evading and smiling and

passing out cheese puffs over a woman we all know was terribly dysfunctional.

Tony has arrived. He is glaring at Janice.

CARMELA
Who spread no cheer around. At all. Who's main function in life was to reject and to undermine.

MARY
Carmela, be quiet –

CARMELA
(thunders)
This is <u>my</u> house.

MARY
I'll leave if –

HUGH (O.S.)
Let her talk, Goddammit.

All turn. He's up out of his chair.

MARY
Sit down, Hugh!

HUGH
I'll speak if I want to, goddammit. Who are you, the minister of propaganda?
(trembling with rage)
We suffered for years under the yoke of that woman. Years! She estranged us from our own daughter, ruined how many goddamn Christmases I don't even want to begin to count –

JANICE
All right, Hu –

HUGH
Naaah, don't hand me that. Bullshit! You wanted it, you got it.

TOM
(quietly)
Hear, hear.

CARMELA
(to Janice)
Look at the effect. This is what I'm talking about. From beyond the grave even.
(beat)
I'm gonna catalogue her faults? Who's got the energy for that? At this late date? I should have – somebody should have – done that a long time ago, once and for all, while she was here.
(beat)
The point is this is a woman who didn't want a funeral. You all – her children – you ignored her wishes.

Her eyes meet Tony's.

CARMELA (cont'd)
Only after she's dead, by the way.
(disgusted; to all)
Everybody walking around all day with these long funeral faces. And then laughing in the bathroom. What a parade.
(glances at Meadow and AJ)
And listen, it's not, who was a villain, who was a witch –

> *(to all)*
> – she <u>didn't</u> <u>want</u> <u>a</u> <u>funeral</u>. She didn't want a remembrance of any kind.
> What does that tell you?
> *(beat)*
> She didn't think anybody would come.

Total silence. No coughing, no fidgeting.

CARMELA (cont'd)
> How sad is that?
> *(beat)*
> She wouldn't write down her memories for her grandchildren because
> she figured, somewhere inside, nobody loved her enough to read them.
> *(beat)*
> She <u>knew</u> there was a problem. Who knows why she was like she was.
> *(beat)*
> If anybody needs to rest <u>in</u> <u>peace</u> it's that woman.

Nobody knows where to look. Tony has his eyes on Carmela. She looks right back at him. Silence in the room.

ARTIE
> There's... desserts in the dining room if anybody wants some.

CHARMAINE
> Yes. Um... all of them from Vesuvio. Our new pastry chef, Bobby Vasquez.

63: EXT. SUBURBAN HOME – NIGHT

A city vehicle pulls into the driveway. On its door the 'City of Raritan Township, Department of Recycling' seal. A MAN gets out, steps toward the path to his home. A battered florist's van pulls to a stop.

EUGENE
> Joe Zachary?

The Man turns. Ralph Cifaretto, still in his wake shirt and tie, is behind the wheel. EUGENE PONTECORVO rides passenger and BOBBY ZANONE is stuffed in the middle. Zachary has a bad feeling.

ZACHARY
> Yeah...?

Eugene gets out – Zachary breaks for the house – Eugene and Bobby chase him with bats. It's a BLUR. Eugene and Bobby deliver a vicious rapid-fire beating with bats and feet. Ralph watches.

EUGENE
> Where you gonna steer that fuckin' contract? Heh? Heh? Where you
> gonna steer that fuckin' contract?!

64: TV SCREEN

Cagney/Tommy in the pouring rain. He leers. It's unnerving, old fashioned as it is. Gun in each hand, he walks into the Burns gang's hide-out. SHOOTING and SCREAMING erupt.

TONY

watching. The rest of the house is dark and silent.

MOVIE

The shooting stops. Some dying screams. Tommy comes out, blood coming from his mouth. Amazing BACKWARD TRACKING shot through rain. He sinks to his knees.

TOMMY
> I ain't so tough.

He pitches face-forward into the gutter.

TONY

staring into his glass, jiggling the cubes in his scotch.

                    MA POWERS (O.S.)
          Tommy...? Mike's here.

                    TOMMY (O.S.)
                    (feeble)
          Hi, Mike. I been wantin' to see ya. There's something I been wantin' to
          say to you – I'm sorry.

MOVIE

                    MIKE
          Sorry for what?

*Tommy is in a hospital bed, close to death. His head and body are wrapped in
immaculate white bandages.*

                    TOMMY
          You know, just... sorry.

                    MA POWERS
          Oh. Both my boys are gonna be friends again!

                    TOMMY
          Ma... you must... like Mike a lot better than me.

A two-shot. Ma takes Tommy's hand, her eyes filled with tears.

                    MA POWERS
          No, no, Tommy boy. You're my baby.

TONY

Haunted. His face slack from all the scotch and grappa.

                    MA POWERS (O.S.)
          You're comin' home, ain't ya, Tommy? To stay?

                    TOMMY (O.S.)
          Sure... coming home.

MOVIE

                    MA POWERS
          You're going to get well and strong. Both my boys, home again. All of us.
          Together. Oh! I'm almost... glad this happened.

*She bows her head, crying, against her wounded son. Cagney reaches out feebly, gives
her a feathersoft loving 'ya knucklehead' punch on the head. Cut to: a hand lifts a
phonograph needle onto a lacquer 78. "I'm Forever Blowing Bubbles" starts. A phone
in the movie rings.*

TONY

lets the scotch burn going down.

                    MIKE (O.S.)
                    (answering phone)
          Yeah? This is Mike. When? You are?!
                    (hangs up; excited)
          Ma, they're bringing Tom home. Right now. He's on his way.

                    MA POWERS
          Is he all right?

                    MIKE
          He must be or they wouldn't be bringing him home.

MA POWERS
Oh, it's wonderful! I'll go get his room ready. I knew my baby would come home!

The sweet guileless woman goes running upstairs. Into Tommy's room, singing a happy nonsense song. Downstairs Mike waits. "I'm Forever Blowing Bubbles" scratches on. A KNOCK at the door. Mike excitedly runs and opens it. Tommy stands swaying, bound by rope and his hospital blanket. He is still bandaged like a mummy, blood and dirt now stain the bandages. His eyes are dead, unseeing. He is dead.

TONY

no expression, focussed helplessly on the TV.

MOVIE

Tommy/Cagney sways in place. Then topples forward into CAMERA – THUD. Face down on the floor. Seventy years later it is still horrific, electrifying.

TONY

numb.

MOVIE

Cut: upstairs Ma, unaware of what has happened to her son, sings her happy song, pulls a pillow out of it's case with childlike glee. She sings.

TONY

tears spring to his eyes.

FADE OUT:

THE END

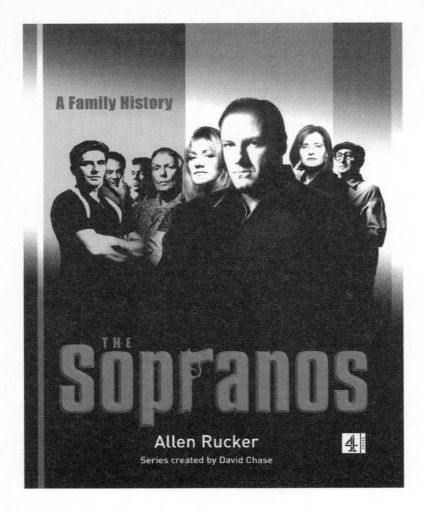